A Global
Mennonite History

Volume One

Africa

The Global Mennonite History Project

The Global Mennonite History Project (GMHP) was established by Mennonite World Conference at its 13th Assembly held in Calcutta, India, January 1997.

The purpose of the GMHP is "to tell the story of Mennonite and Brethren in Christ churches in their regional and global relationships with the goal of nurturing a sense of belonging together, promoting mutual understanding, and stimulating the renewal and extension of Anabaptist Christianity world wide." In order to achieve this goal the GMHP has set out to produce a five-volume history of the worldwide Mennonite and Brethren in Christ churches. These volumes, one for each continent, will be written by persons from the respective continents, and will reflect the experiences, perspectives and interpretations of the local churches. The present volume on Africa is the first in the series to be published.

1. Africa (2003), by Alemu Checole assisted by Samuel Asefa, Bekithemba Dube, Doris Dube, Michael Kodzo Badasu, Erik Kumedisa, Barbara Nkala, I. U. Nsasak, Siaka Traore, Pakisa Tshimika. General editors: John A. Lapp and C. Arnold Snyder.
2. Asia (Projected, 2004)
3. Latin America (Projected, 2005)
4. Europe (Projected, 2006)
5. North America (Projected, 2006)

GMHP Organizing Committee Members

Premanand Bagh, Asia	Gerhard Ratzlaff, Latin America
Doris Dube, Africa	Pakisa Tshimika, Africa
Adolf Ens, North America	Walter Sawatsky, North America
Alle G. Hoekema, Europe	Aristarchus Sukharto, Asia
Hanspeter Jecker, Europe	Paul T. Toews, North America
Juan Francisco Martinez,	Takanobu Tojo, Asia
Latin America	Larry Miller, MWC

First Printing: 1250 copies printed at Baptist Publishing House, Bulawayo, available to participants of the 14th assembly of MWC, August, 2003.
Second Printing (plus index): Pandora Press, September, 2003
Reprints and the French and Spanish editions are available from Pandora Press and Herald Press. **www.pandorapress.com**

A Global Mennonite History

Volume One

Africa

John A. Lapp and C. Arnold Snyder
General Editors

Published by Pandora Press
Co-published with Herald Press

National Library of Canada Cataloguing in Publication

A global Mennonite history / general editors, C. Arnold Snyder, John A. Lapp.

Includes bibliographical references.
Contents: v. 1. Africa.
ISBN 1-894710-38-X (v. 1)

1. Mennonites—History. I. Snyder, C. Arnold II. Lapp, John A., 1933-

BX8115.G44 2003   289.7   C2003-903871-8

A Global Mennonite History. Volume One: Africa
Copyright © 2003 by Pandora Press
33 Kent Avenue
Kitchener, Ontario N2G 3R2

Co-published with Herald Press,
Scottdale, Pennsylvania/Waterloo, Ontario

International Standard Book Number: 1-894710-38-X

Book Design: Nathan Stark
Cover: Brethren in Christ baptism in the Ginqa river, Zimbabwe.

10 09 08 07 06 05 04 03   12 11 10 9 8 7 6 5 4 3 2

Table of Contents

List of Maps

Abbreviations

AEC Evangelical Alliance of the Congo
AIC African Independent Churches
AEMSK Evangelical Mennonite Association of South Kasai (later CEM)
AIM Africa Inland Mission
AIMM Africa Inter-Mennonite Mission
AJPR Ecumenical Peace Association – Congo
AMBCF Africa Mennonite and Brethren in Christ Fellowship
AMBM American Mennonite Brethren Mission
AMBS Associated Mennonite Biblical Seminary
BIC Brethren in Christ
CCT Christian Council of Churches of Tanzania
CCZ Christian Council of Zambia
CEM Evangelical Mennonite Community (Communauté Evangelique au Congo)
CETP Centre of Theological Studies for Peace (Centre d'Etudes Théologiques pour la Paix – Congo)
CIM Congo Inland Mission
CMCo Mennonite Community of Congo (Communauté Mennonite au Congo)
CMS Church Missionary Society
COMAS Congo Mennonite Agricultural Service (later Service de Développement Agricole – SEDA)
CONIM National Inter-Mennonite Committee (Congo)
CPC Congo Protestant Council
CPRC Council for Peace and Reconciliation in the Congo
DESADEC Department of Health and Development (Congo)
DRC Democratic Republic of Congo
EBI Ekuphileni Bible Institute (Zimbabawe)
ECC Church of Christ in the Congo

EEMBF Evangelical Mennonite Church in Burkina Faso
EMBMC Eastern Mennonite Board of Missions and Charities (EMM, 1993)
EMC Mennonite Church of Congo becomes CMCo (Communauté Mennonite au Congo)
EMM Eastern Mennonite Missions
ETEK Evangelical School of Theology
FEM Fraternity of Mennonite Students (Congo)
INAK African Institute of Conciliation (Institut Africain de Conciliation)
ISTK Superior Theological Institute of Kinshasa
KMC Kenya Mennonite Church
KMT Kanisa La Mennonite Tanzania
MBC Canadian Baptist Mission
MBMSI Mennonite Brethren Mission Service International
MCC Mennonite Central Committee
MEDA Mennonite Economic Development Associates
MKC Meserete Kristos Church of Ethiopia
MPR Popular Revolutionary Movement (Congo)
MRC Mennonite Relief Committee
MWC Mennonite World Conference
PAP Programme Agricole Protestant (Congo)
PEPR Program for Peace Education and Conflict Resolution (Programme d'Education à la Paix et Résolution des conflits – Congo)
SBI Sikalongo Bible Institute (Zambia)
SMM Somalia Mennonite Mission
SRHC Sikalongo Rural Health Centre
TMC Tanganyika Mennonite Church (becomes KMT)
TMCYL Tanganyikan Mennonite Church Youth League
UCKin Christian University of Kinshasa (Université Chrétienne de Kinshasa)
UTM Unevangelized Tribes Mission
VIM Inter-Mennonite Volunteers

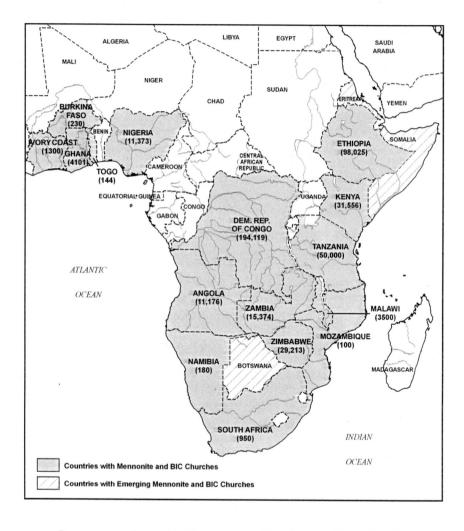

Countries in Africa with Mennonite and Brethren in Christ churches.
Total baptized membership (2003): 451,341

Editors' Foreword

The Mennonite World conference in 1994 reported that for the first time in Mennonite and Brethren in Christ history more baptized members lived in Africa, Asia, and Latin America than in Europe and North America. This stunning news created widespread discussion in the church press about the significance of such a development. This story is all the more remarkable when we recall that only one African church had been established before 1900 with only a few dozen communicants. The most recent survey from Mennonite World Conference lists more than 450,000 baptized members in Africa—451,341 to be exact—surpassing the membership of Mennonite and Brethren in Christ in North America.

Scholars and missiologists have been predicting for several decades that membership in the fast-growing churches of the global South would soon surpass that of the older northern heartlands. The Roman Catholic missiologist Walbert Bühlmann coined the label "Third Church" in a book first published in German in 1974.[1] This new era in church history, he noted, would be world-wide but its center of gravity would be in the South. In the early 1970s he expected this shift to be in full force by the beginning of the present century. While the South would become numerically dominant Bühlmann emphasized the interdependence of the world-wide body: "The third (church) needs the second (Euro-American church) for support and the second needs the third for renewal."[2]

These earlier projections have been confirmed in numerous articles and books in recent years.[3] The most recent statistical summary by David M. Barrett and Todd Johnson in the January 2002 *International Bulletin of Missionary Research* says that of two billion Christians in the world more than 1.2 billion live in the South—approximately 60% of the total.

An international group of historians convened at the Associated Mennonite Biblical Seminary in April 1995 to explore this new reality for understanding Mennonite history. The keynote speaker for this meeting,

Professor Wilbert Shenk, now at Fuller Theological Seminary, observed that the populous new Brethren in Christ and Mennonite "heartlands" are in Africa, northern Andra Pradesh India, central Java in Indonesia and the Paraguayan Chaco. Taken together this represents "a massive redefinition of identity."[4] By the time this consultation ended, historians from Colombia, Costa Rica, Zimbabwe, Zaire, India, Indonesia, the United Kingdom, and the Netherlands as well as Canada and the United States urged "that a comprehensive account of the Mennonite and Brethren in Christ experience as a global community should be published by 2005."[5]

This present volume represents the first fruits of that recommendation. It took almost two years to finalize the Global Mennonite History Project (GMHP). At Calcutta in January 1997, the General Council of the Mennonite World Conference (MWC) decided to sponsor the project. It was decided to have one volume for each continent written by representatives from those areas. Each volume would focus on the development of the church of its global area, on the context in which each church lived and the character and life of each church. At the strong urging of the Executive Secretary of MWC work was concentrated on getting the Africa volume prepared in time for the 14th Assembly of MWC scheduled for August 11-17, 2003, in Bulawayo, Zimbabwe.

With the assistance of the African members of the sponsoring committee, Doris Dube of Bulawayo, Zimbabwe, and Pakisa Tshimika, Kinshasa, DRC and Fresno, California, a team of writers was organized early in the year 2000. In the course of three meetings held in Fredeshiem, Steenwyck, Netherlands (Nov. 2000), at AMBS, Elkhart, IN (June 2001) and Bulawayo, Zimbabwe (Aug. 2002), outlines were developed and initial presentations of the material shared. The writers faced the difficult task of reconstructing the church's story with few published materials and little documentary evidence. Many oral sources were used, and writers were assisted in travelling to a wide variety of churches in far-flung areas.

This present volume is written by African writers describing their own churches.[6] Certain themes re-appear throughout the narrative, even though the authors choose different narrative emphases. The multiple stories supplement each other, broadening and deepening insight relevant to each other's experience.

A common theme running through all these stories is a deep appreciation for the missionaries who brought the Gospel to the African continent. At the same time, it is clear that the African encounter with God began long before the arrival of the first missionaries. The story of "God in pre-colonial Africa" recurs in the accounts. This message needs to be appreciated: the story of God's work in Africa did not begin with the arrival of the missionaries, but rather from the African perspective, their arrival continued, reinterpreted and re-shaped an ancient story.

The encounter between western Christianity and African religion raised a central question that faces all churches in all cultures: What is the heart of the Christian message, and what are non-essential cultural expressions? Readers will find the African churches struggling with these questions. Increasingly the African churches are expressing their faith in Christ in ways that reflect who they are as Africans, winnowing out some of the cultural trappings brought by the western missionaries.

Not all cultural expressions are easily assimilated. The profound religious importance of the veneration of ancestors in African religion remains problematic for Mennonite and Brethren in Christ churches. So does the practice of polygamy, widely practiced in traditional African society. Some lingering uncertainty remains (although fading) about the use of African instruments, song, and dance as appropriate expressions of Christian worship. African Mennonite and Brethren in Christ churches continue to grapple with these issues, testing and discerning God's will for their lives in the context of their own culture and reality.

Missions were based on a spirit of self-sacrifice and giving, both on the part of the missionaries and the sending churches. The stories told by Africans shed a new angle of light on the legacy of mission generosity. While the churches, schools and hospitals were of great benefit to the African population, their manner of founding, funding, and administration did not have entirely positive long-term results. A colonial mentality sometimes lodged control of these valuable institutions in the hands of the missionaries. A painful theme that re-appears in this narrative is a legacy of dependency in finances and personnel. The African churches faced a difficult struggle in achieving self-reliance and self-sufficiency when political circumstances changed.

A final, hopeful theme to be found in these narratives is the discovery of the human and material resources to be self-sufficient and self-reliant. The painful adjustments of growing beyond the colonial legacy are receding into the past, and the Mennonite and Brethren in Christ churches of Africa are blazing their own trails in popular education (religious and practical), church administration, responsible tithing, church planting, grass roots evangelism and witness. In their creative use of local resources, the African churches are demonstrating that God's work is established on faith and trusting action, more than on dollars and cents. If such a faith explosion is possible with such few resources and under such difficult conditions, what might be accomplished with more? The story of Mennonite and Brethren in Christ churches in Africa leaves us chastened, but with the light of hope.

We are pleased to put forward this first volume of a Global Mennonite History. We believe the insights expressed by these African writers tell the story of the African churches in fresh and perceptive ways.[7] We also know this is more like the first word—rather than the last word—on these African churches. Indeed we hope this project will encourage deeper research and investigation; we expect and welcome revision.

This present book is dependent on the support of numerous church bodies and many individuals. We are grateful to church conferences and leaders in all the countries represented for assisting the writers. We are especially beholden to the support of the African members of the Mennonite World Conference executive committee: Fimbo Ganvunze, DR Congo; Bedru Hussein, Ethiopia; and Joram M. Mbeba, Tanzania. Thanks also to the individuals and groups who provided photographs.

Each of the writers had readers for their sections. Those who assisted the editors in reading the entire volume are James Bertsche, Elkhart, IN; Nancy Heisey, Harrisonburg, Va.; Susan Godshall, Mt. Joy, PA; Bedru Hussein, Addis Ababa, Ethiopia; Harold and Annetta Miller, Nairobi, Kenya; Larry Miller, Strasbourg, France; Bishop Danisa Ndlovo, Bulawayo, Zimbabwe; Garry Prieb, Elkhart, IN; Morris Sider, Grantham, PA; Paul Toews, Fresno, CA. Special mention should go to Richard Derksen, Lancaster, PA and Pakisa Tshimika, Fresno, CA, who not only translated French materials into English but also did extensive editing.

The project has been supported by major donors including Mennonite Central Committee, United Service Foundation, Mennonite Mutual Aid, Goodville Mutual Casualty Company, Oosterbaan Foundation through the Algemene Doopsgezinde Societeit, Mennonite Brethren Historical Commission, Mennonite Foundation, Canada, a number of Mennonite Historical Societies, several regional conferences, and individuals in Canada, the Netherlands, and the United States.

As editors we feel privileged to have had the opportunity to work with this group of dedicated and talented writers. Along with them we offer this volume as a testimony and record of "the great new fact of our time," the coming of the global church.[8]

John A. Lapp and C. Arnold Snyder

Notes

[1] Walbert Bühlmann, *The Coming of the Third Church* (Maryknoll, NY: Orbis Books, 1977).

[2] *Ibid.*, 23

[3] See especially two significant books by Andrew F. Walls, *The Missionary Movement in Christian History* (1996) and *The Cross-Cultural Process in Christian History* (2002) both published by Orbis Books, Maryknoll, NY and T. & T. Clark, Edinburgh, Scotland. Also Philip Jenkins, *The Next Christendom: The Coming of Global Christianity* (New York: Oxford University Press, 2002); Wilbert R. Shenk, ed., *Enlarging the Story: Perspectives on Writing World Christian History* (Maryknoll, NY: Orbis Books, 2002); John McManners, ed., *The Oxford History of Christianity* (New York: Oxford University Press, 1993); Adrian Hastings, ed., *A World History of Christianity* (Grand Rapids, MI: Eerdmans, 1999); David Chidester, *Christianity: A Global History* (San Francisco, CA: Harper, 2000); Dale T. Irvin and Scott W. Sunquist, *History of the World Christian Movement*, vol. 1, (Maryknoll, NY: Orbis Books, 1999).

[4] Wilbert R. Shenk, "A Global Church Requires a Global History," *Conrad Grebel Review* (Winter/Spring 1997): 6.

[5] "Consultation Findings," *ibid.*, 132.

[6] Fresh histories of the church in Africa include Adrian Hastings, *The Church in Africa 1450-1950* (New York: Oxford University Press, 1994); Elizabeth Isichei, *A History of Christianity in Africa* (Grand Rapids, Michigan: Eerdmans, 1995); Bengt Sundkler and Christopher Steed, *A History of the Church in Africa* (Cambridge and New York: Cambridge University Press, 2001). The African theologian Kwame Bediako includes rich historical referencing in *Christianity in Africa: The Renewal of a Non-Western Religion* (Maryknoll, NY: Orbis Books, 1995).

[7] So far as we know there are only two Africa-initiated histories of these churches: Barbara Nkala (ed.), *Celebrating the vision: A Century of Sowing and Reaping* (Bulawayo, Zimbabwe: ZBIC Church, 1998) celebrating the 100th anniversary of the Brethren in Christ in Zimbabwe, and Tilahun Beyene Kidane's fifty-year retrospective on the presence of Mennonites in Ethiopia, *I Will Build my Church* (Addis Ababa, Ethiopia: Mega Printing Enterprises, 2002), published in Amharic.

[8] Archbishop William Temple used this phrase to describe the growing world wide ecumenical movement on his accession to Canterbury in 1942. Lesslie Newbigen, "Mission to Six Continents," in Harold E. Fey (ed.), *A History of the Ecumenical Movement, Volume Two 1948-1968* (Geneva: WCC, 1993), 176-77.

Introduction to Mennonite and Brethren in Christ Churches in Africa

by Pakisa K. Tshimika and Doris Dube

An African leader once said, "To be an African is to sing and dance." For him singing and dancing are two expressions that encapsulate the essence of African life, values and worldview. For Africans, singing and dancing take place in a community and usually as a shared activity. Even though songs and dances are sometimes conducted in relationship to events, they are usually in relationship to people. Through singing and dancing we express and share our joys and sorrows knowing that we are not alone— we belong to a larger community. Through song and dance we share our dreams, our longings and belonging, our frustration, pain, and our hope. The songs and dances are diverse because even though we belong to one continent, the people of Africa are diverse. It is through our songs and during our dances that strangers and aliens are welcomed to celebrate with us.

Writing about Mennonite and Brethren in Christ churches in Africa is like writing about our songs and dances. When one sees us from a distance our stories seem simple; however, when viewed closely a diverse, complex, energizing, and powerful reality emerges. As we tell our stories, readers will realize how our history is that of complex and intertwined stories— the songs and dances of our people. The stories tell of the joys and struggles of being committed Christians while remaining Africans. These are stories of people with many opportunities and dreams who face difficult economic and political environments that make their dreams nearly impossible to realize. Our stories are of people torn by civil and tribal wars and stories of people who have seen God's hand at work and His grace being sufficient. Finally, our stories are about a people who—in spite of the important contribution of African teachers, evangelists and pastors throughout the period of western missionary efforts—for a long time were perceived to

14

be on the receiving end of the Gospel. Africans today are increasingly seeing themselves as active partners in God's mission.

Today Mennonite and BIC churches in Africa are approaching half a million members in 16 different countries. We are organized in 23 different church bodies where those who were once enemies due to tribal or language barriers are now brothers and sisters. We are no longer strangers and aliens. How did we get here? The story begins before the missionaries arrived.

It would be very misleading to tell our stories beginning from when missionaries from the West came to Africa during this past century. Any person who takes time to listen to elders in African villages can report stories about African spirituality and the role God played in our lives before the arrival of missionaries; scholars of African religions report the same thing. Africans knew about a Higher God, the creator of everything that exists in the world. He is the God who gives gifts to individuals and to communities. He blesses and punishes. He reveals Himself through His creation. We owe all we have to this God who created people and all the environments in which we live. This understanding of God's revelation is echoed in Paul's writing to the Romans when he reminded them that they did not have reasons for not knowing God. His creation, eternal power, and divine nature were all known to Africans.

However, for many African societies the spiritual relationships we could understand were with the ancestors, those who had lived with us but were now living in the world of the living dead. The ancestors understood our joys, struggles, and dreams. They could relate to us because they had lived among us, and at the same time they could also relate to God because they now had direct access to Him. When missionaries from the West brought us the story of Jesus Christ as Mediator between God and humanity, in the words of Kwame Bediako, "Christ replaced our ancestors as the Supreme Ancestor," and we came to know Him as the one who could offer healing, hope, and salvation. We experienced what Jesus said to his fellow Jews who thought he had come to destroy their tradition in Matthew 5:17: *I have come not to abolish, but to fulfill.*

If there is one word that best describes Mennonite and Brethren in Christ churches in Africa, it would be diversity—diversity of geography, in the genesis and growth of different churches, in ethnic make up, and ways of adapting to change.

15

A careful look at a map of Africa (see page 8) shows Mennonite churches located in Central, Eastern, and Western Africa with several emerging churches in the Southern region. The Brethren in Christ, on the other hand, are almost exclusively located in the Southern region of the continent.

The birth of Mennonite and Brethren in Christ churches in Africa began with the arrival of missionaries from North American Mennonite and Brethren in Christ churches. This work was picked up by African nationals and today the African churches make up one of the fastest growing parts of the Mennonite and Brethren in Christ family.

The Emerging Churches

The first group of African churches emerged out of missionary efforts in the beginning of the past century, when individuals heard and accepted the call from God to evangelize people from other lands. Some were sent directly by their home mission agencies but many went under other agencies and were later incorporated and supported financially by their denominational mission agencies. In certain regions, such as in the Democratic Republic of Congo, some of the work was begun by non-Mennonite missionaries, but due to financial difficulty, these ministries were turned over to Mennonites.

In many cases, Mennonite and Brethren in Christ missionaries from North America arrived in Africa after other Protestant denominations had already been given their "piece of the pie" by the colonial powers of the time. In some of these cases, Mennonite and Brethren in Christ missionaries had no choice but to go to areas other missionaries had not yet reached.

The first missionaries were faced with a lack of social institutions. They responded by creating primary, secondary, Bible and nursing schools. They founded hospitals and health centers, and in some cases university level theological training courses and publishing houses. Establishing these institutions seemed a positive thing to do at the time. However, sometimes what seemed to be assets turned into liabilities and a cause of pain and frustration for those in leadership in Africa, North America and Europe.

Many of these African churches today have kept a strong relationship with their North American counterparts. These relationships usually are marked by what we would call a rollercoaster kind of partnership. The downside of the relationship has usually been caused by questions regarding financial and material resources—who controls the church's resources and who has the final word in terms of their use in the church? The up-side is marked by new partnerships in evangelism and church planting, and responding to the social needs of the communities outside the churches. The creation of training institutions during the founding era is contributing to the emergence of new leadership for the African churches today.

Nearly every Mennonite and Brethren in Christ conference in Africa has been involved in national struggles for independence, or internal conflicts. In Angola and the Democratic Republic of Congo several conferences emerged as a result of such conflicts. In Angola there are three national bodies today, each maintaining a Mennonite name. All three church organizations have their roots in the Democratic Republic of Congo, where Angolans fled as refugees during times of internal conflict and years of civil war. While in Congo, several of them came into contact with Mennonite churches and decided to start their own churches when they returned to their homeland. Unfortunately, with time a leadership crisis led to the splitting of the one Angolan Mennonite Church into the three we know today.

In the Democratic Republic of Congo, ethnic conflict forced one tribal group to move back to a location that was known as their place of origin. Without another Mennonite church in the region, they felt compelled to start one. More recent examples are the newly forming Mennonite churches in eastern Congo following the influx of refugees after the 1994 genocide in Rwanda, as well as the church planting work in Congo-Brazzaville following the civil war in that country. These "satellite" churches tend to have a very weak link to North American or European churches, but they have strong links to Congolese Mennonite churches.

Sometimes the movement of people between neighbouring countries leads to the founding of churches. This was the case when church planting efforts in Tanzania gave birth to the Mennonite church in Kenya, and the efforts in church planting by Brethren in Christ from Zimbabwe gave birth to the Brethren in Christ church in Zambia, Malawi, Botswana and South Africa. This also is how the Angolan Mennonite churches were planted along the border regions of Kasai and Bandundu provinces of the DRC. As many African Mennonite and Brethren in Christ churches reach out beyond their own borders, they are establishing Mennonite and Brethren in Christ churches in other African countries.

The diversity of African Mennonite and Brethren in Christ churches increases when other faith traditions join the Anabaptist family. This phenomenon is often related to churches receiving social assistance from Mennonite Central Committee or other Anabaptist-related groups in times of war or natural disaster. The Mennonite churches in Burkina Faso, Mozambique, Nigeria, and South Africa came into being in this way.

A new phenomenon in African Mennonite and Brethren in Christ churches relates to the movement of young people, especially those involved in the diamond trade or general commerce, who settle elsewhere in search of a better life. Thousands of Zimbabwean brothers have worked in the mines and industries of South Africa during the past fifty years. Many of them start small prayer cells which have the potential to become well-established churches. This phenomenon is particularly notable in the Eastern and Southern regions of Africa. Some young people are organizing similar meetings in Europe and Asia. Undoubtedly, more will emerge from this movement.

Diversity through Ethnic Make up of our Churches

To those who are new to African culture and African people, we look the same from a distance. As will be indicated in more detail in another section of this volume, Africa is a mosaic of many cultures, ethnic and tribal groups as well as languages. This mosaic is also reflected in our churches. In some, one ethnic group might constitute the majority of members. In others, one will find more than a dozen ethnic groups. All have been brought together because of the redeeming blood of Jesus Christ. In general, Mennonite churches in Central Africa tend to have more ethnic variety in their congregations than those from other regions. This is likely due to the multiplicity of ethnic groups already present in that region. The result is a multiplicity of languages used for worship and song in many African Mennonite and Brethren in Christ congregations.

We can say with certainty that our songs are a better reflection of the reality of ethnic diversity of African Mennonite and Brethren in Christ churches than anything else. It does not take very long for a foreigner travelling to any of our churches to realize that rather than hearing one language during a church service she ends up hearing three or four languages used in the same service. The diversity of language is most often expressed in song, thus making our songs a powerful unifying force for our diversity and ethnic divisions.

Ethnic diversity is not always celebrated in churches. It has often been a source of conflict, pain, and grief, as a close look at conflicts in Mennonite and Brethren in Christ churches demonstrates. Ethnic loyalty becomes divisive especially when new leaders must be selected for the church. In some cases conflicts have lingered so long and caused so much tension that government officials have had to intervene. In most of these cases the issues were eventually sent back to the church for final resolution. Where conflicts were not resolved, a division took place and another Anabaptist-related church emerged.

Diversity in Ways of Adapting to Changes

The challenge for African Mennonites and Brethren in Christ has been to know how to be truly African and truly followers of Jesus Christ in the African context. For example, singing and dancing have always been a part of being African. Stories are told about missionaries prohibiting local people from dancing, singing their traditional songs and using African musical instruments. Instead, Africans were taught hymns translated from English and German. For these early Mennonites and Brethren in Christ, to be followers of Jesus Christ also meant being and doing church in the American, Canadian or European way. But how does one discern what is Christian, as opposed to what is culturally North American or European? Mennonite and Brethren in Christ churches in Africa and in the rest of the world are still challenged by these issues.

The wave of political independence from colonial powers in the late '50s and early '60s brought new breath to the churches. Some church members began expressing their new-found freedom by celebrating their spirituality in African ways. Dances, drums and local songs were introduced during church services. Unfortunately even today, our churches are divided in this regard. In some churches using drums during a service or when the choir is singing is no longer an issue, but for others drums remain a sign of a sinful nature. How the offering is received also distinguishes our churches. Should a basket be passed around (as the missionaries taught us) or should the offering be collected in the front of the church so members can come forward and present their offering while singing, clapping hands, and dancing? Some young people have left churches because their leaders would not allow them to express the African way of giving offering or singing during Sunday morning service.

Another challenge is related to the role of women and youth in churches. In some churches women are gradually finding more room to exercise leadership. But thus far, there is only one Anabaptist-related church in Africa where women can be ordained following the same procedures as men. Despite the fact that Mennonite and Brethren in Christ churches in Africa have made efforts to train women in biblical and theological schools, they have not been able to clearly define the role of women in the churches. Many young women finishing theological training have expressed their frustration at the way churches choose men over women for leadership positions. Some have complained that some of their male colleagues were chosen for leadership positions just because they were men.

This issue is dealt with in many different ways in Mennonite and Brethren in Christ churches in Africa. In some cases, women are scheduled to preach just like all the other members of the pastoral team. In other cases women are allowed to speak in front the church only on certain special occasions, usually related to women's day. There are also churches that only allow women to preach if they are standing beside the pulpit and not behind it. The extreme cases are churches that will not allow women to do anything in the church unless it is approved by the male leadership.

Mennonite and Brethren in Christ churches are made up mainly of young people, but the youth have not been able to find a place in their churches beyond singing in choirs and providing logistical services during meetings and large gatherings. The future of the Mennonites and Brethren in Christ lies with these young people. They are responsible for the high energy found in the African churches. They are also to be given credit for many positive changes taking place in the churches, such as lively songs, the messages contained in these songs, and reaching out to other youth with the Gospel. They provide a sign of hope in the African continent torn by war and conflict. Our churches still have a long way to go in preparing these young people to continue the work begun by current leaders. The fact that many of our young people are well educated and highly skilled is perceived as a threat by some leaders. Much effort is needed to include the youth and to use their energy to further the mission of the church.

A Common History and Challenge for Being Church

One day, during a conversation about early mission work, a Mennonite pastor shared a story about a discussion he had had with a Mennonite missionary in the late 1950's. They were talking about life in the city and European languages. This missionary told the pastor that it was not a good idea to send his children to the city, because it was a sinful place. The pastor also should not let his children learn French, which was the national language of that country. According to this missionary the French language would be harmful to the pastor's children, especially for their walk with the Lord. The missionary was also careful in making sure that the pastor knew how awful the French people were, with their lustful literature and how French people could be found kissing in public places without respect for other people around them.

A couple of years later the missionary returned to North America and the pastor continued his church planting work in rural areas of his country, and continued teaching young people how to read and write in a local language. After a long stay in North America the missionary returned. This time he was assigned to the capital city. In the meantime he had gone to a French speaking country in Europe to learn French so that he could communicate with government officials and other city dwellers. A year later, during a church meeting the two men met again. The pastor asked the missionary if God had completely cleansed the cities, the French language and French-speaking people from all their sins. The missionary had forgotten what he told the pastor several years earlier, but the pastor had not forgotten.

Stories like this one can be found in all Mennonite and Brethren in Christ churches in Africa because the majority of these churches started in rural areas. In most cases missionaries worked among the poor and in the marginalized regions of the country. The move to the cities came about after independence in the 1960s. It also coincided with many people moving to cities in search of a better life, since the rural areas did not have much to offer them beyond involvement in agricultural production. That is why it is not unusual to find churches in cities made up of one dominant ethnic group. Those who first arrived in the cities started churches and were joined later by people from their respective regions or ethnic groups. Mennonite and Brethren in Christ coming from rural areas had to face the dilemma of how to live in the city, keeping in mind that their early spiritual formation had included the teaching that the city was an evil place.

The challenges did not only have to do with the early teaching of the missionaries. Many members who moved from the rural areas joined their relatives and formed a system that preserved their tribal and ethnic practices. It was easy to be a church in a rural area because one only had to deal with one, two or at the most three tribal groups. In the cities, the church had to face the challenge of including everyone, no matter what their ethnic group, inviting all to become part of the family of faith, where strangers and aliens can become one in Christ.

Africans know that through songs and dances, even foreigners and aliens can participate freely. However, can foreigners and aliens participate freely in leadership? This critical question continues without answer in practically all the African Mennonite and Brethren in Christ churches. It is even more crucial and critical today than ever before because of our desire to reach beyond national borders and because the future outreach for Mennonite and Brethren in Christ churches will be in the cities.

It did not take very long for Mennonite and Brethren in Christ members to discover that the city also brought a high level of vitality to the church. The freedom found in the city introduced new ideas and practices to the church. Young people introduced new songs written by Africans. With time, drums and dances entered Mennonite and Brethren in Christ churches. I recall attending a very heated debate at one of the Mennonite churches where the issue of the use of guitar and drums was being discussed. The bottom line was that the congregation had been taught not to use these instruments, and some people felt that using them would constitute a sin. The same national church is now freely using these instruments in all its congregations.

Many churches were founded by missionaries from North America, who also ran these churches. Political independence movements raised leadership questions. National leaders began to question missionary control of church affairs. In some churches, missionaries were willing to relinquish control of the church, but in others it was not so easy. The language used during these times is very interesting. National church leaders used the language of independence from the mission; the missionaries and their agencies used the language of turning over responsibilities to nationals. The first phrase implied the right to self-governance; the latter implied willful transfer of power.

Despite struggles related to power there was remarkably fast growth among African Mennonite and Brethren in Christ churches. Growth seems to have happened faster in countries with a high level of economic and political hardship than in countries where life was easier. A young pastor, when asked why there was such an increase in the number of people attending the churches, replied that many people in his country used to think that when they were in trouble, help would come from the outside. Now they had been disappointed by their national as well as international governments, and they realized the only hope left was in God and God alone.

The African Mennonite and Brethren in Christ churches that are growing the fastest are also those whose strategies for church planting include ministries that reach out to the whole person. Schools and medical institutions, community development activities, and a strong push for leadership development are contributing enormously to church growth in Africa. It is not unusual to find churches that have developed because of people who left their own countries to go to neighbouring countries for medical care. Upon return to their villages these people started Anabaptist-related churches based on what they had learned through morning services organized by the hospital chaplain or the Sunday morning services at the local church. Not enough credit has been given to people involved in school systems in Africa. Both during the missionary era and today, schools contribute enormously in helping young people come to Christ and grow in their Christian faith. When many national institutions and infrastructures are falling apart, schools and hospitals provide spaces where people are put in touch with the message of the Gospel.

During the past several years, several of the African Mennonite and Brethren in Christ churches have had to face the challenge of violence in their respective countries. Such conflicts raise issues of discipleship in the churches. How well are members trained? During a conflict in the Democratic Republic of Congo and Angola, several young people from the churches were found among those stealing from stores being looted by other young people from the neighborhood, or participating in burning the bodies of people considered enemies. Stories are told of people praising God during a church service because they now had food "taken" by their young people during the looting, and also because their children had not been killed by soldiers shooting at looters.

The question of identity, what it really means to be Anabaptist in Africa, is becoming a major challenge for African Mennonites and Brethren in Christ. In many parts of Africa religious groups were divided in such a way that no two Protestant groups could be found in the same area in order to avoid conflict among them. The result is that people from rural Africa became Mennonites, Brethren in Christ, Baptists, and Presbyterians by virtue of where they lived, rather than by choice. The exception was mainly with Catholics in some countries who could be found anywhere even if Protestant churches were already established in the region. Another exception was in the cities where any Protestant group could be established even if another Protestant church was already present.

The result of this situation has been a strong ecumenical tendency among African Mennonite and Brethren in Christ churches. It was more critical for survival to work together with other Protestant groups than to focus on denominational distinctives. Today, because of this history of division, those who became Mennonite by virtue of location are asking the critical question of what it actually means to be Mennonite or Anabaptist.

In the past few years when the question of what it means to be Mennonite/Anabaptist is asked, one immediately begins to reflect on the sixteenth-century European context. The question has historical interest, but it is not where we as Africans will find out who we are. One of the urgent needs of the African church—particularly from the perspective of the global church—is for African Mennonites and Brethren in Christ to bring the gifts of our diverse and particular cultures and histories to the world-wide Anabaptist peoplehood. What are the "roots" of Anabaptism that can be found in Pende, or Xhosa, or Ibo, or Luo, or Ndebele or Chokwe culture? If we say that we Anabaptists are a peace-loving people, what can be found in each cultural heritage and each societal history that sustains that value? The way forward lies in the dialogue between African insights and Anabaptist principles.

The need to define an Anabaptist identity in African contexts is especially acute given the rapidly changing and sometimes volatile socioeconomic and political situations in many countries. African answers to questions of identity will help define what it means to be Mennonite or Anabaptist not only in Africa, but in the world as a whole.

Opportunities in Africa and Beyond

When seen through the lens of the economic, political, and health problems of the past several years, Africa seems to be in a mess. However we Africans are a people of hope. The vitality among youth and churches is a sign of that hope. Mennonite and Brethren in Christ find the recent situations in Africa to be opportunities for outreach in the continent and beyond. Many young Mennonites and Brethren in Christ are travelling to numerous parts of the continent for economic or political reasons and introducing the Anabaptist interpretation of the Bible in their newly-found homes. Moreover many people of non-Christian faiths are also accepting Christ through the outreach of Mennonite and Brethren in Christ churches, especially in African cities. As a result, these people are also reaching out to others from their communities and in some cases to their countries of origin.

The Mennonite and Brethren in Christ churches in Africa were founded quite independently of each other. Orie O. Miller, Executive Secretary of both Mennonite Central Committee and what became Eastern Mennonite Missions, was one of the few Mennonites who sensed the positive benefits of more conscious inter-relatedness. With his encouragement, MCC hosted a meeting of all the churches at Limuru, Kenya in 1962. In 1964 representatives of the Congo Mennonites visited Tanzania churches. Tanzanians visited Brethren in Christ churches in Rhodesia and Zambia. At Bulawayo, Rhodesia (now Zimbabwe) the Africa Mennonite and Brethren in Christ Fellowship (AMBCF) was formed. Due to distance and expense there have been few meetings of the group, except in conjunction with Mennonite World Conference assemblies. An elected executive committee organizes these meetings. AMBCF released a major peace statement in 1979 and has worked on study materials for leadership training. This volume is very much a product of the continental consciousness created through AMBCF.

The desire to reach out beyond their national boundaries is also pushing Mennonite and Brethren in Christ churches to seek partnerships with other churches from around the world, based on mutual respect and accountability. Many young professional leaders are also ready to serve Christ in other countries, either as missionaries sent by their churches or in self-supporting or "tent making" ministries. In a context of churches with limited financial resources and with a desire to rediscover the essence of the Anabaptist vision, tent making ministries might just become the future of church planting in Africa.

Conclusion: Our Songs and Dances Go On

Our people's stories teach us that even strangers and aliens in the land are welcome to participate in our songs and dances. Their participation, with time, will also shape our songs and dances. New forms of songs and dances are being introduced in our communities. The old and the new are practised depending on the context. When our people leave the villages, they are expected to carry with them the songs and dances they learned there. The goal is to share them with people in their new homes, otherwise our songs and dances will die.

Mennonite and Brethren in Christ in Africa have much to share with the global Anabaptist family through songs and dances. Because we are a part of this global family our songs and dances will continue to be shaped by how we relate to the rest of the family; the rest of the family, in turn, will be shaped by our stories of joy and sorrow, pain and celebration, by our hopes and dreams. Our sincere desire is that our vision to be actively involved in the global family will continue to be a reality, in spite of current economic, political and social problems. There is vitality in our churches, our young people are optimistic and energetic, and the opportunities are limitless for our churches to reach out within and beyond our own boundaries.

The Africa Context

by Barbara Nkala

Introduction

The early African histories of the twentieth century were often derived from records of explorers and colonisers who depicted Africa as a dark continent infested with bad-mannered, superstitious savages that needed to be tamed. As a result of such ill-informed reporting by foreigners observing Africa from only one angle, many inhabitants of Africa almost came to believe that they were truly an inferior people. These reports bring to mind the story of the six blind men of India, who each touched a different part of the elephant's body, trying to discover what it looked like. The blind men, however, were only able to impart partial truths because each held on to only what they had experienced. Some people say ignorance is bliss, but more poignantly it is worse than a curse and can cause untold damage. Later historical records have tried to be more scholarly and accurate in painting African life authentically and in its entirety.

The purpose of this book is to give a record of the Mennonite and Brethren in Christ Church history in Africa. But before these stories can be told, first there is a need to understand something of the background of the African continent.

The African continent encompasses a wide range of climatic and geographical features. The climatic conditions traverse the dry Sahara Desert and the Sahel region in the North, as well as the dry Kalahari Desert in the south western region of the continent; the tropical rain forests, the grasslands of Central and Southern Africa, the Mediterranean region in the extreme north and southern tip, and the highlands of the East.

The history of Africa before and during the nineteenth and twentieth centuries was very diverse socially, culturally, economically and politically. This introduction will highlight different themes in African history, from the Africa of the Stone Age period up to the arrival and impact Western missionaries and the rise of nationalism.

Africa is populated by almost 600 million people of diverse cultural hertiage. There was no one way of doing things or governing behaviour before the nineteenth century. The same variety subsisted even within one country or within a tribe or a clan. Though a great deal of material has been documented from archaeological records and from the oral tradition concerning many of these cultures, not all the traditions can be considered. Our spotlight will be focused mainly on Central and Southern Africa, and will only briefly touch on other areas in an effort to capture the broader general picture of the African Context.

Stone Age People

Stone Age people lived in various regions on the African continent between 20,000 and 12,000 years ago. Archaeologists have excavated numerous caves to find out more about the way of life of these people. In their rock paintings, the artists of the Stone Age period captured different scenes such as men hunting and women gathering fruits, vegetables and nuts, dances and various family scenes, providing insights into life as it was lived by the people of that age. The belief systems, mythical stories and legends depicted in these rock paintings constitute a rich heritage.

Hunting and Gathering Societies

The hunter-gatherers lived mainly from fishing, gathering wild fruit and hunting wild animals. They are often described as later Stone Age people, namely the Khoisan of South and Central Africa. The Khoisan lived in small communities, in family groups of about twenty people. These communities moved from place to place following the trail of game which was their basic food source. They carried their meagre belongings with them. When they set up camp, they would build shelters out of twigs and branches, then cover the frame in animal skins. Some of the camps were set up under overhanging rocks, where they painted depictions of animals and hunters. Many such paintings have been located and added to the fascinating list of African tourist attractions.

The women in these communities spent a lot of time looking for food for the family. Sharing food enhanced community spirit and with time, organised communities began to farm rather than continuing to move from place to place. Parsons describes their activities as follows:

> They regularly left the camp to pick plants, wild fruit and nuts, as well as to dig up roots and tubers. They would gather firewood for cooking. Children might assist their mothers, and men would assist in digging up termite nests and collecting honey, caterpillars and plants for medicine or poison. Men and boys would make traps from grass, twine and sticks in order to catch birds and edible rodents or reptiles such as lizards.[1]

Henry Ellert explains that the men organised communal hunting parties from time to time, but that most of the fresh meat was caught in simple yet ingenious traps, each designed and suited to the kind of prey they were after. In later times, when village settlements and agriculture had come into being, traps would be laid in and around the fields near the village to capture field mice and any other rodents that were attracted to grain and other crops. For larger animals, traps were set along the paths to drinking places. Sometimes hunting was dangerous, as hunters were susceptible to attacks from marauding or venomous predators. For this reason, hunting was preceded by ceremonial dances and certain medicines were applied to the bodies of the hunters. Dangerous animals were tracked and shot at from a distance with poison-tipped arrows, disabling the game and allowing the hunter to deal with it with ease.[2]

Herders

Some of the hunter-gatherers domesticated sheep and cattle and became herders. They domesticated dogs as well which they used for hunting. They drank milk and ate meat mainly from sheep. Sheep tails provided the fat they used in a variety of ways. Cattle were primarily used for transporting goods and for riding. The herders sought good pasture for their livestock, but instead of moving quickly from place to place, the herders settled in one place and built more permanent houses.

During the period known as the Iron Age, cattle became a very important economic resource. Families that owned numerous livestock were richer and had more prestige, and any village that had a big herd of cattle which raised a lot of dust as they went to or from pastures was considered a very rich clan. Cattle were the means for paying the bride price. With the advent of western education, cattle were sold to pay school fees, in order to be able to educate one's children. Debts and fines were settled in the same way. Cattle were also used as beasts of burden, pulling carts or ploughs and for other transport purposes. During various traditional ceremonies, rituals and rites such as births, weddings, funerals, feasts, initiation rites and other important events, cattle were an indispensable commodity. Cattle were slaughtered for meat or used as mediums for ancestral spirits. From cattle came meat and milk for food, skins for various leather products, horns for different ornaments. Cattle dung was smeared on the floors of houses for a fresh, clean smelling surface.

The Iron Age Civilization

Iron Age civilisation seems to have evolved from the north and moved southwards, eventually covering all of Africa south of the Sahara. Iron Age civilisation came to Africa as one of the first aspects of technological development, leading to the production of more effective tools and implements. Basil Davidson notes that the "… use of iron enabled people to move into a mainly agricultural economy, to penetrate dense forests, to live in settled and large communities…" Davidson notes further that the emergence and growth of the modern states during the ninth and tenth centuries was intimately related to the skill of the people in making and using iron tools and weapons for farming, hunting, mining, or for defending themselves or fighting against their enemies. The new technology paved the way for crop cultivation, rearing of livestock and mining.[3]

Iron Age people lived in organised communities where they kept livestock and started crop farming. They produced enough food for subsistence and extra for bartering with neighbours. Some of the major crops cultivated were millet and sorghum, which became staple foods. Beans and various kinds of melons were also grown. In the north-western countries the staple foods were yams, rice, maize, millet and cassava. When a community settled in a place, thick bush was cleared to build houses and to cultivate crops.

Village communities thus became preoccupied with plant cultivation, which necessitated clearing new fields, growing a variety of crops, reaping, storing and starting all over again with the changing seasons. Each household had a plot of land given by the chief to cultivate their own crops. In many communities, women cultivated the land for subsistence. They also took care of the children, found firewood, fetched water, stamped or ground grain for mealie-meal, cooked for the family, and did all the other tasks that promoted the well being of the family.

Men built the stronger and longer lasting houses, hunted animals for meat, did some farming and cared for the livestock. The tsetse fly, which thrived under the cover of thick bush, particularly in the valleys of big rivers such as the Zambezi and Limpopo, was a menace to the livestock. They were found around the great lakes as well. Clearing the bush lessened the breeding of these pests that caused a disease called sleeping sickness.

With the advent of trade, grain and other crops were sold in exchange for other products. From this trade came a cash economy. For example, in southern Ghana, cocoa became one of the best sources of cash income. The proceeds financed schooling, housing, as well as other investments.

Slave Trade

Between the fifteenth and eighteenth centuries, rich merchants began trading in slaves. Traders travelled throughout West and East Africa in a quest for slaves and ivory. Thousands of villages were hounded and brought to destruction in the process of capturing slaves. Traders ventured far into the interior of Africa as interest in the slave and ivory trade increased. Weller and Linden tell how

> the Bemba grew powerful and prosperous by raiding for slaves. On the shores of Lake Malawi, the last Karonga was murdered and his ancestral shrine destroyed, but the Yao grew rich and converted in large numbers to Islam—a religion which seemed to suit their new role as powerful men of business selling others to the Swahili. In 1863, the Portuguese reopened Zumbo, at the confluence of the Luangwa and the Zambezi, as a collecting point for slaves and ivory, to be sent on to the ports of the Indian Ocean. From Zumbo, the Chikunda slaves could range far into Central Africa.[4]

Slave trading was also done on a small scale to provide cheap labour. Slaves were used in household work, and many others were conscripted for military service in Muslim armies. But after the discovery of the Americas, "only hard work could open mines and make plantations flourish; and work was the last thing envisaged by the conquerors. . . ."[5] Africans were resilient, hard working and strong. They were used to tropical farming and mining and so were able to endure the tough work.

So began a regular trade in slaves which went on for over 300 years. Some 12 million Africans were taken captive and transported across the Atlantic Ocean to labour in the Americas. The slave trade thrived particularly in the West of Africa, where slaves were captured and taken across the oceans in big ships to work in sugar and tobacco plantations in America and in Europe. To this day the West African coast has many forts, called Slave Castles, that were built by Western powers as depots where ships stopped to pick up slaves, gold and ivory. They also served as warehouses for captured Africans. Many African Americans visit these places—now tourist sites—and tears are shed in memory of what these forts represent.[6]

Bantu Languages

Records show that before colonial times, the people of Africa were divided into hundreds of different nationalities and ethnic and tribal groups. These ethnic groups differed greatly in their way of life and language. Basil Davidson says there are more than 1000 distinctive languages from only a handful of root languages.[7] One useful way of classifying African societies is by the languages they speak. Some languages are spoken by millions of people, and yet others are spoken by only a few hundreds to a million peoples. Joycelyn Murray says that some languages "like Mandinke, Igbo, Yoruba and Hausa in West Africa, Swahili in East Africa, Zulu and Sotho in the south of Africa and Arabic in northern Africa, have millions of speakers."[8]

The languages spoken by people in the central regions of Africa and also south of the equator are referred to as the Bantu languages. The spread of Iron Age culture also had a hand in the spread of these Bantu languages across Africa. Aneas Chigwedere, a Zimbabwean historian, contends that "Before the second half of the nineteenth century, there were no Africans anywhere in Africa who were called Bantu. They were all previously called Negroes . . . only the Arabs, and in earlier times, Greeks and Romans, called them the Ethiopians. The name Bantu did not exist in the vocabulary of world writers."[9]

The name Bantu is linguistically derived, given to people from different ethnic backgrounds because of similarities in their language group. Parsons explains the origin of the Bantu languages, saying:

The Bantu languages, spoken over most of Africa, south of the equator, are classified as a single language group because every language has a noun root similar to *-ntu* for 'person', and a prefix similar to *ba-* for that noun class. For example in southern Africa there is *abantu* (isiZulu), *bantfu* (siSwathi), *batho* (seSotho and seTswana) and *vhathu* (tshiVenda), *vanhu* (chiShona), *avandu* (tjiHerero), and *antu* (ciChewa), *bantu* (iciBemba) and *watu* (kiSwahili), further north.[10]

It is curious though, that some languages have actually taken this root to mean their specific ethnic grouping. For example, when the Ndebele people of Zimbabwe speak of *umuntu* (a person) or *abantu* (people), it is with specific reference to their own people-group, though broadly speaking the words refer to human beings in that language. For example, they might ask, "*Ngumuntu?*" ("Is he/she a person?") It seems a ridiculous question, because indeed, a person is a person. What they mean in essence is, "Is he/she a Ndebele person?" or "Is he/she one of us?" Such a question is usually posed when the identity of the person in question is not clear.

This singular root *-ntu* thus refers to humanness. Lovemore Mbigi gives the most definitive perspective of *ubuntu* (humanness) as offered by Archbishop Desmond Tutu in 1994.

Africans have a thing called *ubuntu,* it is about the essence of being human, and it is part of the gift that Africa is going to give to the world. It is about embracing hospitality, caring about others, being willing to go that extra mile for another. We believe that a person is a person through other people. That my humanity is at once caught up, bound up inextricably in yours. When I dehumanise you, I inexorably dehumanise myself. The solitary human being is a contradiction in terms, and therefore you seek work for the common good, because your humanity comes into its own in community and in a sense of belonging.[11]

Ubuntu is therefore a unifying force among the Bantu-speaking groups. The term values personhood, interdependence and love. It speaks of human dignity.

Patrilineal Kinship

In patrilineal communities, each household had a man of the family as head. Most men in these societies were husbands of several wives. A man had as many wives as he could support; having many wives was considered a sign of wealth and prosperity. A poor man could not afford to marry that many wives, since the *lobola* (bride price) had to be paid to the in-laws of each wife. Poor households sometimes resorted to giving their daughters to rich men to become new wives in exchange for foodstuff or other property. This, coupled with a general custom to give away young girls in marriage to old men, caused conflict between some of the early missionaries and the parents of the girls given away. Missionaries saw it as a violation of human rights. Mtshabezi Mission in Matabeleland, Zimbabwe, was started by Brethren in Christ missionaries originally as a school that was a place of refuge for girls fleeing such bondage.

Lobola was paid in the currency of livestock. Lobola gave a husband legal rights over his wife and children, including any other household or crop farming aspects. A new bride moved to her husband's village where she was to remain for the rest of her life.

A man's wealth was also measured by the number of children he had. It was prestigious to have many children who would in turn strengthen one's political power and economic prosperity. There definitely was power in numbers. Labour was carried out faster and there was more production. Children were also treated as a kind of bank, where one deposits money which can be drawn out at a later date, when needed. Parents always depended on the fact that it was mandatory for their children to support them in their old age. In times past, parents would indeed die and be buried by their children, unlike today, where because of the scourge of HIV/AIDS, many parents in their old age are forced to bury their young children, and many of the young men and women who are dying are leaving little children behind.

Each wife from a household owned her own hut, which she built herself. Her role was to enlarge the clan by bearing children and caring for the family. As a result, her life completely revolved around her home and family. She had practically no power or authority except over her own children. From the headship of her father, she was passed on to the headship of her husband. If her husband died, she was passed on to the headship of her husband's brother, or her own brother, even if he might be younger than she.[12]

When households began to farm, it was the wife who tilled her husband's land; she did not have any firm land rights either in her husband's household, or back in her village of birth. A woman who bore her husband many boys was well-loved and respected by clan members. Boys were considered very important, as they would carry on their father's name. A family which only had girls was despised.

Matrilineal Kinship System

There were also matrilineal African societies that traced kinship allegiance and inheritance through the mother's family. In these societies, only daughters could pass on the family line to their offspring. Inheritance of land or maternal positions were transferred by maternal uncles, who also had the authority to organise the marriages of their sisters and children. For example, in Central Ghana, a king would never pass on his title and status to his own offspring. That was the prerogative of his sister's offspring. This is because he was not by right a member of the ruling matrilineal family group.

The matrilineal inheritance system did not by any means bestow any inheritance rights on wives, sisters or daughters. Ironically, patriarchal rule still reigned. Men remained in full control of the land, marriage, dependants and politics without consulting the females involved. But, if a woman divorced, her children remained with her, only because their kinship subsisted with their maternal relatives and not with their paternal relatives. Some such societies are those of the Senufo people of the northern Ivory Coast, the Yao of Tanzania, the Bemba of Zambia and the Ndembu of the Democratic Republic of Congo. The women in these societies retain the right to live in the compounds in which they were born. They also have the right to be provided for from their land of birth. In certain instances, men who married were to live in the homes of their maternal uncles.

The Socio-cultural Setting

Governments as they are known in the modern era were unknown in Africa south of the Sahara. Yet there were clearly defined rules that closely governed each family and community. The way of life differed for each ethnic grouping scattered across the continent. They were small stateless communities ruled by chiefs, and very large areas, empires controlled entirely by kings. Neil Parsons differentiates kingdoms and chiefdoms.

> The Kingdom was a much larger state consisting of a number
> of chiefdoms under a paramount ruler or King, who was often

also chief-Priest and doctor for the whole nation. Such sizeable states, which we may call kingdoms first, appeared in Southern Africa and around the middle Limpopo Valley by the 13ᵗʰ Century.[13]

Historians suggest that a leader's power stemmed from heroic prowess in warfare or some outstanding skill. The rest of the people in that society then respected and placed total confidence in that individual. It seems that there always is a need for someone to plan, control, organise and lead the rest. Therefore, whenever serious disagreements occurred, there were battles for supremacy, with the defeated becoming subservient to the victor. This is exactly how Shaka Zulu rose from being chief to king in South Africa, rising from being a rejected boy born in about 1778 out of wedlock, to being a chief, and finally a king. His focus and vision was to unite all African tribes in the southern half of the continent under a single empire.

Chiefdoms were smaller states governed by a chief whose position was hereditary from a lineage of tribal rulers. The chief relied on tribal headmen or village leaders to rule his subjects. The hierarchical structure comprised, in ascending order, the family, village headmen, the chief and then the king. Even the stateless societies had leadership in the form of elders, who were respected for their age, wisdom and experience. A council of elders discussed important decisions, dealt with conflicts and any other socio-cultural issues until a consensus was reached.

Senior citizens were well respected in many African societies. Their voice carried power. In Ndebele there is a proverb, which says *"Ilizwi lomzali aliweli phansi."* Literally translated this means that the voice of an elderly person should not be neglected, since it carries a lot of wisdom. Elderly people have travelled the windy, rugged, rocky, bumpy, hazardous road that the young are still travelling. Therefore, they have earned the authority to advise others on how to negotiate such trails in order to arrive at a destination.

It should be noted, however, that women were never part of the council of elders. Women of any age were considered minors. Only the heads of households would sit among the council of elders. In a household where the man in charge was deceased, another male relation had to stand for that family. The young men in kingdoms were called together and trained in regiments to be valiant warriors who fought to protect their kingdom. Many times they were on the offensive and raided other communities, bringing home loot to enrich their kingdom. Captured communities were also taken as subjects of the captor kingdom.

Traditional African Beliefs

African peoples have diverse religious beliefs. However, a common denominator is that all peoples of Africa believe in a supernatural being, the creator and controller of all things. This is the one God who is above all else, who is called *uNkulunkulu* (Zulu and Ndebele), *Modimo* (seTswana and Sotho), *Mwari* (Shona), and *Mulungu* (Chewa and Nyanja). Murray observes that " Belief in a high God, creator of the universe is almost universal in Africa."[14] Turaki also says, "The conception and the attributes of God as expressed by African theology were rooted mainly in God as the Creator."[15]

When Western voyagers, traders and even some Christian missionaries first came into contact with Africans, they described African culture and belief system as savage, primitive, pagan animism, heathen, spiritism and all sorts of other negative terms. As Westerners from Europe rushed to occupy different parts of the continent of Africa in the early part of the nineteenth century, they convinced the indigenous people that everything African was primitive and that what was Western was civilised. African academics of the last century are striving to paint a more representative picture of the way life actually was for the African people. Msiska says,

> The African therefore has left his religion, and rightly so, but he had so many other things that were good for him as an African. He has lost his whole religious past and background on which the Christian faith could have flourished through all time. The African has rightly thrown out his dirty, torn old shirt, but he has at the same time, lost his golden buttons with it.[16]

African people talk of experiencing the presence of the supernatural and the mighty being who reveals himself in different situations. People have always needed the intervention of this mighty being when they are faced with the challenges of life. What differed was the way this Supreme Being was approached. In many African cultures, the Supreme Being was approached through the ancestral spirits who were referred to as the living dead. From their spiritual domain they exerted a powerful influence upon the living.

Belief in Ancestral Spirits

The general belief among Black African people is that when a person dies, his or her spirit does not die. The spirit is the part of the person that remains alive even after the physical body stops functioning and dies. The spirit of the dead person is believed to wander about until it is time to call it to come back home. This ritual is called *umbuyiso* (Ndebele) or *kurova guva* (Shona). The spirit of an adult person is called *idlozi* (Ndebele) and *mudzimu* (Shona). The spirits of departed adults are the ones that are termed ancestral spirits. They are contacted concerning every aspect of life during various pertinent ceremonies, since they are considered to be much closer to the Supreme Being. Messages to and from God are therefore communicated via the ancestral spirits.

The example of how children make their requests to their parents in the African setting is often used as an example to demonstrate how ancestral spirits function in the process of communicating with God. Children in the home did not normally approach their fathers with requests. Their needs were shared with their mothers, who in turn would then express them to the fathers as petitions. A child was considered too much of a minor to make requests directly to its father. The mother became a mediator between the two parties. Similarly, living beings were considered too insignificant to talk directly with God. They therefore communicated their needs to God through the ancestors who were their intermediaries.

It was considered that those who died earlier were nearer to God than the recently deceased. Therefore, a family would petition the ancestral spirits according to seniority. The spirit of the divine dead father was passed on to the living dead grandfather, which was in turn passed on to the living dead great grandfather who would in turn pass it onto the Supreme Being. This would be done through a special organised ceremony to consult with the ancestral spirits. The message from God or the Supreme Being was expected to come back through the same route, communicated to great grandfather, who would communicate it to grandfather who would communicate it to father who would eventually communicate it to the family. The ancestral spirits were therefore considered a very important link between human beings and their God. They were considered guardians or keepers of the community.

Westerners interpreted the communication with the ancestral spirits as worship and, therefore, as an act of idolatry. Turaki, an African scholar and theologian contends differently. He says that it is generally accepted that God is not worshiped directly but only through

> It is my hope that my children and the African children, will not allow the process of globalisation to make them forget who they are and to keep them from celebrating their culture.
> —Phinda Mzwakhe Madi[17]

the intermediaries who are the ancestral spirits. He goes on to pose some theological questions about traditional African religion that African theologians continue to debate. He questions whether the African worship of divinities is an end in itself (and so idolatrous), or whether it is God who is ultimately worshiped through them.[18] Are African divinities considered gods in their own right, or are they only mediators between God and man? Is traditional religious belief and practice idolatry, or true worship of God? In the context of African religion, these are questions that will continue to be debated and pondered.

Traditional Ceremonies

In the traditional African context, nothing simply happened; religious belief explained life. There was always cause and effect, whether it was a good phenomenon or a bad one. Various spirits were believed to cause every event: there were spirits that caused good things to happen and those that caused bad things to happen. The latter were aggrieved and vengeful spirits. Whenever good things happened there was always need to call for a ceremony to thank the Supreme Being through the spirits. Such important occasions included the birth of a baby, a marriage, setting up a new home and many other happy events. When misfortunes and suffering occurred, spirit diviners were called upon to detect the cause of the misfortune. After the consultation, corrective action was taken through the ancestral spirits. Families, clans or tribes did all this in religious ceremonies. The direct family members of the deceased were the only ones who could access the ancestors. The function of some ceremonies was to make petitions for supernatural protection. What will follow are examples of what occurred in some traditional ceremonies in some parts of central and southern Africa.

First Crops Ceremony

The "first crops ceremony" was held to celebrate the readiness of new crops for harvesting and eating. It was taboo for any member of the family to just start harvesting any new crop, be it maize, sorghum, melons, pumpkins, vegetable, marrow, sweet reeds or groundnuts. This was done to prevent people from taking unripe crops that might make them ill and to give thanks to God for a good harvest and for God's providence. Dedicating the first crops to God was done via the ancestral spirits. Some ethnic groups such as the Shona of Zimbabwe, held the ceremony beneath a tree, and the Ndebele also of Zimbabwe held this ceremony either at the king's cattle kraal or at a place in the village designated by the chief. When the crops were ready, a date was set for the first crops ceremony. A medicine man was always present to prepare the medicines used during the ritual, either to cleanse or to strengthen the people.

Different ethnic groups give detailed accounts explaining how the ceremony was conducted. M. M. Mlambo says that among the Shona, an area around a tree was cleared and swept. Only old men and women were allowed to enter that area. One of these old people offered a prayer to the ancestors thanking them for the good harvest. After this assembly, people returned to the chief's home where they spent the day dancing and drinking. A bull and several goats were killed so that the people could eat and be merry.[19]

The Rain Making Ceremony

Water is life. The one season that people anticipated in most Southern African countries was the rainy season that would give life to crops and the grazing land, water the livestock, and provide water for various needs. Rainfall was a most welcome phenomenon in due season. When the rain did not come, it spelled doom for the people, the livestock and the natural vegetation, and rain-making ceremonies were undertaken. Dominic Mandaza says, "If there is no rain after these ceremonies, then it is obvious that something is wrong in the area; some people have committed incest or some other kind of immorality and the spirits are upset."[20] The belief was that the gods were angry and had caused the drought. They needed to be appeased.

Other conditions also worked against getting good rainfall. Nyathi explains that such conditions "could include nests or crows on trees, rotting carcasses, stones on trees and barkless trees. Exposed bones, whether of humans or animals, are also thought to militate against rain falling."[21] Such substances had to be removed and destroyed to clean up the veldt.

If rains still failed to materialise, then the custodian of the land was approached and he called for a ceremony to bring rain to the community. Different tribes perform this ceremony differently, but usually there is a diviner or rainmaker who is the key to the whole performance. Gifts are brought to the rainmaker and the ceremony is conducted with a lot of singing and dancing. When the request for the rain is granted, there is an immediate downpour and people are happy.

Marriage

In many places, marriages were arranged between families. Families approved marriages between young men and women whose families were known to them. Parents needed to know that the home that the son was marrying into, or where their daughter was bequeathed was a good home where there was no witchcraft, thievery or other characteristics that were not deserving of respect. The tendency was to marry from nearby, where prospective in-laws were well known to one another. In some tribes, heavy tasks were given to the groom so that he could prove that he was a hard-working man who would be able to support his family. This is similar to Jacob working for his uncle Laban to win Rachel.

When boys and girls reached the courtship stage, the young man openly visited the young woman at her home. He was vetted by his in-laws to be, before marriage, who would ply him with questions about himself and his family. This established for the parents whether or not he was deserving of their daughter. In the Ndebele culture, a girl did not accept a young man's advances immediately, even if she was interested in him. She would ward him off for a few months before she accepted his proposal. A girl who accepted courtship quickly seemed to be cheap, and the suitor might lose interest in her. The one who dragged out the courtship was more prized, like a precious stone which took a lot of energy to find. Once the proposal was accepted, simple gifts were exchanged. The girl would then inform her grandmother, who would then communicate the news to her parents. The young man would inform his own parents through his aunt or uncle, and the process of seeking the girl's hand in marriage would begin. It was a long process where dowry or bride price charges were made.

41

In the Ndebele culture, the bride price was not paid before children were born to the young couple.

In some cultures, such as the Shona, the groom worked hard at his in-laws' fields as payment of the dowry. Others went to the bush with their dogs, to hunt and bring good game to their in-laws, to make the payment for the bride. Before the marriage ceremony to welcome the young woman at her new home, she took time to visit each of her relatives to let them know that she was getting married. She received counselling from each place, as well as farewell gifts in the form of mats, baskets, pots, plates, chickens and goats. The young bride was treated with herbs and ancestral spirits were implored to accompany her and care for her where she was going. She left her home from the cattle kraal and was expected not to look back, but to focus on where she was going.

The wedding day at the groom's place was a big affair. There was a lot of singing, dancing and eating to receive the bride. More counselling of the bride by close elderly relatives took place before those accompanying the bride returned to their homes. Some of the key points in the counselling included telling the bride to be very patient, to avoid gossip, to be very kind and to block her ears to any unfair insults or criticisms directed at her. She was there to build and not to destroy.[22] At her new home, she was introduced to her new relatives in the extended family. A woman wasn't just marrying her man but was coming to the new home to serve all the members of the new family without complaint. If she was kind and gracious to all, her mother-in-law would become the envy of all the other women in the area. Each marriage made the family grow bigger as new relationships were created, extending the family.

Elopement

In arranged marriages, if the girl did not love the man to whom she was betrothed and loved another instead, she eloped from home. In other cases, a girl eloped when she became pregnant before her lover had approached her people to ask for her hand in marriage. In such a case, the young woman would elope to his house. In the Shona culture, the young man would tell his parents that his bride was coming over, and arrangements would be made to receive her, and she would be accompanied by a friend.[23]

The messenger had to be discreet and on guard as he delivered the message announcing where the girl was; if he was caught, he would be beaten up by the girl's relatives. The groom's parents would prepare payment for appeasement of the girl's parents as reparation for the "damages" done to their daughter. After that was settled, the rest of the bride price was charged. Meanwhile, the new wife had to work very hard at her new home in order to impress her new people and to become a recognised wife of the son in the family.

Children

Childlessness was considered a curse. A barren woman was most miserable, as was Hannah of the Bible. A home without a child was not considered a home at all. Therefore, a woman who conceived and bore children was honoured. The birth of a child, especially the first child, was cause for much rejoicing because it enhanced the propagation of the family: the clan was growing bigger and the ancestors were also told of the good news, so they would bring protection for the child and the family. Traditional medicines were used on the baby to protect it from evil and to make it grow strong.

The first child in a new family was always delivered at the new wife's home of birth. She would be taken back to her birth home a month or so before delivery, where she would be attended by her mother and other close relatives. They prepared concoctions of medicines for her to take to make delivery easier. Capable midwives were alerted to await the day of delivery. Women who were barren were permitted to bring into the marriage younger and fertile relatives to have babies for them. When a man could not have children, a convenient arrangement was made where he went away and a brother came in to "raise seed for him." The whole arrangement would remain a closely-guarded secret of the family. The offspring from this arrangement belonged to the husband, who was told by his wife of her condition. This arrangement was only meant to happen once, and was not supposed to be perpetuated. This was to prevent the two parties becoming attached.

It was very important to have at least one son in the family to perpetuate the family name. Sons were therefore more esteemed than daughters. When there already was a son, having many daughters meant riches for the father that would come in the form of the bride price. Girls grew up under their mother's and grandmother's tutelage. They learned to do all the domestic tasks such as grinding corn, stamping mealies, finding firewood, fetching water, cooking, cleaning the home, feeding the hens and field work. Boys were under the instruction of their fathers and grandfathers. Herding and caring for the livestock and other domestic animals, hunting, fishing, milking cows and goats, fencing, field work and building homes were the boys' chores.

At puberty both boys and girls would be given instructions by their guardians. They were carefully trained for future roles as men and women who would continue producing children for posterity. At puberty, boys and girls were considered to have reached marriageable age. During that stage, girls were given lessons on how to become good wives, how to care for children, how to behave towards men, sex education, home economics and the regulation of one's sexual desires. Boys graduating from childhood to manhood would learn to build a home, be trained for combat and prepare for all other roles done by men in the community.

Among the Yao of Tanzania, when girls reached puberty—around age 15, 16 or 17—they were taken to a camp in the forest where older women gave instructions on matters of sex, manners and customs. The rites ceremony lasted the whole night with dancing and singing. Later they were accorded respect as women. Among the boys, initiation took place during the dry season in August. An all-night dance was performed and the boys or the candidates who were ready for initiation were not allowed to sleep. They had to listen to the songs and watch the dances. The initiation rites were performed in a forest where the drums were beaten very loudly and accompanying men shouted and sang very loudly to drown out the cries of the boys who were being circumcised. The area chief then addressed them, telling them they were now full men of the tribe. A camp site was made for them where they remained till their wounds were healed. The boys did not bathe until their wounds had healed. At the camp, the elders taught them customs, manners, sexuality and dress. They also were well fed during this time. When a person wanted to find out if a boy had been circumcised they would ask, "Has your son been danced to?"

Death Ceremonies

Turaki says an African community is a place where life and death co-exist communally and in interdependence and solidarity. When a person died, many rituals were conducted relating to burying the deceased, memorials and the coming home ceremony. It is well to note that in African culture, no one was thought to have died just of natural causes. In many cultures, soon after the burial, a number of relatives of the deceased would go to a diviner to find out what had killed the person. This was often the cause of unending feuds as there were accusations and counter accusations of relatives or neighbours about causes of a death in the family.

When a person died, those on the scene would wail loudly and unmistakably to announce the death. Relatives and members of the community would gather together to grieve with the family. In the Ndebele culture in Zimbabwe, children were taken away to another relative's house and would only be brought back when the burial was over.

Burial ceremonies differ from tribe to tribe. In the Shona culture in Zimbabwe, mourners wail loudly as they approach the relatives of the deceased. Some of them dash themselves against walls or the ground in grief. Some tribes even hire professional mourners to mourn loudly. Traditional songs are often sung, accompanied by drums, with people singing and dancing all night before the burial, in a celebratory manner. Close friends mimic what the deceased used to do to entertain the guests. In the Ndebele culture, the opposite happens. Mourners sit quietly and solemnly, and some weep softly in sympathy with the relatives of the deceased. Death ceremonies still occur in this form, even among those who profess Christianity.

The Burial

If the grave was dug the day before the funeral then some of the men would keep vigil there. Other cultures dig the grave very early on the morning of the burial. In the Ndebele culture, a man was buried by the cattle kraal, and a woman behind her granary, in identity with the kinds of activities they were associated with. While the men dug the grave, the women brought stones to cover over the mound of soil. Quite a procession would be seen trooping to and from the grave because each person was supposed to carry one stone at a time, using the left hand. The biggest stone would mark the position of the head of the deceased in the grave.

Usually a beast was slaughtered, usually a bull for a man's funeral and a cow for a woman's funeral. The meat would be cooked and served to the people after the burial. The skin was used to wrap up the dead body for burial. When a man was buried, his heir stood at the head of the grave, holding his dead father's spear with the blade stabbing the ground. Nyathi says this spear was broken and the handle was placed on the grave after the burial.

> The bit with the blade is kept at home to use the following year during the bringing home ceremony, *umbuyiso*. The breaking of the spear symbolises the tree that has broken. The tree shall "resurrect" during the *umbuyiso* ceremony, when the spear is restored fully and given to the heir.[24]

The elders of the family usually remain behind after the burial to present the spirit of the deceased to the ancestors. Certain words are spoken by the key person. Among the Shona these words are used: "Here is your person whom you have taken from us. We now hand him to you, welcome him in the spirit world, and also look after us who are left outside."[25]

Meanwhile, consultations are made with mediums to learn the cause of death. After the burial, beer is brewed for a ceremony to cleanse the people who dug the grave and those who carried the stones to place on the grave. It is a cleansing ceremony so that those people are not beset by misfortunes. It is during this ceremony that the cause of death of the deceased is revealed. Relatives from afar would continue to arrive to pay their condolences to the family and they would be led to the grave to place a little stone on it in order to bid their farewell.

Bringing Home Ceremony

In the bringing home ceremony, the spirit of an adult who died a year before is "brought back" home to be the guardian of the family traditions, to discipline family members who had done wrong, and to be the link between the living and God. Peter Sango says,

> A week before the ceremony beer is brewed and a beast is selected by the closest relatives of the deceased. On the day of the ceremony the beast is slaughtered. The relatives then take a small pot of beer to the grave and a prayer is offered. . . . Before leaving the grave an old man then tells the deceased that he is now a member of the ancestral spirits. . . . Songs are sung, accompanied by drums. Singing lasts all night, beer is drunk at intervals and roasted meat is eaten without salt. After the ceremony, the deceased is now a member of the ancestors and prayers and sacrifices can now be offered to him.[26]

After the bringing home ceremony the family members talk to the ancestral spirits and God, using the recently deceased as the closest link. Nyathi says the spirit was summoned by the words, "This family is vulnerable, come to the children. Bring them luck. Speak to our ancestors, that you may all intercede with the Creator, who we cannot speak with, but you who are now spirits can now speak on our behalf."[27]

After the bringing home ceremony the widow underwent some cleansing, discarded mourning clothes and was free to be remarried if she so chose. Normally, she was inherited by one of the brothers of the deceased husband. If she was not keen on that, she would just remain single and live with her children. This decision constituted a ceremony in itself. Nyathi describes the Ndeble ceremony as follows:

A spear and a knobkerrie are placed across the doorway. The widow is asked to jump these forwards and backwards. If she manages to jump over them, this means she did not indulge in sex. Her success is met with wild ululation. She then picks up the two items and gives them to whoever she decides to be her husband, from among her late husband's younger brothers. If she decides not to get married, she hands these things to her eldest son.[28]

This ceremony differs from tribe to tribe.

At times, when an adult died, his or her name was given to someone else to perpetuate it. This someone was usually a grandson or a granddaughter of the deceased. A black cloth and black beads were given to the selected person who was designated to guard the family, future ceremonies to communicate with the ancestral spirits were done through this person. This was the occasion when the heir was presented with the deceased father's spear, fitted with a new shaft. This signified that he was from then onwards the head of the household, responsible for all decisions to be made and problems to be solved.

Evil Spirits

In African religion, evil spirits bring harm or destruction to people. The ancestral spirits, the spiritual protectors of the land, are benevolent spirits, who pour their blessings liberally on their relatives. But when angered, they allow their wrath to reign and withhold their protection from evil influences that bring harm. It was believed that there were benevolent spirits who did good, and also malevolent spirits that brought a lot of harm and destruction. This compares to the Christian principles expressed in the words of Jesus Christ, "The thief comes only to kill, steal and destroy. I have come that they may have life and have it to the full" (John 10:10). Misfortunes, illnesses, sufferings, deformities, insanity and death were all attributed to forces of evil. These forces of evil were practised and spread by witches and wizards who were purported to possess magical powers that could bring about suffering. They were greatly feared and still are feared. Many Christians in the present day still believe in and fear the powers attributed to evil people, just as believers are aware of the rulers, principalities and authorities of this dark world and spiritual forces of evil in the heavenly realms (Ephesians 6:12).

Witches were said to be very active at night, carrying out their evil exploits under the cover of darkness. It was supposed that they travelled at night, visiting all those they wanted to bewitch. In both the Shona and Ndebele cultures, a witch was said to ride on the back of a hyena. The wheel of witchcraft is oiled by hate, jealousy and other similar negative traits. It is vindictive, destructive and merciless. Witchcraft belonged to the spiritual realm; spiritual means had to be used to detect and fight it.

Witches were said to pass on their attributes to the next generation by teaching their own children to carry on the skills. Witchcraft is supposed to be inherited from ancestors. Those who practice witchcraft are said to be able to direct even forces of nature such as lightning to strike a person, livestock or property of the intended victim. The witches were said have powers to cause incurable illnesses, great misfortunes or even death. Turaki says, "witches kill their victims by casting spells, by direct use of poisonous substances, by tampering with the victim's hair, nail cuttings or any articles worn by the victim, killing from a distance."[28]

Families did all they could to protect themselves against the powers of these forces, calling on spiritual diviners or mediums who were supposed to be possessed by ancestral spirits. They used divination to diagnose the problem, after which family members would go to a medicine man who would attend to the prescription by preparing protective or curative medicines to protect their babies and children from evil. A newly-born baby would have a mixture of medicines applied to the head to prevent the fontanelle from collapsing, concoctions taken by the mouth, medicinal powders and poultices tied around the neck or waist or wrists to ward off evil. Adults were treated with medicinal bands or necklaces for the same purposes.

Witchcraft is still strong in the mind of the African people. Even today there are villagers who believe that many diseases cannot be fully treated in the hospitals. The belief is that doctors cannot treat certain ailments because they are caused by witchcraft. It is believed that these ailments can only be suppressed by roots and drums after a divination by spirit mediums and appeasement of ancestral spirits.

Sometimes villagers would meet and agree to rid their community of witchcraft. Spirit mediums would coax the witches and wizards to rid themselves of their magic properties by confessing before a crowd the witchcraft items they possessed. They would be asked to bring those items before the crowd where they would be burned and destroyed, neutralising the powers of that person to bewitch others. If the witch or wizard refused to give up his/her witchcraft, or if the community felt it was dangerous for that person to continue living in that area, then that family would be driven away and would have to start a new life far away where their evil influence was not known. At times, when a witch committed what the community considered to be an unforgivable act of witchcraft, family members of the offended, or all the people in the community, might take the law into their own hands and kill the witch or wizard. Turaki says,

> Both the belief and the dread of witchcraft and sorcery in Africa are pervasive and very powerful. The death of young people, mysterious deaths, accidents, incurable diseases, are usually attributed to witchcraft and sorcery. There are many reported cases in modern Africa where old people have been beaten to death by the youth on account of this strong belief in witchcraft and sorcery.[29]

He notes that there are also reports of urban dwellers in the twentieth century who would "secretly sneak out without bidding farewell to relations and kinsfolk for fear of witchcraft and sorcery."[30]

In Rhodesia (now Zimbabwe), the government of the day had to introduce the Suppression of Witchcraft Act in 1899 to prevent such acts, though at the time the law was enacted as an attempt to suppress African nationalism that was spearheaded by the confidence people had in the spirit mediums. Some of the glorified spirit mediums who were hanged by the white settlers were Sekuru Kaguvi and Mbuya Nehanda.

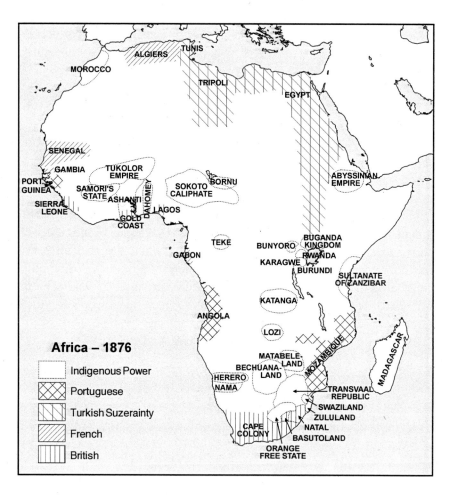

Africa – 1876

☐	Indigenous Power
▨	Portuguese
◪	Turkish Suzerainty
▨	French
▥	British

Africa before the Colonial Scramble

Enter Colonial Rule

There is a proverb that says *"Impethu ingena ngenxeba"* literally meaning "a maggot worms its way in through a sore." The proverb aptly describes how colonial power moved in, first by providing useful footholds all along the coast of West and East Africa, followed by explorers such as Mungo Park in the eighteenth century, who had set out in pursuit of science. History records do not seem to hint that Park also set out on an ambitious exercise to seize, colonise and engage in trade. There were others as well, such as Sir Joseph Banks of the British African Association, founded in 1788, who had purer motives and wished to understand better "the shape and layout of the African continent."[31]

For the most part, the justification for colonial infiltration was less than honourable. It was argued that the primitive peoples of Africa needed to be civilised. The habits, customs and beliefs of the indigenous peoples were condemned. Those who developed and extended the myth claimed that the "tribal chaos would continue to reign supreme unless and until it was stopped by European intervention."[32] Sadly, even most of the Christian missionaries who travelled to Africa to spread the Gospel in the nineteenth century did not really make an effort to understand the African way of life. They only saw dire poverty and backwardness, from which the African could only be saved by European Christian civilisation. They therefore set out to change the African way of dress, prohibited aspects of traditional African marriage and other cultural activities such as polygamy, bride price, beer brewing and drinking, and tribal dancing and singing.

By the nineteenth century, colonial powers were competing relentlessly to provide help and benefits to peoples of their protectorate colonies. It had started simply as trade in the first century AD, with Arabian merchants who exchanged goods such as "Cinnamon, tortoise shell, ivory, rhinoceros horn, a little palm-oil and a few slaves, selling in exchange Arabian made iron spearheads, axes, glass, wine and wheat..."[33] Later, as trade grew, there was an exchange of cotton, luxury goods, pottery and porcelain, and life began to change in the interior, with far reaching political changes.

Meanwhile, the explorers who traversed Africa discovered that it was a land very rich in natural resources. The Dutch, for instance, settled at the Cape of Good Hope about 1652. They started farming in the interior and needed cheap labour, which they obtained from migrant village workers. Some Africans were taken from village life to work on plantations, as well as in the diamond and gold mines discovered in the 1880s. In the process, traditional systems were being compromised and destroyed. Colonisation grew by leaps and bounds. Western European countries such as Britain, Germany, France, Spain, Belgium and Portugal competed incessantly to possess the land and natural resources in what was termed the "Scramble for Africa." The term "scramble" has connotations of rushing and showing greed without consideration for others' feelings.

While all this jostling occurred, Basil Davidson says, African leaders looked on helplessly. "They watched the erratic course of European policy and action and could seldom make head or tail of it. They accepted the alliance of friendship of this and that European country, seldom seeing how they had thus opened the gate to later conquest."[34] This is proved by the numerous concessions the African kings and chiefs were made to sign, granting the colonial settlers mineral rights, land rights and other rights. Most of the concessions were couched in deceitful terms, taking advantage of the lack of book knowledge of the incumbents, as well as lack of knowledge of the legal rights coming in with the new settlers.

For example, when the Ndebele King Lobengula realised he had been deceived in signing the Rudd Concession of 1888, he sent two of his chiefs as envoys to London to refute the deal that was grabbing his country. He said, "A king gives a stranger an ox, not his whole herd or [*sic*] cattle."[35] His plea was completely ignored.

In Southern and Central Africa, the Portuguese occupied Angola and Mozambique. The Germans took southwest Africa. There was a protracted conflict between he British and the Boers (Dutch Settlers) in the 1880's in the imperial rulers' quest to acquire more land and cheap labour from the African communities of southern Africa, who were the Zulu, Swazi, Xhosa, Bapedi, Bavenda, Tonga, Ngwato, Shona and the Ndebele to the north. Shreuder says,

> On the eve of the scramble, this is exactly what was happening in colonial South Africa. The area was already rife with European agencies of empire and expansion penetrating the remaining lands, markets, resources and authority of the African politics in the region. The aims of these groups could be couched

in the terms of the strategic or economic expansion of the European states in the underdeveloped world.[36]

While all this exertion and extension of power took place, the indigenous peoples were pushed to the margins of their lands and colonial societies. Their energies were needed only to expend in making colonial masters prosper. Their own hopes, aspirations and needs were pushed to the back of the stage. The best and most fertile pieces of land were taken over by the colonial powers while the indigenous people were relegated to poorer and unproductive areas, in what was called the reserve land. Neil Parsons says, "Many rural families became peasant farmers of crops for the new mines and towns—until capitalist farmers took over production, and peasants were forced to become farm workers or were expelled to overcrowded tribal reserves."[37]

The indigenous communities no longer had the liberty to rule themselves, or to live as they pleased. They had become subjects of their colonial masters, working hard for minimal wages. In addition, colonial rulers imposed taxes and laws enforced by colonial police, making life unbearable. Under the harsh conditions of the new reserve areas, poverty became the rule. Many people escaped the severe rural conditions for industrial towns and cities where they did domestic work or performed other menial tasks. Many young men migrated to the gold and diamond mines where they laboured for most of the year, visiting their families on the reserve only once a year. They would stop working only when they were either disabled or too old to cope with the heavy labour in the mines. No gratuity had been laid aside for them. Such privileges were the prerogative of the White masters.

The indigenous people noticed the unfair labour practices, and were not happy at being second class citizens in the land of their mothers. This state of affairs led to the Zulu war of 1879, and also the Ndebele and Shona uprisings of 1893 and 1896, respectively. The rebels eventually were subdued. After the Ndebele uprisings in 1896, Cecil Rhodes met with the chiefs and tried to appease them by promising them land. One angry young chief is said to have interjected sarcastically, saying, "You will give us land in our own country! That is good of you!"[38] Though defeated and dishonoured, the indigenous people had proven to the settlers that they were not fools. However, similar concessions pacified indigenous leaders in many of the southern African countries, and armed resistance was squashed.

Impact of Western Missionaries

Colonial governments did not support or promote African education. Consequently, Western missionaries worked very hard to establish mission schools and hospitals in the nineteenth and twentieth centuries. Although the main purpose of missionary education was biblical knowledge, nevertheless the education offered at the mission schools provided people with enlightenment and awareness of human inequality. The missionaries taught school, provided health facilities and propagated the Gospel at the same time. Many African leaders of the 1950s to the 1990s had been educated at such mission schools. Precisely these leaders began to show dissatisfaction at the contempt of the white settlers and their unfair land allocation policies.

Cattle, the traditional African means of wealth, could only be maintained in small numbers on the overcrowded land reserves. The indigenous people were forced to look for work in order to get money to pay colonial taxes and to purchase the many consumer goods that were being introduced. They became prisoners in their own land. The worst of the segregation laws was witnessed in South Africa with the apartheid system of government, which set out to promote White supremacy. The result was discontent among the Black people in both rural and urban areas.

Missionaries did try to oppose the injustices meted to the indigenous people, with little success. It takes the one wearing the shoe to experience the painful pinch and to react in a manner that will ease the pain. In Ndebele there is a proverb that says, *"Umntwana ongakhaliyo ufela embelekweni"* (A child who does not cry dies in its mother's back). The indigenous people received education from mission schools, and the knowledge gained made them realise acutely the unfair conditions and other social injustices to which they had been subjected. They began to react, and this contributed to a rise in nationalism.

The Rise of Nationalism

Nationalism became a major force all over the African continent. National giants led liberation wars that brought about independence for many

African countries. These leaders never lost hope, but encouraged their followers to keep their eyes fixed on the goal. Among them were Kwame Nkrumah of Ghana, Haile Selassie I of Ethiopia, Jomo Kenyatta of Kenya, Kenneth Kaunda of Zambia, Abu Bakar Tafawa Balewa of Nigeria, Patrice Lumumba of Congo, Julius Nyerere of Tanzania, Joshua Nkomo of Zimbabwe and Nelson Mandela of South Africa, possibly the best known and the best loved of the African leaders who pioneered Nationalism. Most of these leaders had been educated by missionaries.

Many missionaries quietly supported the liberation movements in solidarity with the people. Some were killed in the process, together with the thousands of indigenous people and many Christian converts who were greatly involved in the task of evangelism. Some, like Bernard Mizeki of the Anglican Church in Zimbabwe, even became martyrs. Most African countries attained their independence from the colonisers only after much blood was shed. The first Black African state to attain independence was Ghana in 1957, and the last of them was South Africa, which attained its independence in 1994 with the former political prisoner, Nelson Mandela, at the helm.

The colonial battle is long past for many African countries, but Africa continues to suffer a different kind of struggle: neo-colonialism, economic dependence, civil strife and wars, lack of good governance, oppression, ethnic conflict, poverty, hunger and disease. Lately, the HIV and AIDS scourge continues to take its toll. Ironically, about twenty years ago, one of the struggles was to keep the population of Africa under control. At present, AIDS has ravaged millions of people on the continent ruining the economy by depleting the labour force which was blooming in certain areas. One of the darkest clouds hovered over Africa during the Rwanda genocide of 1994 when some 800,000 Tutsi people, who were in the minority, were massacred by the ruling Hutu majority. The consequences have been devastating for the population. After the United Nations set up a tribunal, leaders were tried for their complicity in the genocide. Sadly, some of them were church leaders. Despite this gloomy picture, there is hope.

Hope for Africa

Hope is in the Light of the World, who is Jesus Christ. This book tells the story of how Christianity came into Africa, and how the Mennonite and Brethren in Christ churches have emerged and grown as part of the African reality. In Africa, about 65% of the population are young people, and they are not despairing. Africa's hope lies in the young people of the continent who are embracing education and the Gospel.

We hear this hope in the words of Sane Dube, a sixteen-year-old Bulawayo student who prepared the following essay for the Rotary Youth Exchange Programme in 2002.

The Beauty of Africa

Picture this:

1848-Matabele Territory, Kwa Bulawayo

It is *'inxwala'*—the festival of the first fruits, and a beehive of activity at the heart of the king's kraal is evidence of the excitement in the midst of the Ndebele people. The sound of drums beating can be heard echoing in the surrounding hill land. The king approvingly looks on as a group of young, well brought up girls raise the dust to the heavens in a passionate dance! They energetically stamp their feet, all the while baring white-toothed smiles to the world, as if to advertise for sale the extent of their joy. On the side lines, the young men watch in admiration whilst clapping their hands with equal enthusiasm. A scene reflecting joy, a scene reflecting tranquillity, a scene emphasizing the beauty of Africa. Africa—vibrant, alive and beautiful!

The scourge of poverty, underdevelopment, civil wars and ethnic disputes has led to Africa being permanently labelled "The dark Continent." Where other countries develop technologically, Africa seemingly remains at a stand still. With over 70% of her countries considered Third World, many have given up the hope of ever seeing any beauty in this land. And yet, beauty does not only lie in advancements. Sometimes it's in what others choose to ignore. Underdevelopment has given Africa the advantage that she retains much of her natural beauty. For example, in the north, the sun rises over the serene scene of an African jungle. Its orange rays are reflected on the calm surface of a lake, numerous creatures ranging from the rock lizard to the towering giraffe rise with the sun and prepare to begin yet another day. The creatures represent the wealth of Africa in the beauty of nature.

From the mist covered Drakensburg mountain range to the absolutely stunning pyramids!

From the East African Rift Valley to the rolling hills in the Matopos, from the captivating Lake of stars in Malawi to the rumbling smoke that thunders along the Zambezi River, Africa is the word Beauty embodied!

Culture shapes who we are and what we become. Africa is blessed in being able to maintain it. It is this culture that has ensured that those suffering from HIV and AIDS are taken care of. In African culture it is almost taboo to permanently hospitalise the sick. As a result, they are kept and cared for in the home. This means that over the years, many have been educated on the basics of home-based care whilst also learning about the risks and dangers of the deadly disease. Isn't this a beauty indeed?

Africa is a thing of beauty. The continent may be torn apart by civil wars, underdevelopment and sickness, but there is a way around this. We need to teach ourselves to look beyond misery to the point of hope and beauty. Africa is beautiful! *Viva* Africa!

Notes

[1] Neil Parsons, *A New History of Southern Africa* (Harare: The College Press, 1984), 8.

[2] Henry Ellert, *The Material Culture of Zimbabwe* (Harare: Longman Zimbabwe, 1984), 113.

[3] Basil Davidson, *Africa in History* (New York: Simon & Schuster, 1995), 86.

[4] John Weller and Jane Linden, *Mainstream Christianity to 1980 in Malawi, Zambia and Zimbabwe* (Gweru: Mambo Press, 1984), 5.

[5] Davidson, *Africa*, 207.

[6] Some of the well-known "slave castles" are Elmina Castle, Cape Coast Castle and Fort Coromantine, all found along the Ghanaian coast, and Gore island off the coast of Dakar.

[7] Davidson, *Africa*, 62.

[8] Jocelyn Murray, ed., *Cultural Atlas of Africa* (Oxford: Phaidon Press, 1981), 24.

[9] Aneas Chigwedere, *The Roots of the Bantu* (Marondera: Mutapa Publishing House, 1998), 86.

[10] Parsons, *New History*, 16.

[11] Cited in Lovemore Mbigi, *In Search of the African Business Renaissance* (Randburg, South Africa: Knowledge Resources, 2000), 7.

[12] This custom was only crippled by the introduction of the Legal Age of Majority Act, introduced in many African states in the early 1980s, which gave any person above 18 years of age the right to be able to enter into a contract on his or her own.

[13] Parsons, *New History*, 3.

[14] Murray, *Cultural Atlas*, 33.

[15] Yusufu Turaki, *Christianity and African Gods* (Nigeria: IBS Nigeria Press, 1999), 27.

[16] Stephen Kauta Msiska, *A Kachere Text* (Malawi: Christian Literature Association in Malawi, 1998), 19.

[17] Phinda Mzwakhe Madi, *Leadership Lessons from Emperor Shaka Zulu, the Great* (Randburg, South Africa: Knowledge Resources, 2000), vii.

[18] Turaki, *Christianity*, 34.

[19] M. M. Mlambo, "The Importance of Ancestors," in Clive and Peggy Kileff, *Shona Customs: Essays by African Writers* (Gweru: Mambo Press, 1970), 62.

[20] Dominic Mandaza, "Traditional Ceremonies Which Persist," in Kileff, *Shona Customs*, 60. Pathisa Nyathi, *Traditional Ceremonies of AmaNdebele* (Gweru: Mambo Press, 2001), 86, says "When normal rains did not materialise the Ndebele interpreted this to mean that God or the living dead were angry."

[21] Nyathi, *Traditional Ceremonies*, 86.

[22] "This marriage counselling was the corner stone of all stable marriages among the Ndebele. Most of the problems she came across would have been alluded to during the counselling session. This was her survival and fall-back-on-kit." Nyathi, *Traditional Ceremonies*, 116.

[23] "Little boys and girls wait up for the two women, even if they arrive after midnight. They are greeted with singing and drums. . . . After about two weeks, the husband's

parents send a messenger to the girls parents." Lydia Janhi, "Roora and Marriage," in Kileff, *Shona Customs*, 36.

[24] Nyathi, *Traditional Ceremonies*, 129.

[25] Dominic Mandaza, "Traditional Ceremonies Which Persist," in Kileff, *Shona Customs*, 56.

[26] Peter Sango, "Some Important Shona Customs," in Kileff, *Shona Customs*, 72.

[27] Nyathi, *Traditional Ceremonies*, 18.

[28] Turaki, *Christianity*, 196.

[29] *Ibid.*, 198.

[30] *Ibid.*, 281.

[31] Davidson, *Africa in History*, 281.

[32] *Ibid.*, 276.

[33] *Ibid.*, 279.

[34] *Ibid.*, 280.

[35] Parsons, *New History*, 177.

[36] D. M. Schreuder, *The Scramble for Southern Africa, 1877-1885* (London: Cambridge University Press, 1980), 6.

[37] Parsons, *New History*, 223.

[38] *Ibid.*, 182.

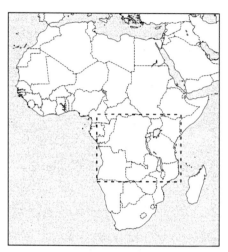

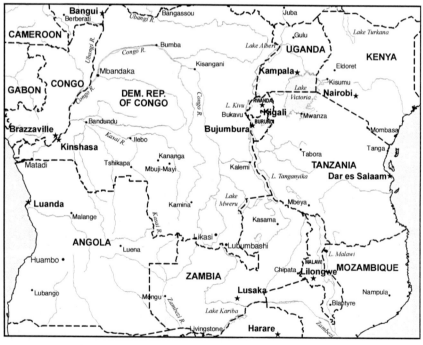

Central Africa

Mennonite Churches in Central Africa

by Erik Kumedisa

Introduction

The history of Bantu migrations in the geographical area covering the Democratic Republic of the Congo (DRC) and the Republic of Angola has been discovered thanks to the hypotheses of linguists, pre-historians, and anthropologists. The term Bantu was introduced in 1862 by the German linguist William Henry Bleek to note the ties that exist among the languages spoken by the majority of peoples in sub-Saharan Africa. The conceptual unity represented by the word "muntu" is the key to the linguistic, anthropological and ethnological relationships among these peoples. Their fundamental cultural traits are similar when it comes to philosophical and religious institutions, political and social structures, and languages and traditions.[1]

It has been established that the first inhabitants of the geographical area now covered by the DRC and Angola were the Twa peoples, commonly known as Pygmies. Generally speaking, these peoples are smaller in size than Bantu peoples and for the most part they continue to live separately as hunter-gatherers in different parts of the equatorial rain forest. They are monogamous and, in terms of dress and tools, their way of life appears to remain largely intact.

Following the original inhabitants, there were several waves of Bantu migrations from the North and West starting well before the time of Christ and continuing to move South and East right up through the fifteenth century AD. These peoples are the ancestors of those currently settled in Angola and the DRC. Most were sedentary farmers with crops and small livestock who knew how to use iron, wood and ivory; they used animal skins and raffia cloth for clothing and wore jewelry. They were polygamous and organized themselves into both matrilineal and patrilineal societies. Apart from the Twa or Pygmy peoples of Central Africa, the Khoi and San peoples of southern Africa, and certain Sudanese and Nilotic peoples, the groupings of sub-Saharan Africa are made up of Bantu peoples.

All of the peoples of Central Africa, without exception, believed in God and used various names for the Creator. In addition to the Creator, there were mediators or intermediaries between God and human beings. This is one area where we see the richness of religious and cultural diversity in Africa. For certain peoples such as the Kongo and Luba, ancestral spirits played the role of mediator between God and the living. For others such as the Tio, the spirits of nature played this role. For yet others, the king played the role of intermediary. Different persons were designated as chiefs, priests, diviners, and healers in order to ensure the health, harmony, and prosperity of the community.

In all of these societies, supplementary powers also protected people against evil, helped them to succeed, and in some cases to destroy. And so one hears of fetishes, sorcery, magic and witchcraft. All of these beliefs and practices were based on a certain notion of equality, sharing, and cooperation, and they manifested themselves in rituals of birth, rites of passage represented in some cases by circumcision, rituals of marriage bringing together two families, two clans, and sometimes two kingdoms, fertility rites, installation ceremonies for chiefs and kings, healing rituals, and many different rituals around death. Very often it was through these rituals that the traditions of the clan, the ethnic or tribal group, or the kingdom were transmitted from one generation to the next by way of dances, music, visual symbols such as masks, and teachings. In all of these diverse peoples and cultures, one might say that God was present in Africa before European missionaries arrived.

When Europeans first arrived in Central Africa, most Bantu societies were organized in the form of kingdoms or empires. For the purposes of this introduction, we will mention the western cultural grouping represented by the kingdom of the Kongo and the North Katanga cultural grouping represented by the Luba and Lunda empires, as well as the Kuba kingdom. The Kuba kingdom was situated primarily in what is now West Kasai and is best known for its weaving and sculpture. The Luba empire of North Katanga had a well-developed political system that was further adapted by the Lunda empire, an empire that was eventually divided up among three European colonial powers: the British in Zambia (Northern Rhodesia at the time), the Belgians in the Congo, and the Portuguese in Angola.

As for the Kongo kingdom, it was founded by the Bantu peoples close to the mouth of the Congo River. This kingdom had a remarkable capital, Mbanza Kongo, and was ruled by a king, the Mani-Kongo. Diego Câo, a Portuguese navigator, was the first European to enter into contact with the Kongo kingdom in 1485. Diplomatic relations were established between the kingdoms of Kongo and Portugal. The Portuguese ambassador suggested to the king of Kongo that it would be good to ask the king of Portugal to send missionaries; the king of Kongo did so, and Portugal sent the first Catholic missionaries in 1491. The king of Kongo, Nzinga Nkuwu, was baptized as a Christian the same year. The capital was renamed San Salvador and the son of King Affonso, a successor to Nzinga, was ordained as the first Congolese bishop around 1520.

Tragically, this first initiative in evangelization by the Portuguese also facilitated the beginning of the slave trade. What followed was a period of conflict with local chiefs who were enriching themselves thanks to this shameful commerce, as well as rupture with Portugal when the king of Kongo could no longer tolerate the occupation and dismantling of the kingdom by a foreign army. At one point the Mani-Kongo sent an envoy to the Pope in Rome to ask for protection against Portuguese domination. Curiously, it took four years for the envoy to reach Rome and he died the very day of his arrival!

Needless to say, this initial attempt at evangelization was unsuccessful due to a number of factors: the slave trade; the interference of the Portuguese, including the missionaries, in the affairs of the kingdom of the Kongo; internal conflicts; wars with other peoples; the eventual military conquest of the Kongo by Portugal; the mortality rate among missionaries and so on. In the late nineteenth century, when the kingdom of Kongo was divided up among the colonial powers, with France controlling in Congo-Brazzaville, Portugal in Angola, and Leopold II of Belgium in Congo-Kinshasa (DRC), the only visible signs of the early attempts at evangelizing this part of Africa were the remains of crosses here and there near the mouth of the Congo River. Evangelization had quickly turned into the buying and selling of human beings.

The Slave Trade

One of the consequences of contact between Europeans and Africans was the Atlantic slave trade. This trade began towards the end of the fifteenth century and took off in the sixteenth century, considered the "Century of Gold" among the peoples of the Iberian peninsula. The slave trade reached disastrous proportions during the early part of the sixteenth century. Slaves were bought from local chiefs in exchange for products such as cloth and wine by agents who criss-crossed the kingdom. These agents would return to Luanda or Benguela with bands of hundreds of slaves chained together, often malnourished and in pitiful condition after a long march. On the coast, they were better fed before being put on ships in order to make the ocean crossing; they were baptized en masse by Catholic priests. By 1530, the Portuguese were exporting between four and five thousand slaves each year. It is estimated that the population of Angola was reduced from approximately 18 million in the fifteenth century to 8 million in 1850 due to the slave trade and wars. The slave trade finally was abolished but only after Central Africa had lost a significant number of its human resources.

> **Petition from King Ndo Funsu to the king of Portugal, 1526:** There are many traders in all corners of the country. They bring ruin to the country. Every day people are enslaved and kidnapped, even nobles, even members of the king's own family.[2]

Evangelization and the Colonial Policies of Missions

The evangelization of Africa south of the Sahara followed the ebb and flow of European imperialism and colonialism in the nineteenth century. Europe had undergone major political and cultural changes as a result of the industrial revolution that started at the end of the eighteenth century. One of the consequences of these changes was a renewal of Europe's interest in Africa: economic interest in the search for primary resources and markets, scientific interest (e.g., in the discovery of the source of the Nile), religious interest in the evangelization of Africans, and a stated social or humanitarian interest in ending slavery.

European explorers began to travel the African continent to "discover" the peoples of Black Africa. The best known of these was a Protestant missionary, David Livingstone, who traveled from southern Africa up to central Africa from 1852 to 1873. It was there that Henry

Morton Stanley, an American journalist, met Livingstone just before his death. Stanley was employed by King Leopold II of Belgium to follow the Congo River from Boma close to the mouth of the river in the west all the way to the east. At about the same time that Stanley was helping Leopold lay his claims to the Congo, a French explorer, Brazza, was exploring the land to the north and west of the Congo River on behalf of France.

In order to establish the rules of the game and put an end to the divergences among themselves, the European powers organized the Berlin Conference (1884-85). At the end of this conference, the delegates signed the Berlin Act, carving up the map of Africa and, for the purposes of this history, determining the policies of colonial missions in article 6. This article guaranteed the freedom of conscience, religious toleration, freedom of worship, and the right of the colonizing powers to organize Christian missions.

The first Protestant missionaries in the Congo—mostly British and American—had arrived in 1878, just a few years before the Berlin Conference. The Berlin Act of 1885 opened the Congo River basin to the activities of missions and in April of the same year the Belgian Parliament granted Leopold permission to accept the title of Sovereign of the Congo Free State which had been conferred on him by the Berlin Act, with the Congo as his private domain. Leopold did as he wished with evangelization. In July of the same year, the king published a law declaring himself owner of all of the "vacant" lands in the Congo.[4] In accordance with this law Leopold distributed vast concessions of land to

Berlin Act of 1885, Chapter I, Article 6.
[Relating to the Congo River Basin and adjacent territories]
All the powers exercising sovereign rights or influence in the aforesaid territories bind themselves to watch over the preservation of the native tribes, and to care for the improvement of the conditions of their moral and material well-being and to help in suppressing slavery, and especially the Slave Trade. They shall, without distinction of creed or nation, protect and favor all religious, scientific, or charitable institutions and undertakings created and organized for the above ends, or which aim at instructing the natives and bringing home to them the blessings of civilization. Christian missionaries, scientists, and explorers, with their followers, property, and collections, shall likewise be the objects of especial protection. Freedom of conscience and religious toleration are expressly guaranteed to the natives, no less than to subjects and to foreigners . . .

E. Belfort Bax, in *The Commonweal* in 1885: "The plunder continues joyfully. The explorer identifies the land, the missionary prepares the terrain, the trader exploits . . . Stanley is the pioneer of the purveyors of the market, the precursor of the Gospel and cheap goods, both for himself and all of his fellows in armed robbery."[5]

trading and industrial companies as well as to Catholic missions. Leopold's land policy especially favored Catholic missions and prevented the expansion of Protestant missions. The king made his intentions very clear concerning the evangelization of the Congo in a letter addressed to his friend, Baron Lambermont, in 1886: "I insist that our Congo be evangelized by Belgians."[6]

It is important to understand that Belgian Catholic missionaries arrived in the Congo well before the first Protestant missionaries, not as a result of their own initiative nor as a result of an initiative from the Vatican, but because their king pushed them to enter the apostolic field he had opened for them. Upon their arrival in the Congo, these missions were assigned a specific territory according to the division of the country among the various missionary orders. In addition to receiving land concessions, Catholic missions received financial subsidies from the colonial government. Leopold could not refuse entry to Protestant missionaries without violating the agreements he had signed at the Berlin Conference, but by not granting Protestants the same rights to land and subsidies that he granted to Catholics, the king was sowing the seeds of future tension.

At the same time, Leopold was providing the motivation for Protestant unity. In order to confront the challenges of colonial policies, Protestants organized a Mission Conference in 1902 in Leopoldville (Kinshasa). Conscious of their extreme diversity, representatives of the Protestant missions discussed common problems in the areas of evangelization, education, literature distribution, medical service and their relations with other organizations and the government. This initial cooperation made it possible for Protestant communities to achieve together what no single group could have done on its own. Of one mind, it was decided that they would organize other similar gatherings in order to work together in planting an indigenous, local church unencumbered by the divisions originating in their home countries.

In 1908, Leopold's Congo Free State was annexed by Belgium's Parliament as a Belgian colony, at least partly as a result of a campaign in Great Britain and the United States publicizing some of the atrocities committed by Leopold's regime in the Congo.[7] The policies that the king had put in place with regard to the missions continued. In fact, he signed a concordat with the Vatican, making the land concessions to the Catholic orders free of charge and permanent. This agreement also included the promise of financial subsidies for Catholic missions in exchange for certain services such as geographic, ethnographic and linguistic studies.

Following the international missionary conference in Edinburgh, Scotland in 1910, the Protestant mission organizations working in the Congo formed a Continuation Committee that gave birth to the Congo Protestant Council (CPC) in 1924. In 1935 the members of the CPC agreed to give mutual recognition to each other's church members and, at the General Assembly of the CPC at Luebo in 1942, the Protestant missions adopted a plan of organic union. This mutual recognition created a sense of unity among the various Protestant churches in the Congo. The early missionaries understood that the Bible is the unique reference that teaches, transforms, edifies and nourishes. That is why they presented the centrality of Christ over and above the theologies and doctrines that divided them in the West.

Observers often note that Congolese Protestants feel united by their faith as brothers and sisters. Each pastor or evangelist, regardless of denomination, is recognized as such and can be invited to preach in any of the member communities of the Church of Christ in the Congo (ECC). Neither the baptism of adults as practiced by Anabaptists, nor the baptism of infants as practiced by Presbyterians and Methodists, nor the action of the Holy Spirit as understood by the Salvation Army has ever been the subject of contention within Congolese Protestant Christianity. Of primary importance for Congolese Protestants is the Gospel.

As was the case in the Belgian Congo, the story of missions in Portuguese Angola had its share of ups and downs. Catholic missions that had been in the hands of Portuguese and Italian Capuchins during the early period of evangelization were assigned to the Holy Ghost Fathers of France in 1865. In 1879 members of the Baptist Missionary Society of Great Britain, who had arrived in the Congo the previous year, visited San

Salvador, the capital of the kingdom of Kongo in Angola. In 1880 the American Board of Commissioners sent missionaries to the Ovimbundu people further to the South following an appeal by a British army officer in South Africa. The Congregational Church of Canada joined this work in 1886. By 1897 the New Testament was already translated into the Umbundu language. In the meantime, American Methodists had begun work around Luanda and Malanje in 1885.

The Portuguese, like the Belgians, were obligated to allow Protestant missionaries to work in their colony, but they were suspicious of the Protestant foreigners. The fact that British agents with the help of Protestant missionaries exposed the exploitation of Angolan plantation workers in Sâo Tome and Principe in the early part of the twentieth century did nothing to diminish these suspicions. In order to limit the influence of these "anti-Portuguese" foreigners, the colonial government promulgated a series of laws such as the "Organic statute of Catholic missions in Africa" in 1926, the colonial charter in 1933 to 1935, the missionary agreement of 1940, and finally the decree of 1941 granting Portuguese Catholic missions protection and subsidies along with a virtual monopoly in education. These policies, together with a marked increase in the number of Catholic missionaries, resulted in rapid growth of the Roman Catholic Church in Angola to the point where, according to some estimates, up to 50% of the population was considered Catholic in 1960.[8]

In contrast to the Roman Catholic missionaries, the Protestants did not benefit from government subsidies and protection, but the focus on indigenous languages, including the translation of the Bible, along with the tendency to concentrate on one people enabled the Gospel to take root in the local culture, and close relationships with the people developed. It is no accident that the early leaders of the nationalist movements in Angola came out of the Protestant churches. In fact, Agostinho Neto, the first president of Angola following independence in 1975, was the son of a Methodist minister. Tragically, Angola was torn by the war for independence from 1961 to 1975, followed by a civil war from 1975 to 2002. It was in this context of war, however, that Mennonite churches were born in the 1970s and '80s both along the common border between Angola and Congo and among Angolan refugees in the Congo.

Genesis of Mennonite Churches
in Central Africa, 1911-1945

The history of Mennonite evangelization in the Congo starts in North America where, in 1910, God sparked a missionary vocation to go and announce the Gospel in Africa. Two American Mennonite groups—the Central Conference of Mennonites and the Defenseless Mennonite Church—examined the possibility of opening a common mission field in Africa by creating a mission committee for the Belgian Congo. It was officially named Congo Inland Mission (CIM) on January 24, 1912.

The first Mennonite missionaries, Lawrence and Rose Haigh, arrived when the Congo was under Belgian rule in 1911. At the time, the geographical divisions created by the colonial administrations corresponded to the geographical areas occupied by those who came to evangelize. The territories visited by the first missionaries were vast and unevangelized, that is, unoccupied by any other Christian mission organization. With the help of American Presbyterians and a Congolese evangelist named Mutombo from Luebo, Lawrence and Rose Haigh established two mission posts, Kalamba Mukenge among the Lulua people and Djoko Punda among a diverse population, many of whom worked for the Kasai Company (Compagnie du Kasai). They began by organizing what were called "school-chapels."

This early method of mission work had its beginnings in a decree issued by King Leopold II in 1892. According to the decree, Leopold authorized religious and philanthropic organizations working in the Congo to take in those children who had been liberated from Arab slave traders, as well as abandoned and orphan children, for the ostensible purpose of educating them. The mission posts thus created were called "Ferme-Chapelles," or chapel-farms.[9] These posts were established with the permission of local chiefs and usually brought together a group of children under the supervision of two or three catechists. The young people engaged in agriculture and at the same time received intellectual instruction and a Christian education, all of which was crowned by baptism and later by a Christian marriage following the western model. Although this method of evangelization was intended specifically for Catholics, it had a significant influence on Protestant missionaries as well.

Djoko Punda Mennonite Church, built on the first CIM/AIMM mission station (now part of the Mennonite Community of Congo—CMCo).

By 1915 the CIM missionaries had trained the first Congolese teacher, Isaac Luaba, and in 1917 they baptized 17 persons at Djoko Punda. Early on, Djoko Punda became an important center from which the various programs of CIM work were coordinated. In 1921 Congo Inland Mission founded a third station at Nyanga among the Pende people of the Kasai. While the first two missionaries to Nyanga were Agnes Sprunger and Raphael Valentines, responsibility for the station was given to Aaron Janzen. Two years later, CIM created a fourth mission post at Mukedi among the Pende of Bandundu. The first contacts at Mukedi were made by Joseph Songomadi, a Congolese catechist/evangelist from Djoko Punda, who opened the way for the arrival of the first missionaries, Lester Bixel, Henry and Emma Moser, and Erma Birky, in 1923. By 1930, according to a report given to the CIM board by A. M. Eash, there were 800 church members and 6,675 pupils in the four mission stations of Kalamba, Djoko Punda, Nyanga, and Mukedi. In the meantime, Agnes Sprunger set out to translate the Scriptures into Giphende with the help of Isaac Khenda and other local consultants. The first Giphende New Testament was published in 1935.

At the beginning of the 1920s, Aaron Janzen, who had been working under CIM, resigned and left to start a strictly Mennonite Brethren mission post. Janzen started his mission in a Baphende village about seventy-five kilometres from Kikwit in the Kwilu district called Kikandji. Like the other missionaries of that period, Janzen also started by opening a "school-chapel." One of the first graduates was Djimbo Kubala, who went on to become the first Congolese Mennonite Brethren teacher and played an important role in the early development of the Mennonite Brethren church in the Congo.

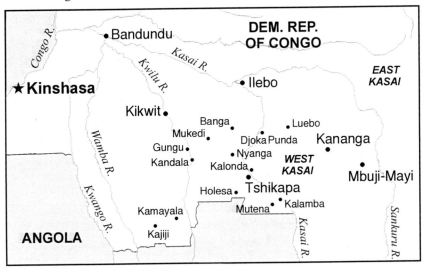

Area of early Mennonite Mission Activity in the Congo

Unfortunately, the village of Kikandji was situated on a hill and therefore far from a source of water. The need for a water supply within easy reach motivated the transfer of the mission station to Kafumba, about ten kilometres from Kikandji in a valley. Because the occasional gifts that he received from friends were not sufficient to support the work that he was doing, Janzen realized that preaching the Gospel would depend on local resources. He started an agricultural plantation together with the villagers from Kafumba and the surrounding area. During the first years, they planted two large plantations of coffee and palm trees for palm oil. The work of evangelization advanced slowly. It was not until 1926 that the first Kafumba convert, Luka Sengele, was baptized, but thanks to his witness thirty-seven others were baptized later that same year, thus creating a core group for further evangelization. Thus it was that by the 1920s there were two branches of Mennonites in the Belgian Congo, one supported by a mission committee and the other evolving as an independent mission effort carrying the Mennonite Brethren name.

Ernestina Janzen, Aaron's spouse, began research on the Kituba language spoken by most of the inhabitants of Bandundu province. By 1930, with the help of Congolese consultants, the gospels of Matthew and Luke as well as the book of Acts had been translated into Kituba. A team made up of Djimbo Kubala, Nganga Diyoyo and Ernestina Janzen continued translating the New Testament until Ernestina's death in 1937. Following her death, Martha Hiebert joined the translation team that went on to complete the manuscript of the New Testament in 1943.

> **Account of an early Mennonite missionary (unattributed):**
> During our first Christmas at Mukedi, we went to the village of Nzaji. During the prayer time, we asked people to close their eyes. When we opened our eyes at the end of the prayer, everyone had left. The only ones left were us missionaries and our assistants. Our assistants explained that the people thought that by praying with their eyes closed they would get sleeping sickness. For those villagers, the missionaries were sorcerers.

Meanwhile, in 1933, a second Mennonite Brethren missionary, Rev. H. B. Bartsch from Canada, also began an independent work in the region of Dengese and Bololo. The two Mennonite Brethren mission efforts started by Janzen and Bartsch continued separately until 1943, when the Conference of North American Mennonite Brethren Churches decided to take responsibility for the independent initiatives and created the American Mennonite Brethren Mission (AMBM). Although there were clear advantages to being under the umbrella of a North American mission organization, the shift from depending on local resources to depending on North American resources had far-reaching implications that would be noticed by Mennonite Brethren church leaders in the Congo many years later.

For all of the early missionaries, the first contacts with indigenous people were difficult for many reasons: the traumatic effects of the slave trade, the perception of white skin as a symbol of the misfortune brought about by colonization, and the myth according to which white people were the spirits of the dead returning to cast a spell on the local population. There were times when the indigenous population fled the missionaries because there was no way to distinguish between missionaries and colonial administrators, who were the symbol of oppression and with whom the missionaries shared the same Western culture.

It was in this climate of mistrust that the first missionaries formed Christian enclaves known as chapel-farms, school-farms, or mission stations. A station was separate from the customary village, with a chapel building, a dispensary or hospital, a maternity, a school, houses

> **An early reaction to the missionaries.** Much to their surprise, our ancestors saw missionaries take photos of them. They concluded that these missionaries, much like African sorcerers, were looking for the shadows of those they wanted to kill and, therefore, that the missionaries were there to kill them, they were white sorcerers who were more dangerous than the Congolese sorcerers. They would have either have to flee from them or chase them out of the country.
> —Makanzu Mavumilusa[10]

for missionaries, housing for Congolese Christians, and other buildings for various uses. The large number of children and young people who came seeking protection obligated the missionaries to plant crops and raise livestock on a large scale in order to feed everyone.

The construction of a mission station started in the following manner. A favorable site was chosen close to a village and the missionary together with indigenous people at his service and local villagers would clear the area and begin to build a house for the missionary, a dispensary, and so on. It wasn't long before sick people started to come for medical care. The station quickly became the hub of a wheel whose spokes reached out to the surrounding villages. Schools, chapels, and other buildings were constructed, often with straw roofs and mud walls at first, with more permanent structures replacing the original structures later on.

Only adults were baptized as church members and baptism was administered on confession of faith and after a period of catechetichal instruction. Those who became Christians were expected to leave their old way of life and begin a new one, which meant abstaining from any sort of indigenous celebrations such as dancing and other traditional practices. They were also to abstain from tobacco and alcoholic beverages and begin the practice of tithing as outward signs of their new life in Christ. In this way the Gospel began to take root among the indigenous populations of the Congo.

First missionary dwelling at Kalonda station, built by Archie Graber in 1949.

Mission Schools

The creation of schools provoked fear, because the young people were learning to speak the language of those from the other side. Initially no one wanted to send their own children to the white missionary's schools, so they sent children of slave origins. For example, according to Congolese Mennonite historiography, when missionaries asked Congolese families to send their children to the school at Mutoto, Pastor Lukengu, the first black pastor at Mutena, was willing to send children from slave families or children that had been captured during tribal wars, but not his own sons.[11] Consequently, missionaries needed to redeem slaves in order to start with a small core of Christians who would spread the Gospel in the country.

The catechism classes based on the "chapel-farm" model were the only means of spreading the Gospel and implanting it in the minds of these young converted slaves. The opening of mission schools was a cultural shock for our ancestors, who saw it as a trick on the part of the White missionaries to take away their traditional powers. When the missionaries taught the pupils to read and write, our ancestors trembled with fear, believing that their purpose was to teach the children to read and write the names of those who had remained in the village in order to devour them or sell them by means of magic to the White missionaries.

When the missionaries delivered certificates to those who completed their studies at the end of the school year, our ancestors believed that the certificates were receipts attesting that the pupils had indeed sold the souls of their brothers in the village to the missionaries. When these pupils left the mission schools, they had a different social status from those who had remained in the village and they were referred to as "Mindele-Ndombe," or "black-whites," or "evolved." They were, therefore, excluded from certain customary practices. Missionaries arranged for male students to marry female students and observe monogamy. It was primarily through these schools that the missionaries evangelized both children and adults through the reading of the Bible and the teaching of trades and crafts.

In addition to these challenges, Protestant-Catholic tensions were never far away. Colonial policies favoured Catholic missions with land concessions and subsidies. At times there was open hostility and at other times there was hidden opposition and resistance on the part of colonial administrators. In certain cases there was a spirit of competition between Catholic and Protestant missionaries. For example, a certain Father Bouve from the Catholic mission at Luebo, wrote in a report in 1914 that missionaries from Djoko Punda were competing for converts with a Catholic catechist at a place called Ndombi. In other cases, Belgian Catholic missionaries closed Protestant schools and colonial authorities would refuse justice to indigenous Protestants and threaten chiefs that favored the presence of Protestant missionaries. Melvin Loewen notes that the degree of tension differed according to the region. For example, there was more tension between CIM missionaries and Jesuits in Bandundu than between CIM missionaries and the Scheut missionaries in Kasai, but everywhere there was tension.[12] Perhaps more than any other factor, this tension motivated Mennonites along with other Protestants to work towards Protestant unity during this time, something which inevitably entailed stressing what they shared in common, rather than emphasizing their distinctive characteristics.

Missionary Precedents

The context in which missionaries worked created precedents that predisposed Congolese Christians towards paternalism. Today this is observed in the centralized and hierarchical structures of the Protestant churches in the Congo. Just as the Belgians thought and reasoned in place of the Congolese, so the missionaries did in the case of Congolese churches. Among the precedents created by missionaries was the provision of free services to the Congolese. A Mennonite church leader in the Congo remembers this phenomenon in the following terms:

> The missionaries did a lot of things, but we didn't know the origins of what they had. . . . The missionaries did much to help us. But for us, all of that was like an illusion. It wasn't until 1960 that we understood what they were saying when they would repeat the Baphende proverb that says, "Gana ga ndjila gadi hakianzu, gadi munenga khuta gudia gwa ginendji; uvi gabetsha gawambelele anendji gamba: anami! Hagenu mahambu uvi temu mbadihia tshwiya, uvi lamba mbadidi muza," which means, "the little birds are in the nest, they are pleased that their parents always feed them, but the lark is a wise bird who said one day to its young: my children! You must grow your wings quickly, because soon there will be a brush fire since the dry season is approaching. Our nest will burn, but with wings you will be able to escape this calamity."[13]

It is important to note that the CIM and AMBM missionaries settled in rural regions without basic services among populations without adequate financial resources to assume responsibility for themselves. In responding to the call of Christ to feed the hungry, clothe the naked and give water to the thirsty, they built schools, provided health services, established printing presses, etc. This spirit of self-sacrifice is embedded in the collective memory of Congolese Christians.

Missionaries had the necessary financial and material means to accomplish their task. Mission agencies

---

An African Mennonite Brethren church leader recalls the missionaries:
We do not stop giving thanks to God for placing a call among Christians in North America to come and announce the Gospel to us. We remember with great respect the services rendered by the pioneer missionaries who gave their lives for the Lord in our country. We are not ignorant of the difficulties faced by these valiant servants of God at the beginning of their work here with us: sicknesses, lack of roads, indecent housing, problems of adapting to the food, climate, etc. Many died here in the Congo and others died in America.[14]

provided their means of transportation. The early catechist/teachers were paid by the missionaries, and Bible and pastoral training was financed by the mission agencies. In every area of work missionaries led and controlled the church more or less on their own, and the indigenous people believed that the Church was the exclusive property of the missions. This belief created a psychology of dependency. Here are the words of a Congolese Mennonite doctor who talks of the manifestation of this dependency in medical work:

> Generally speaking, our church inherited work that was started by American missionaries. During their time, there were white doctors who had the means to do their work without too many difficulties. They were supported by their home churches and benefited from the financial help of the Belgian colonial government. Today we often hear that our hospitals should operate on the basis of compassion for the sick with no financial means as was the case during the time of the missionaries. This option is no longer possible. We know that from the beginning of the medical work in the Congo, the sick received free health care. Missionaries worked with the funds that they received to help sick people who were poor, funds that were given to them to administer medicine to the sick. . . . A huge mistake was made in the past and that is the cause of the paternalistic mentality that characterizes our church members who hope that everything will come from somewhere. But I am happy to see that even the preaching in our churches has started to combat this paternalistic spirit. The preaching that we hear now is different from what we heard during the missionary period. At that time we were told, "You can work without pay for God, but your salary will be paid in heaven."[15]

The decision of AMBM to subsidize the mission work in the Congo in 1943 had negative implications.

When Aaron Janzen received insufficient gifts to continue his work, he began an agricultural plantation with the villagers of Kafumba, introducing the idea of local people assuming responsibility for meeting the needs of their own church. Unfortunately, this arrangement was discouraged when subsidies began to come from the American Mennonite

Brethren Mission in 1943. A Congolese Mennonite Brethren recently commented:

> This contributed significantly to reinforce the psychology of dependence of the churches in the Congo vis-à-vis the missions out of which they came. Missionaries got indigenous Christians to believe that everything had to come from North America to support the Church in the Congo and the attitude of the Brethren of North America was such that they considered the Christians born as a result of their work as children rather than as responsible partners. Today we have trouble getting over this mentality of dependence.[16]

Two additional precedents going back to this period merit attention. The first is the predominant role of the missionary in the churches. Even though missionaries were involved in a variety of ministries in the early period, generally speaking those who exercised the pastoral ministry occupied the positions of responsibility in the mission stations and in conferences. In addition, biblical, pastoral and theological education was provided by the mission in such a way as to prepare Congolese catechist/evangelist/pastors to likewise assume positions of responsibility in the church. Secondly, just as male missionary pastors and evangelists played a dominant role in church affairs, so it was that male missionaries had positions of leadership and not female missionaries. There is, of course, a paradox here. Women such as Alma Doering, Agnes Sprunger, Erma Birky, Ernestina Janzen, and Martha Hiebert played very important and even critical roles in the early stages of planting Mennonite churches in the Congo through their recruitment, translation and educational work. Perhaps it is thanks to these and many other examples that the Mennonite churches in the Congo today have dynamic women's movements. Nevertheless, despite the important role played by missionary women, men were in charge of the decision-making bodies of the church. All of the above-mentioned precedents continue to influence the life of Mennonite churches in the Congo today.

Involvement of Local Preachers

Precedents notwithstanding, one of the most significant observations concerning this early period is the active involvement of indigenous Christians in the work of evangelization. Missionaries did not see themselves continuing in the role of church planters forever. They saw themselves as instructors, as pioneers who had come to start the work of evangelism, whose goal was to start classes and train catechists, evangelists, and pastors to preach the Gospel to their fellows. The Congolese would be much more able and effective in this work than the missionaries. This first generation of catechists contributed greatly to the

> **Some early Congolese Mennonite catechist/teachers:** Mutombo, James Kamba, Badiasa, Katalayi, David Mundeke, Makusudi, Isaac Luaba, and Joseph Songomadi and his spouse Beneka at Djoko Punda; Kleinboy Mutoto at Kalamba Mukenge; David Mundeka at Holesa; Daniel Kitamba, Pierre Mazemba, and David Kipoko at Nyanga; Joseph Kitenge, Jacob Kitugu, Philippe Kafuatu, and Jean Kapenda at Mukedi; Djimbo Kubala at Kafumba; Abel Shangalula, Kabongo, Elie Kahanga, Marc Kandumba, Emmanuel Shambuyuyu, Paul Mwatshikele, and Emmanuel Wayindama at Kamayala; Pierre Kikandji and Pierre Khelendende at Kandala; Pedros Lusangu and Lusoki at Panzi; Isaac Tshimika at Kajiji; Gédeon Lumeya and Temo Malwano at Lusemvu, and others.

expansion of Mennonite witness in the Congo. With a profound knowledge of their own languages and cultures, the indigenous Congolese were better equipped to do the job of church planting than were the missionaries. So it was that almost from the start, Congolese themselves were in the forefront of the work of evangelization.

The central role played by the first catechist/teachers in the growth of the church reminds us of another part of the history of Christianity in Central Africa, that of African Independent or Instituted Churches (AICs). These were churches founded not by western missionaries, but by Africans themselves. Almost at the same time as Mutombo and Isaac Luaba were working with the first CIM missionaries and Aaron Janzen was beginning the Mennonite Brethren work with Djimbo Kubala, another Protestant catechist, Simon Kimbangu, began a large movement in Bas Congo.

Simon Kimbangu was born in 1889 in the village of Nkamba, studied in a Baptist school, was baptized in 1915, and taught for a time in a Baptist school. Eventually he became an evangelist in his home village. While working as a Protestant evangelist, Kimbangu received a vision and call from God. In April 1921 he responded to God's call by healing a sick woman. This healing marks the beginning of his prophetic ministry of preaching and healing. When the Kongo people responded en masse by flocking to Nkamba, Catholic missionaries accused the Protestants of inciting their evangelist to rebel against the Belgian colonial government.

Seeing the popularity of the movement, the colonial government arrested Kimbangu in September 1921, only a few months after the start of his ministry. In October of the same year, a Belgian military tribunal convicted him and condemned him to death, but this sentence was commuted to life in prison by King Albert of Belgium. Simon Kimbangu died in prison thirty years later, but even though the movement he had started was banned, it experienced extraordinary growth during the colonial period. According to the history of Kimbanguism written by the former spiritual head of the Kimbanguist Church, Diangenda Kuntima, the movement has five million members in the Congo, Angola, other African countries, and Europe. Today, the Kimbanguist Church is the largest of the AICs.

The critical role played by Congolese catechist/evangelists in planting Mennonite churches is tied to the role of translation in the evangelization process. Dr. Lamin Sanneh, an African professor at Yale University in the United States, notes that translation work sparked a process in which indigenous people played a primary role and Western missionaries played a secondary role, regardless of intentions. He gives the example of a white missionary named Schmidt who arrived among the Khoi people in South Africa in 1737. His goal was to bring the message of salvation, but he quickly realized that he would have to learn the language in order to communicate with the people. Following is the conversation he had with one of the local people after telling them why he had come:

"That is good, baas [master]."
I asked them, Schmidt says, if they knew that there was a great
Baas, who had given them their cattle and all they possessed.
"Yes," replied the tribesmen.
"What do you call him?"
"We call him Tui-qua," was the reply.
Schmidt then stepped back to announce to them that he had come to tell them about Tui-qua, as if they had never heard of him.[17]

For Africans, the preaching of the Gospel was a confirmation of the presence of God in Africa before the arrival of missionaries. In addition, as soon as the Bible was translated into the vernacular language, Africans realized that there was a discrepancy between colonialism and the behaviour and attitude of certain missionaries on the one hand and the biblical message on the other hand. It was this realization that eventually gave birth to the various nationalist movements leading to independence.

By the beginning of World War II, CIM and AMBM were firmly implanted with Congolese catechist/evangelists and teachers playing a critical role in evangelization. Significant parts of the Bible had been translated into several vernacular languages, but there were only a few mission stations in the rural areas of Kasai and Bandundu. The war in Europe and subsequent events, however, were about to bring dramatic changes to the Mennonite churches in the Congo.

Expansion and Transition, 1945-1970

Colonial Subsidies

In 1946 the Belgian government granted equal treatment to Protestant missions in the Congo thanks in part to the election of the Socialist party and a request by the United States government, which had just supported Belgium during World War II. The impact of this decision on the growth of Protestant churches in the Congo cannot be exaggerated. From 1947 on, as long as colonial government policies and programs were respected, all Protestant mission schools were subsidized with government money.

With these subsidies Mennonite missionaries were able to build a significant part of the infrastructure of their mission program in the Congo—that is, schools and hospitals. The Belgian colonial government's offer to subsidize Protestant mission work also planted the seeds of the Congolese state's power to legislate certain affairs of the Church even today. Mennonite missionaries accepted the government subsidies, even though in America their churches had nothing to do with the government. As a former missionary has said, "in the end we said yes like almost all the missions in the Congo, because refusing to accept the subsidies would be like preventing our people, our young people, from receiving assistance from the government through us as intermediaries."

Something that Congolese Mennonite Christians never quite understood was how Mennonite missionaries could put up with the colonial government to the point of accepting subsidies while this same government was engaged in supporting a systematic structure of violence against the indigenous population. A former CIM missionary explains:

> Yes, we must recognize the fact that at times we collaborated with the colonial government and did things that the government should have done itself. . . . The policy was to ask Christian missions to provide education and health care to the indigenous population that they were evangelizing. We didn't see how we could do otherwise. Also, I must say that it is thanks to those subsidies that amounted to hundreds of thousands of dollars that we were able to greatly expand the network of schools and medical services at all of our mission stations. . . . We were able to create teacher-training programs where we trained hundreds of teachers each year and it was thanks to those teachers that we were able to open centers, schools and churches in the areas surrounding each of our mission stations. These schools became very a fruitful means of evangelization because where there was a center in the bush, there was a teacher, or a catechist, or an evangelist. Often there were baptisms in those centers. It was the same situation in the medical work, where we were able to build maternities, infirmaries, and hospitals. We were able to buy medicines and medical equipment that we could not have bought before 1947, the date when we started to benefit from the colonial government subsidies, because the mission organization did not have sufficient means to undertake social programs. We were able to train nurses and midwives who were placed in the bush and provided services to rural populations far from our mission stations. All of this was thanks to the significant subsidies that we received from the government.[18]

The decision to accept colonial government subsidies, therefore, made it financially possible to multiply mission stations, which in turn led to the multiplication of schools. The creation of a large number of schools together with the requirements of the government necessitated establishing training schools for Congolese teachers. Both CIM and AMBM founded Ecoles d'Apprentissage Pédagogique (EAPs) at several of their stations. In the beginning of the 1950s, the two Mennonite mission organizations also began to cooperate formally in joint projects for the first time. They started a higher level teacher-training school at Nyanga called Ecole de Moniteurs, and they also founded a school for missionary children at Kajiji called Ecole Belle Vue.

Establishing and Acquiring New Stations

The financial stability that came after World War II was accompanied by an increase in the number of missionaries. Abraham Kroeker of AMBM founded a new mission station at Matende among the Mbunda people in 1946, creating a school and a medical service. Two years later, Mennonite Brethren missionary J. B. Kliewer opened a station at Kipungu in Masi-Manimba among the Mbala, Ngongo, and Suku peoples. CIM missionaries founded two new mission stations in 1950: one at Banga among the Lele people in the Ilebo district following threats to the Lele children in the school at Djoko Punda, and the other at Kalonda just outside of the mining center at Tshikapa.

Thanks to the presence of Forminière, a Belgian mining company formed after the discovery of diamonds around Tshikapa in the 1900s, Tshikapa became a commercial and administrative center. It was there that the colonial government established territorial headquarters. From the time of the first visit of Forminière in 1907, agents of the mining company had cooperated with Belgian Catholic missionaries, the Scheut Fathers. In order to improve production and stabilize the workforce, Forminière built hospitals, dispensaries, and schools. The teachers in these schools were Catholic. The growth of Tshikapa provides a perfect example of what some have referred to as the triple alliance between the colonial state, capitalist interests, and the Church.

The CIM missionaries who arrived at Tshikapa were motivated by the opportunity to evangelize and minister to the Protestant employees of Forminière. Although there was significant resistance to the entry of Protestant missionaries on the part of the Catholic missionaries, the Belgian colonial administrators, and agents of the mining company, Archie Graber and Elmer Dick of CIM, along with Congolese evangelist Tom Kabangu persevered until they convinced the agents of Forminière to allow them to settle there. Diamonds had brought Forminière to Tshikapa and the presence of Protestant workers in the mining company brought Mennonite missionaries to establish a mission station at Kalonda. This diamond centre would later become the headquarters of the Mennonite Community in the Congo (CMCo).

At the same time that Mennonites were building new stations, schools, and hospitals, they also took over stations that could no longer be

Eudene Keidel with a women's sewing class, Kalonda Station.

maintained by other mission groups, such as Kajiji and Panzi for AMBM and Kamayala and Kandala for CIM. Kajiji, Panzi, and Kamayala had been created by Unevangelized Tribes Mission (UTM). UTM had been founded in 1926 by Alma Doering, a dynamic woman who had played a critical role in the creation of CIM and had worked as a CIM missionary for a number of years. She had resigned from CIM in 1925 as a result of differences between herself and other missionaries. She had wanted the mission to be non-denominational, whereas the CIM board decided to remain Mennonite. Alma Doering and the other UTM missionaries were supported through the voluntary gifts of Christians in North America under the banner of "faith missions," but without any coordinating structure. When hard economic times hit the donors at the beginning of the 1950s, and the Belgian colonial government came out with new requirements, the UTM missionaries saw no choice but to transfer the stations to AMBM and CIM, agencies that were the closest to UTM in faith and practice.[19]

Since missionaries were in control, transfer arrangements were made among missionaries. However, it was certainly in the interests of Congolese leaders of that period to ensure continuity and stability in the development of the region. Leaders such as Etienne Matshifi, Jean Tshinyama, Simon Mangala, Tshimika Mutondo, Lusoki Kituku, and Lusangu Kapenda at Kajiji and Panzi as well as Emmanuel Shambuyuyu and Emmanuel Wayindama at Kamayala no doubt participated in one way or another in the transfer decision. In any case, after all of the discussions among missionaries and Congolese, official transfer documents were signed by Arnold Prieb in 1953. AMBM took over Kajiji and Panzi and CIM took over Kamayala.

The following year CIM also received the station at Kandala from Rosalind and Percival Near, a missionary couple working under the Canadian Baptist Mission (MBC). This couple was no longer able to meet the requirements of the colonial state to place their assets in the Congolese bank and were consequently forced to cede the station to another mission. Kandala was situated close to Gungu among the Pende and not far from the Sonde, Tshokwe, and Lunda peoples of Feshi. Being part way between the stations of Mukedi and Kamayala, Kandala was a strategic location for CIM. Here again, Congolese leaders such as Pierre Kelendende and Jacques Kindumba most probably played a role in the transfer of this station

---

Mennonite Mission Activity in Evangelization, Education, and Health, 1956

Evangelization

AMBM: 7 stations – 39 missionaries – 8 ordained pastors – 249 evangelist/catechists – 12 monitor/instructors – 4,843 church members – 2,576 baptismal candidates

CIM: 8 stations – 82 missionaries – 16 non-ordained pastors – 532 evangelist/catechists – 254 monitor/instructors – 18,024 church members – 7,783 baptismal candidates

Education

AMBM: 249 primary schools/1,104 pupils – 1 Bible school/68 students – 1 monitor school/10 students

CIM: 506 primary schools/19,037 pupils – 3 teacher-training schools/116 students – 1 monitor school/28 students – 5 Bible schools/195 students – 1 trade school/20 students

Medical work

AMBM: 1 hospital – 5 dispensaries – 4 maternities – 1 White doctor, 7 White nurses – 4 Congolese nurses

CIM: 2 hospitals – 6 dispensaries – 1 leprosarium – 7 maternities – 3 White doctors, 16 White nurses – 16 Congolese nurses[20]

---

as in the case of the UTM stations, since without the support of the local population, these transfers would have been difficult to bring about.

The late '40s and early '50s were years of expansion and growth for the Mennonite churches of CIM and AMBM thanks to the efforts of Congolese Christians and missionaries, but also thanks to colonial government subsidies and the take over of bankrupt mission stations.

March towards Fusion Begins

According to the famous "thirty-year plan" published by Van Bilsen in 1956, Belgium was planning for the independence of its colony by 1985. Young Congolese nationalists were angered by the plan; they went to Brussels at the time of the World's Fair in 1958. Their reaction influenced public opinion in the Congo, resulting in demands for immediate independence as expressed in "The manifesto of the African Conscience." In June 1956 the bishops of the Congo published a "Declaration" in which they urged participation of the Congolese in their own political affairs:

> All the inhabitants of a country have the duty to collaborate actively for the common good. They have therefore the right to take part in the conduct of public affairs. The trustee nation is obliged to respect this right, and to favor its exercise by progressive political education... It is not for the Church to pronounce on the precise form in which a people's emancipation may come. She considers this legitimate so long as it is accomplished in charity and the respect of mutual rights.[21]

Contrary to all expectations in Belgium, the Congolese launched hurriedly into political activities. In 1957 municipal elections were held in three

---

Recollections of a former CIM missionary, concerning independence:
I came to the Congo in 1952 during the colonial period. Before coming to the Congo, my wife and I were in Belgium for one whole year to study French and colonial orientation classes. ... I remember the question that the students asked me in the school where I taught [after arriving in the Congo]: Will the Congo ever become independent? I don't know exactly how I responded, but I want to believe that I said, "Yes! That could come in the future, but we don't know what that future will be." In the meantime, the Church also began to move towards independence, because at the time this desire to be independent was very evident even in the villages far from Nyanga. The villagers talked about nothing other than independence and how it would bring what they needed.[22]

cities and Patrice Lumumba held his first political meetings in the Belgian Congo.

The aspirations of the Congolese to be independent from colonial rule were expressed not only by nationalist political leaders, but also by peasant farmers, students, and average church members. A climate of malaise and insecurity on the one hand and eager anticipation on the other hand settled over the country. Embassies and diplomatic missions in the Congo advised their citizens to be cautious. When riots broke out in Leopoldville (Kinshasa) in January of 1959, missionaries began to transfer their headquarters from the countryside to the cities in order to be able to evacuate if necessary.

A former CIM missionary tells the story of CIM's executive secretary meeting some Belgian businessmen in New York City. Having met with them on several occasions concerning the situation in the Congo, the executive secretary warned the missionaries: "Change is coming, it will arrive suddenly, and soon the Belgians will leave the Congo, even though they don't want to understand that change is coming. As for us as missionaries, prepare yourselves in light of the coming revolution and changes."[23]

It was after these words of warning that CIM arranged a meeting with Congolese leaders of the church at Djoko Punda in January of 1960, just six months before independence. The CIM delegation made the following statement:

> Our African brothers and sisters, it is time for us to pass the steering wheel of this church that we have helped to plant on to you. In the future, if you want missionaries here among you, it will be by your invitation. If you don't do it, missionaries will not come of their own will. Organize yourselves in order to choose your leaders. Draw up your plan for the future of the work. As for us, we are there to help, but we are not there to lead or control.[24]

As Bertsche says, thank God this meeting took place, because by the time independence came, followed by the evacuation of missionaries, Congolese Mennonites had chosen leaders and drawn up a plan of action.

Two observations can be made regarding the discussions on transfer of responsibility from mission agency to church. The first is that the talks between missionaries and the Congolese concerning the Congolese assuming responsibility were a reaction to the inevitability of a rapidly approaching independence. Secondly, the Congolese were surprised by the CIM delegation's words. The Congolese had not been associated with administering the work of the mission, and so they had little knowledge of programs, finances, and overall coordination. Colonial policies had not facilitated the training of people to assume positions of leadership. The educational and instructional opportunities provided by the government had trained the Congolese to be docile subordinates of the colonial administrators, and Protestant missions in the Congo had the same policies as the colonial government when it came to training. A 1953 study carried out by an international missionary council had concluded that the Congolese pastors coming out of mission schools were not adequately prepared for the non-missionary world, the world of colonial authorities and the government.[25]

Time, of course, did not wait and the Congo became independent on June 30, 1960. A series of unexpected events led to the sudden evacuation of missionaries less than two weeks after independence which, in turn, left a sense of emptiness and abandonment. One of the older Congolese pastors of that time, Rev. David Ngongo, compared the sense of loss to that of the disciples after the death of Jesus. Since Congolese Christians had not been involved in the coordination of missionary work, some wondered if they should just close things down or continue. If they were to continue, how would they do so and with what means? Rev. Ngongo was encouraged by the words of John 4:42: "It is no longer because of what you [missionaries] said that we believe, for we have heard for ourselves, and we know that this is truly the Savior of the world" (NRSV).[26] This conviction gave Congolese Christians the courage to continue the work even after the departure of the missionaries.

Missionaries also remember this page of their history in the Congo with regret, as told in the following account:

> Although we were constrained to leave the Congo, there were many among us who did not want to leave, but finally, under the pressure of events, due to lack of accurate information, concerned about the lives of our wives and children, under orders from the American embassy, and under pressure from our own missionary leaders, we also agreed to leave. We were six couples at Kandala after all of the other missionaries had

Reverend David Ngongo

left the other stations. We discussed and prayed for two days to know if we should leave like the others or stay and risk our lives. Finally, we too decided to leave. But we have always regretted that departure. And when the situation in the Congo returned to normal and we returned, our Congolese friends made the following remark to us, "When things became difficult, you left us to our sad lot." The remarks of our Congolese friends were justified, but they affected me nonetheless.[27]

Following the return of missionaries, there was hesitation and mistrust when it came to working under local leadership. Parallel structures arose, with one structure coordinated by the local church in the work of evangelization and another structure coordinated by the missionaries in medical work and education. The Association of Mennonite Brethren

Churches in the Congo or AEFMC operated alongside AMBM and the Evangelical Mennonite Church in the Congo or EEMC (later changed to EMC) operated alongside CIM.

At times tensions were high. During a meeting at Nyanga in 1961, for example, Rev. Mathieu Kazadi, who had been elected the first President of the EMC criticized CIM honestly and vigorously, when the CIM representative tried to justify maintaining a legal structure for CIM parallel to the legal structure of the EMC, rather than letting go of CIM's structure immediately. Kazadi made it clear that the color of a person's skin was no longer sufficient to impose authority and that if the missionaries were sincere, they should be ready to work under the responsibility of Congolese leaders. The colonial period was a thing of the past.

Birth of a third Mennonite Church Conference

Meanwhile, inter-ethnic tensions, fueled at least in part by colonial policies of divide and conquer, came out into the open in West Kasai, resulting in widespread violence around the Mennonite stations at Djoko Punda, Mutena (the station originally built at Kalamba Mukenge had been moved 10 km to Mutena after WW II), Kalonda, and Nyanga. Luba Mennonite church members, who had moved to West Kasai to work for companies like Forminière, now found themselves in a precarious situation due to ethnic violence directed against them as Luba people of East Kasai. In 1960 and 1961 many fled back to Mbuji Mayi in East Kasai province. This movement included Rev. Matthew Kazadi and his family, who arrived in Mbuji Mayi in July of 1961. Along with Rev. Kazadi came other leaders from Mennonite mission stations, including Tshibangu Mulenga Isaac, Ntambua Tshilumbayi Paul, Kalala Joseph, Tshimanga Etienne, and Ntumba Kalala André.

Those who fled West Kasai found themselves empty-handed in Mbuji Mayi, in need of the very basics of life. At this point Archie Graber, a CIM missionary who had worked with some of them at Djoko Punda, arrived in Mbuji Mayi as an MCC volunteer to distribute humanitarian aid and help displaced Luba people resettle. They were filled with joy to see a missionary with whom they had worked in the West Kasai. Graber's presence renewed hope among these displaced Mennonites. A distribution committee was formed with Pastors Kazadi, Tshibangu, and Ntambwa as part of the team and they began to distribute food and clothing in different parts of the province where there were refugees. According to the comity agreements, wherein the Congo had been divided up among the various Protestant groups, the Mbuji Mayi region was assigned to the American Presbyterian missionaries of APCM, so the Mennonites had no choice but to join the Presbyterian churches that were there when they first arrived. In the course of their work, however, the idea of starting Mennonite churches in Mbuji Mayi was born.

Mennonites had their first meeting at the home of Rev. Kazadi on April 24, 1962 in the presence of the Grabers. Four months later they held their second meeting, during which

Reverend Mathieu Kazadi, first president of CEM (Evangelical Mennonite Community)

they established a program of evangelization and chose a coordinating committee. So it was that the Evangelical Mennonite Community (CEM) was born with Rev. Kazadi as its first president. Together with Pastor Kazadi was Ntumba Kalala, who went on to become the first legal representative of the new church. With the help of the Presbyterians—the same Presbyterians who had helped the first CIM missionaries—they planted their first church at Sangilayi in the Bipemba commune of Mbuji Mayi and their second church at Kabeya Kamuanga. Graber helped them find the necessary funds to build churches and schools in Mbuji Mayi, Kabeya Kamuanga, Mupompa, Dikundi, Ndomba Bowa, and Lake Munkamba. The schools that they opened were placed under the supervision of Presbyterian schools until 1966 when the new church body received official legal status as the Evangelical Mennonite Association of South Kasai (AEMSK). Four years later, the AEMSK became Evangelical Mennonite Community or CEM.

Unfortunately, the new church didn't have enough qualified people to administer the schools, and the AEMSK council launched an appeal to Mennonite intellectuals from the province who had moved to other places to come and help run the schools. Brothers such as Georges Mpoyi, D. Kabongo and A. Muamba responded favorably to the invitation and were subsequently appointed as directors in some of the new schools. Much to everyone's surprise, however, at the beginning of the 1965-66 school year Pastor Kazadi and an education inspector made other last minute arrangements and transferred Mpoyi to another school. This change displeased a group of pastors from Kabeya Kamuanga who saw Mpoyi as their brother and they foresaw an inter-clan split between their group, the Bena Tshibanda and Pastor Kazadi's group, the Bena Tshimanga.

Mishumbi Bukungu, first treasurer of EMC. For sixteen years (1965-1981) he kept church funds in this steel drum "safe" without incident.

The pastors from Kabeya Kamuanga decided to leave the newly formed AEMSK and asked to rejoin the EMC based at Tshikapa. So it is that there are two branches of Mennonites in East Kasai today: the Evangelical Mennonite Church or CEM (former AEMSK) created by the Luba refugees who had come from CIM churches in West Kasai; and those churches affiliated with the CMCo (former EMC) since the '65-'66 split. This third Mennonite church conference or CEM, unlike the other two church bodies, was started at the initiative of Congolese Mennonites due to some of the tragic consequences of post-independence upheaval. From the beginning, Congolese Christians led the church in all aspects of its life and growth.

Other Post-Independence Changes

The inter-Mennonite cooperation that had started in the 1950s with the creation of the higher level teacher training school (Ecole de Moniteurs) at Nyanga and the school for missionary children at Kajiji was reinforced by the creation of a joint AEFMC/AMBM–EMC/CIM theological school at Kajiji in 1963. Along with the school at Nyanga, the theological school at Kajiji played a critical role in training more highly qualified leaders for the Mennonite churches, in strengthening the spirit of co-operation between Mennonites, and in creating a strong sense of unity among students from many different ethnic or tribal groups all over the Kasai and Bandundu provinces. Relationships of mutual respect and friendship were formed. People from Kamayala, Kandala, Mukedi, Nyanga, Djoko Punda, Banga,

Samuel Kakesa, first legal representative of EMC (later CMCo) and Kafutshi Kakesa, president of the CMCo women's department.

Kalonda, Kafumba, Kajiji, Panzi, and so forth came to study at the same school and got to know each other. As a result, rather than envisioning mono-tribal churches, pastors and lay leaders envisioned a Mennonite church that would bring together people from all tribal and ethnic groups and sub-groups.

About the time that Mennonite refugees in Mbuji Mayi were organizing a new Mennonite church conference, a rebellion took over part of the Bandundu province affecting both AEFMC and EMC churches. The Kwilu rebellion of 1964 was started by Pierre Mulele, who had served as minister in the cabinet of the first Prime Minister of the Congo, Patrice Lumumba. Lumumba had been assassinated several months after independence and Mulele wanted to continue the revolution that Lumumba had started. Mennonite churches, schools and stations were quickly caught up in the fighting.

At the beginning of the rebellion Congolese Mennonites around Mukedi and Kandala were divided. Independence had not brought about the desired changes and Mulele made promises to the people. There were Mulele sympathizers among the students, the village chiefs where Mennonite churches and schools were located, and even among the church leaders. Others resisted the rebellion from the start. Samuel Kakesa, the first Congolese legal representative of the EMC, was taken hostage while he was at Mukedi and held for six months. David Kipoko, a lay leader, led the families of the Bible Institute students from Kandala to Nyanga by foot, crossing the Louange River to get out of the territory controlled by the rebels. Pastor Emmanuel Wayindama, who had come from Kamayala to teach

Nicodème Tshilembu, first education secretary of EMC

at the Bible Institute at Kandala, was threatened by rebels at one point and later falsely accused by government forces at Kahemba of being a Mulele sympathizer. As time went on, as a result of arbitrary arrests, executions and the lack of improvement in their lives, many of those who had supported the rebellion in the beginning ended up rejecting it. Eventually, government forces defeated the rebels, and in November of 1965 General Mobutu Sese Seko took over the country in a coup d'état in Kinshasa.

With the end of the rebellion came a certain degree of political stability and Mennonites began to engage in new forms of social ministry. In 1965 the EMC, CIM, and MCC joined to create a cooperative agricultural development project at Nyanga called Congo Mennonite Agricultural Service (COMAS). Later, this program became the Service de Développement Agricole (SEDA). The primary goal of this program was to help farmers increase their agricultural production in order to meet their own nutritional needs and be able to sell the surplus. In 1968 the Programme Agricole Protestant (PAP), a cooperative effort between the CEFMC (former AMBM/AEFMC), CMCo (former CIM/EMC), and the Church of Christ in the Congo (ECC) Bandundu, was formed in Kikwit. Like SEDA, PAP was created to help peasant farmers increase crop and livestock production. Although these programs ran into difficulties later on, their existence was an indisputable sign that the Congolese Mennonite churches wanted to present a holistic Gospel by addressing not only spiritual needs, but also physical and material needs.

Another visible effect of independence was exodus from rural areas. Although there was some movement towards the cities in the 1950s, this movement was controlled by the colonial government. People from rural areas who wanted to go to the cities had to have an identity booklet, a special permit, a resident permit, a housing card, a work card, a business license, etc.

> **Account of a missionary who was at the Kandala station when it was attacked by Mulele's forces, 1964**:
>
> At the Kandala mission . . . we knew that something was being hatched against the mission and we could have departed, but this time we told ourselves that we were going to stay and suffer with our Congolese friends. And so the moment arrived when Kandala was attacked at night time. We spent the night surrounded by rebels and the whole mission station in flames. My wife and I, two other missionary couples each with a child, a single woman, and two fellow missionary men from other CIM stations spent the night in the maternity amidst the noise, the cries, and the crackling of gunfire. . . . We thank God for giving us the privilege of passing through the test of fire together with our Congolese brothers and sisters. Often, later, when we were in consultations with our church leaders, we heard them say in Giphende: "These people here, we walked with them through the fire. Let's see what counsel they have for us."
> —Jim Betsche[28]

After independence these requirements disappeared, and people from rural areas began to leave the countryside for cities like Kinshasa, Kikwit, Kananga, and Mbuji Mayi in search of employment.

The population of Kinshasa in particular exploded. Whereas the capital had a population of 370,000 in 1957, two or three years after independence the population was estimated at anywhere between 700,000 and 1,300,000.[29] Among them were people from Mennonite stations and villages. After arriving in the urban centers these people found each other and began to form prayer groups. In the late 1960s some of these small Mennonite groups formed churches in the capital city, as we will see in the next chapter. In response to the migration, both of the mission-founded Mennonite church conferences established their headquarters in urban centers. The Mennonite Brethren moved their headquarters from Kafumba to Kikwit and the EMC established its headquarters at Tshikapa.

Fusion Realized

The dialogue and negotiations on the fusion of mission and local church structures continued throughout the decade of the '60s, interrupted at different times and places by the events described above. Congolese Christians continued to press for higher levels of education and greater social action than there had been during the colonial period. The Congolese also wanted to see missionaries working with them in the same structures without discrimination. During consultations between the EMC and CIM at Tshikapa in 1967 the EMC delegates again expressed their desire to see everyone, Congolese and missionaries, working together within a single structure, the structure of the church.

Meanwhile, events in the country as a whole had a significant impact on the churches. Under Mobutu, the government moved towards greater centralization and concentration of power in Kinshasa by creating a single-party state under the Popular Revolutionary Movement or MPR. This in turn influenced developments within the member churches of the Congo Protestant Council. The 48th General Assembly of the CPC held in Kinshasa in March of 1969 passed a resolution on the fusion of mission and church structures into one legally recognized structure, the local church. In addition, the General Assembly recommended organic unity among the member churches as a sign of the spiritual unity that already existed.

A year later, in March of 1970 the General Assembly

Excerpt from an early (1962) agreement between AMBM and AEFMC, concerning the fusion process.

For our church in America, known as the American Mennonite Brethren Church, it is a joy and an honor to work with the AEFMC in the responsibilities given us in the Gospel... We hope that the AEFMC will move forward in its relations of communion with us by taking the laws of the land into account in such a way that no misunderstandings or lack of mutual aid will paralyze our ministry . . . once the AEFMC has its own legal status, AMBM will transfer all responsibility concerning the Church to the AEFMC . . . this agreement will be concluded as soon as the AEFMC will be able to take its God-given responsibility and demonstrate that it is capable of starting properly. At the end of this agreement, AMBM will try to resolve all matters of ownership: buildings and properties that it has kept. Nevertheless, AMBM is not promising to give everything to the AEFMC, but AMBM will make all arrangements as will be decided by its board in Hillsboro, Kansas in the United States of America.[30]

voted to become the National Synod of the Church of Christ in the Congo (ECC). Finally, in January of 1971 the Mennonite Church in the Congo (EMC) and the Congo Inland Mission signed an official fusion document at Djoko Punda, where Mennonite mission work in the Congo had started. CIM ceased to exist as a legal entity and EMC continued the work begun by the first Mennonite missionaries to the Congo.

A group of conservative missionaries—including Mennonites and some Congolese pastors—met in Chicago and Bukavu in response to the creation of the ECC in an attempt to destroy the unity and cooperation among Protestants by forming an Evangelical Alliance of the Congo (AEC). Since this initiative did not come from Congolese, neither the government nor indigenous Christians granted them recognition.

The main reason for forming the AEC was the missionaries' frustration with the fusion decision, which put an end to the existence of missions as institutions in the Congo and called for the transfer of all mission property to the local churches. The goal of the fusion was to encourage missionaries and Congolese to work together within the same structure in order to evangelize and edify the young churches. Unfortunately, some missionaries had a hard time understanding how Baptists, Presbyterians, Mennonites, Methodists, Pentecostals, fundamentalists and other denominations that had relations with the World Council of Churches and the World Evangelical Alliance could work together under one national structure. Despite resistance, however, the ECC was born and this birth was a gift from God; it showed that the Gospel has the power to transcend all barriers. Looking back, the decision of the Belgian government to grant subsidies to Protestant missions and allow them to take over bankrupt mission stations allowed considerable expansion to take place in CIM and AMBM in the '50s.

Mennonite Churches
Under Congolese Leadership, 1971–Present

Church – Mission Relations and Dependency

Relations between Congolese Mennonite churches and North American mission organizations were redefined following the fusion agreements. It

Evolution of the three Mennonite Church Organizations in the Congo.

1. The Central Conference of Mennonites (later General Conference Mennonite Church) and the Defenceless Mennonite Church form the Congo Inland Mission (CIM) in 1912.

    After independence in 1960, CIM ceases to be a legal entity in Congo.
        In Africa,
            EEMC formed in 1960, which becomes
            EMC in 1964, which becomes
            CMZa in 1970, which becomes
            CMCo in 1997 (current designation; relates to AIMM).
        In North America in 1972, CIM becomes
            AIMM (current designation, now a partnership of six
            North American Mennonite conferences)

2. Independent mission beginnings by Mennonite Brethren missionaries are taken over by the American Mennonite Brethren Mission in 1943 (AMBM).

    Foreign and national entities integrate in 1971 and AMBM ceases to exist as a separate entity in Congo.
        In Africa,
            AEFMC is formed, which becomes
            CEFMZ in 1971, which becomes
            CEFMC in 1997 (current designation; relates to MBMSI)
        In North America,
             MBMSI created in 1997 (Mennonite Brethren Mission and
            Services International).

3. A group of Congolese Mennonites in East Kasai organized in 1962, obtained legal recognition as
        AEMSK in 1966, which becomes
        CEM in 1970 (current designation; relates to AIMM).

was up to the Congolese churches to decide on their vision of the future, their objectives and their programs. It was up to the Congolese churches to take the initiative in inviting missionaries and requesting funds according to their priorities, and up to the mission organizations to respond according to their means.

Theoretically, the arrangements were simple and clear, but practically speaking it was much more complicated because there were structures, institutions and programs that depended at least in part on personnel and funds that came from Mennonites in North America. As an older pastor and CMCo leader says: "We grew up in this church. It was always led by the missionaries. We saw the work that was done without knowing where the money with which the missionaries built the infrastructure of the mission came from. . . . The missionaries did a lot of things, but we didn't know the source of what they had."[31] After fusion there was a decrease in the activities of many of the institutions and programs of the Mennonite churches. The number of missionaries diminished, and AIMM and MBMSI reduced their subsidies to the programs of CMCo and CEFMC.

Struggles within CEM and CMCo

Evidently, the problem of adaptation to the new fusion situation was understood in the two churches that had been planted by North American missionaries but not in the Evangelical Mennonite Church (CEM), which had been born out of the troubles in the Kasai provinces from 1959 to 1962. Although most of the members of CEM had come from CIM mission stations, they founded their church without missionaries or external funds. From the start, the members of CEM could count only on their own efforts and resources. Since these former CIM people had decided to create a new Mennonite church in Mbuji Mayi in 1962, there was a certain tension between CEM and CMCo at the beginning. Since AIMM was connected to CMCo by virtue of its history and the fusion agreement, there was no cooperation between CEM and AIMM either. In 1974, however, CEM and CMCo representatives reached a compromise in a meeting that included AIMM representatives. As a result of this agreement, AIMM was free to work with CEM.

> **Transition difficulties, recalled by a leader in the church's literature programme.**
> When the missionaries turned the direction of this department over to us in the '70s, giving their departure as the reason, we experienced many difficulties. ... when [the missionaries] left, ... we didn't have sufficient means or funds to continue with the publication of Christian literature as the missionaries had done in the past. Also, when the machines break down, we don't know what to do because we don't know where the missionaries found the money to maintain and repair them all. Presently, all of the machines that they left have broken down. We don't have the means to repair them. When we address our requests to them, they tell us that they don't have a budget for such things. In the meantime, the work is hampered. [32]

Unfortunately, this renewed cooperation would not last long. In 1976 the director of the Bible Institute that CEM had started not far from Mbuji Mayi ten years previously, Pastor Nkumbi Mudiayi, was removed from his

The Kikwit market

functions and excommunicated by the church following reports concerning his teachings on marriage in this institution that was training future pastors.[33] Just a few years later, however, Pastor Nkumbi was recognized by the ECC and the government as the legal representative of CEM. His election was contested for many years by Pastor Kazadi. Because of the division that ensued, AIMM suspended its relations with CEM.

MCC began to work with Rev. Nkumbi's administration in the mid-'80s. In 1989 a CEM delegation and an AIMM delegation met in Kinshasa and agreed to renew cooperation. This cooperation continued until the mid-'90s when there was another split in the church, this time between those who supported Rev. Nkumbi on the one hand and those such as Rev. Ntumba Kalala (who had served as the first legal representative under Pastor Kazadi) and Rev. Misakabo Nzala, who were in favor of change. This time, Rev. Misakabo was recognized as legal representative by the ECC and the government. In 1998 members of CEM from both sides, meeting in a General Council of Reconciliation, asked for mutual forgiveness following teachings on Mennonite identity by Rev. Kazadi Tshinyama (another Kazadi) of CMCo. Today, CEM continues to work in peace and Rev. Nkumbi, who was not a part of the reconciliation, leads another church group that is not recognized by other Mennonites.

Meanwhile, CMCo had experienced a period of relative stability in the '70s under Pastor Moise Kabangy until his death from cancer in 1979. In 1980 Rev. Mbonza Kikunga, a university graduate in theology, was elected president of CMCo. He was a strong leader with certain gifts, but by the mid-'80s there were growing tensions between his administration and certain church districts and regions. These tensions were due to a number of factors, including the centralization of decision-making powers that had started in the '70s, leadership style, a growing sense of ethnic competition tied to the colonial past, and economic and political deterioration under the Mobutu regime.

In 1987 these tensions resulted in a division of the CMCo into two General Assemblies which in turn resulted in two administrations, both of which claimed to be legitimate. One was represented by Rev. Mbonza; the other by Rev. Tshibulenu Sakayimbo. Faced with the danger of a permanent split, the ECC stepped in and called a Special Assembly in Kinshasa in September of the same year. Unfortunately, Rev. Mbonza did not respond to the invitation of the ECC and consequently, the team led by Rev. Tshibulenu was confirmed. Rev. Mbonza contested the decision and took it to the Justice Department, thereby necessitating a fourth Assembly in 1991. Again, the Tshibulenu team was confirmed. Mbonza then took the case to the Supreme Court and lost, after which he formed a new church called the Mennonite Reformed Episcopal Church in the Congo. This church has no official contacts with other Mennonite churches and is not recognized by the three Mennonite church conferences in the Congo or by international Mennonite bodies. It continues to exist in the area surrounding Tshikapa.

Changes in the Life of the Churches

As we have already observed, one of the effects of independence was the movement of the population towards the urban centers. Many Mennonites arrived in the cities of Kinshasa, Kananga, Mbuji Mayi, and Kikwit in search of employment. At the end of the decade of the '60s several Mennonite Brethren started two groups in Kinshasa, one at the home of Tumbula and his spouse Esther Funda at Bumbu and the other at the home of Mbayanvula at Ngaba. In December of 1971, these two groups formed the central committee of the Mennonite Brethren churches for the city of Kinshasa. Today, the result of this initiative by Congolese Mennonite Brethren is the existence of more than forty congregations that are healthy and self-sustaining, despite the economic and political difficulties in the Congo.

Members of CMCo also settled in Kinshasa, but it was especially the opening of the Evangelical School of Theology (ETEK) in 1969-70, a cooperative effort of six Protestant church bodies including CMCo and CEFMC and successor to the theology school at Kajiji, that stimulated the planting of CMCo churches in the capital city. CMCo students at ETEK such as Kabongo Bukasa, Kikunga Mavula, and Malembe Tshingudi, together with professors Peter Falk and Peter Buller, contributed significantly to the opening of the first churches that eventually went on to organize themselves into three ecclesiastical districts: Matete, Ngaba, and Sanga Mamba (Ngaliema).

The establishment of churches in Kinshasa and other cities brought remarkable changes in the life of the church. As was noted earlier, Mennonite Christians found each other in the cities, started prayer groups and eventually formed churches. At first they worshipped as they always had in the rural Mennonite churches that they came from. They sang the songs that had been translated from English and German, songs that had been introduced along with the message of salvation. The use of African instruments was forbidden. For example, the use of a drum was considered a sin, because the drum was associated with pagan practices.

However, these Mennonite Christians in urban centers had planted churches next to other churches such as Pentecostal churches. These other churches

---

A sample of hymns translated by Mennonite Missionaries into local languages.

Blessed be the name
Revive us again
There shall be showers of blessing
Blest be the tie that binds
God is love (Gott ist die Liebe)
Trust and obey
Draw me nearer
What a friend we have in Jesus
More about Jesus
Take the name of Jesus with you
I surrender all
In the harvest field
Bringing in the sheaves
Sweet by-and-by (funeral)
When the roll is called
    up yonder (funeral)
Standing on the promises
The Comforter has come

Song based on John 10, written in January 1991 for the installation service of the new CEFMC leadership team in the National and the Northern District Offices.[33]

Who is the Shepherd? (*Nani Mvungi na nge?*)
By Malumalu

Solo Alto Tenor:
Who is the shepherd?
All: The shepherd is the one
Who takes care of all the sheep.
He must know each sheep by its name
And the sheep know his voice (2x)

Solo: If he enters by the door   Refrain:
All: He is the good shepherd.   The good shepherd must give his life
Solo: If the sheep know him,   For all the sheep.
Solo: If he loves all the sheep,   When a sheep gets lost, he looks for it.
Solo: He leads them to good pasture,   The good shepherd must know
Solo: He leads them to a good spring.   all the sheep
                                          And the sheep must know him.
Solo: If he enters secretly   When a sheep gets lost, he looks for it.
All: He is a false shepherd.
Solo: If the sheep run away from him,
Solo: If he abandons the sheep when a lion comes
Solo: If he doesn't even have compassion on them
Solo: If he doesn't even have compassion on them.

---

prayed and worshipped in a manner different from the Mennonites and Mennonites began to wonder why. In addition, in the '70s President Mobutu introduced the idea of "authenticity" in the Congo. He invited Congolese to be proud of their culture. The Congolese people were invited to use African names and wear clothing that reflected African cultures rather than Western cultures. During the same period, the Minister of Information and Propaganda organized a forty-eight hour festival of dance in the large Kinshasa stadium. Each tribal group was represented in order to exhibit its music and dances. These events were broadcast live on radio and TV. Representatives from other African countries were invited to attend the festivities. It was from that time on that we began to hear the term "animation" in the churches. African songs accompanied by the rhythm of Congolese drums began to appear in church worship services, first in the cities and then all over.

In the 1980s a "renewal" movement manifested itself in many Congolese churches, including the Mennonite churches. Some of the visible signs of the influence of this movement were teachings that stressed the Holy Spirit and its manifestations, all-night prayer and praise vigils (Veillées de Prière), and prayers during worship where everyone would pray out loud simultaneously. In most cases the movement spread spontaneously. Changes in the manner of praying, singing, teaching and worship were not accepted by everyone. Some leaders embraced the changes, others warned against the dangers of excess, and still others excommunicated those members who advocated the changes, saying that these new ways were not Mennonite. All the difficulties notwithstanding, today almost all Mennonite

Women making soap at Kalonda station, 1977.

churches use traditional instruments and permit certain forms of dance, and many have integrated the new ways of praying and singing into the activities of the church.

Important changes were also taking place regarding the role of women in the churches. One of the precedents observed in the first chapter was

Kafutshi Kakesa (R) with sewing project.

the secondary role of women in the decision-making bodies of the church, despite their immense contribution to missionary work. Congolese Mennonite women recognized the importance of the contribution of women to the life of the church and organized themselves. From the '80s on there were departments of women's works in the structures of the Mennonite churches as well as Mennonite women's associations at the level of the local church or parish, the district, the provinces and the national church bodies. These departments and associations organized seminars in evangelism, public health and community development. In the CMCo, for example, Kafutshi Mulebo (spouse of Samuel Kakesa) was a dynamic leader in the church and, beginning in the 1970s, conducted seminars on the role of women in the church. In most Mennonite churches the majority of active members were women who contributed greatly to the life and growth of the churches.

During the 1980s, women started to enroll in the Bible and theological schools. In 1984 Léonie Kelendende (daughter of Pastor Pierre Kelendende of Kandala) was the first CMCo woman to graduate with a degree in theology with honor from the Superior Theological Institute of Kinshasa (ISTK). The first CEFMC woman to graduate with a theology degree was Kadi Hayalume. Slowly, other Mennonite women followed their example

Baba Madiwasa Yongo teaching a women's seminar on leadership,
Kalonda station.

by choosing theological studies. In November of 2001, sixteen Mennonite women theologians gathered in Kinshasa to address the problems of Congolese Mennonite women theologians. At the end of the gathering they formed the Association of Congolese Mennonite Women Theologians (ATMCo). Pastor Kadi Hayalume was elected president, Pastor Ngombe Kidinda was elected vice-president, and Pastor Swana Falanga was elected secretary. These three went on to represent Congolese Mennonite women at a gathering of African Mennonite and Brethren in Christ women held in Bulawayo, Zimbabwe from July 31 to August 1, 2002.

In addition to the women's movement in the Congolese Mennonite churches, we must also note the lay movement. After the fusion agreement in the CMCo at the beginning of the '70s the General Secretary and the Legal Representative were two distinct and separate positions of responsibility at the head of the church. In order to become General Secretary one had to be a pastor, but in order to become Legal Representative one could be a lay person. At some point, there was confusion and tension surrounding the job descriptions of these two positions and in order to avoid such tension, the General Secretary of the time, Rev. Kabangy, convinced the General Council of the church to modify the constitution of the church by combining the two positions into one. From that time on, the same person was both General Secretary (today President) and Legal Representative, and in order to be eligible one had to be a pastor. This decision had far-reaching implications.

To some lay members, this seemed to be a clericalization of the church. One lay member of the church during Rev. Mbonza's leadership wrote:

In 1969 an interest group revised the constitution with the intention of pushing lay intellectuals aside from church administration in order to institute a clerical system in contradiction with the declaration of the Bible in I Corinthians 12:4-11. . . . To refresh our memories, from the beginning of the sixteenth century Anabaptist Mennonites included intellectuals, theologians and university professors who approached the Word of God with simple hearts. So it is that in Mennonite churches one finds lay preachers next to pastors..., all equally consecrated for God's ministry and recognized as such by the local assembly according to their gifts. . . . We are all called to put our spiritual and material gifts at the service of the church according to need. Consequently, we must be prudent with the system of clergy that we are instituting in our Christian community.[35]

This kind of critique did not just come from lay members. In a memorandum addressed to the CEFMC, Kinshasa pastors stated:

We recommend that the General Assembly rehabilitate the position of administrative secretary at all levels of the church. We have to stop bureaucratizing the ministry of evangelization. . . . We also hope that the spirit of teamwork, cooperation, and unity will characterize all of those in charge of the administration of the church.[36]

Several factors help us understand the evolution of the tension between clergy and laity. When missionaries were in leadership, those who engaged in spiritual tasks often (though not always) occupied the positions of leadership. In addition to this precedent, the ECC, under the influence of the Mobutu government that wanted to centralize power even in the churches, exerted pressure on its member churches to adopt more or less uniform administrative structures—a tendency that the Mennonite churches did not escape. Whatever the reasons, feeling marginalized by the structures of the Mennonite churches, starting especially in the '80s, lay members organized themselves to express their views on the problems of the church and to be able to contribute their spiritual and material gifts to the work of the Mennonite churches. Thanks to this movement, dynamic lay movements exist today at all levels of each Mennonite church conference in the Congo. More progress is needed, but today lay members are represented in most of the decision-making bodies of the church.

Lay people had always been involved as teachers, nurses, elders, deacons, ushers, and so forth, but the decade of the '80s marked a turning point for Mennonite churches in the Congo in terms of community development work. Several young people of the CEFMC can be named as examples of this new involvement.

After finishing his master's degree in public health, Pakisa Tshimika returned to Kajiji in August of 1980 to become the first non-missionary and university graduate to work as administrator of a 150-bed hospital, serving a population of more than 80,000 people. Denis Matshifi followed just a few months later to become the first non-missionary physician in the CEFMC medical work. We should note that at about the same time, two young Congolese medical doctors, Makina Nganga and Keta Binze, started working in the CMCo. When Pakisa Tshimika later got his doctorate in public health and Matshifi his master's degree, they helped CEFMC establish DESADEC, the Department of Health and Development. This department helps the church think about ways to minister to the whole person by supervising hospitals, raising livestock, organizing small credit unions, and so forth. Others such as Toss Mukwa, Bertin Adingite, and Albert Tshiseleka became involved, with Tshiseleka replacing Pakisa Tshimika as coordinator of DESADEC. Maurice Matsitsa, who was director of a carpentry school, became Pakisa's assistant when Pakisa was appointed Director for Africa for MBMSI. In 1996 DESADEC expanded to include a woman, Charlotte Djimbo (granddaughter of Pastor Djimbo), in the development service.

In addition to increasing the number of Congolese medical doctors and nurses in church-run public health programs, the CMCo also created a Department of Service and Development which included agricultural and community development, a garage for maintaining vehicles, a cattle raising project, building projects and so on under the leadership of lay members such as Lovua Mujito and Bambedi. CEM also started development work, inviting an MCC volunteer couple to work with the Mbuji Mayi area churches in ox traction and other areas.

A New Vision of Partnership and Mission

One of the most encouraging changes to take place in the three Mennonite church conferences in the Congo since the 1980s is the emergence of a missionary vision accompanied by the planting of new Mennonite churches where there had been none before. In East Kasai, CEM was growing not only in Mbuji Mayi but also in the countryside. The AIMM delegation that visited Mbuji Mayi in 1989, for example, was welcomed by large groups of enthusiastic members of CEM's urban and rural congregations. CEM also planted churches in Katanga province to the south.

CMCo's Mbuji Mayi churches also planted new churches in Katanga as well as in the Mwena Ditu area among the Kanyoka people. In West Kasai CMCo planted new churches along the railroad in Tshimbulu, Kananga, Mweka, and Ilebo. Mennonite Christians from the Tshikapa area also planted churches among the Angolans and Congolese who were in search of diamonds on the Angola side of the Congo/Angola border. In spite of the civil war in Angola, the inhabitants of both countries crossed back and forth regularly. The presence of diamonds in Angola stimulated a population movement that included Congolese Mennonites, resulting in the planting of Mennonite churches along the border by both Congolese pastors and lay members.

Diamonds were in abundance also in Bandundu province and consequently, there was a population movement in search of work. In Bandundu, members of CEFMC and CMCo planted Mennonite churches in Angola, but also around Kahemba and Tembo. At about the time that Mennonite churches were being planted on the Angolan side of the border in both Kasai and Bandundu, Mennonites were also planting churches among the Angolan refugees who had fled the war for independence and the civil war that followed.

The birth of CEFMC churches at Tembo goes back to the '60s when several Christians began to meet in the open air underneath a tree. The

Kinzamba couple and their friend Kilungu were the pioneers. The work was later reinforced by Deacon Kiluma, who had been sent by Pastor Mbedi. Deacon Kiluma was succeeded by Kashitu Mboyi-Mboyi and the number of believers grew. Today the average attendance at the Tembo church is 800 and there are other churches at Ngombi-Ntumba, Nzashi-Mwadi, Zenga, Kabwanga, and Kabela.[37]

Up until the 1980s the Congolese Mennonite churches for the most part concentrated on maintaining the work started by missionaries, which demanded an immense amount of time, energy and resources. During the '80s, however, Congolese Mennonites began to ask questions about the possibility of sharing the Gospel beyond ethnic and national boundaries. Several developments explain this emerging vision— the graduation of a large number of Mennonite students in theology during the '70s and '80s, the active participation of lay members in the decisions of the church, the contributions of Mennonite students who had engaged in cross-cultural ministries outside of the Congo, the creation of a center of missiology by Dr. Nzash Lumeya, the creation of mission departments in the Mennonite churches, and the search for new models of cooperation between Congolese and North American churches.

Over the years Congolese Mennonites became increasingly involved in the Mennonite World Conference. The first evidence of Congolese participation goes back to 1967 when Rev. David Ngongo and Nicodème Tshilembu represented the EMC (now CMCo) at the MWC assembly in Amsterdam. In 1972, Samuel Kakesa and his wife Kaftushi Francoise represented the Congo Church at the Mennonite World Conference in Curitiba, Brazil. Since the '80s all three Mennonite church conferences in the Congo have been actively involved in the Mennonite World Conference. Leaders from all three conferences, such as Rev. Mbonza of CMCo, Rev. Nkumbi of CEM, Rev. Masolo of CEFMC, and Rev. Fimbo (current president of CMCo) have served as members of the Executive Committee of MWC. Currently, Dr. Pakisa Tshimika is on the MWC staff.

Meanwhile, the three Mennonite churches in the Congo—CMCo, CEFMC, and CEM—have created a new structure for cooperation, the National Inter-Mennonite Committee (CONIM), due in part to the inspiration of Pastor Mukanza Ilunga. Representatives of the three churches participated in the sessions of the MWC Council in Filadelphia, Paraguay in July of 1987. There they issued a joint statement to Council members expressing their desire to create an organization in the Congo that would serve as a channel for promoting the Anabaptist Mennonite vision of the Church and society and a means of coordinating activities, such as mutual aid and fraternal gatherings, in order to strengthen the ties of unity among Congolese Mennonites. This idea was reinforced by an inter-Mennonite seminar on peace organized by Rev. Mukanza Ilunga at the Bondeko Center in Kinshasa in October of 1987.

On December 11, 1987, the National Inter-Mennonite Committee was officially formed

Rev. Mukanza Ilunga

under the impetus of Rev. Mukanza.[38] Since its inception, CONIM's staff has organized a variety of programs and activities such as peace education, training and information on the Anabaptist vision, research and documentation on the identity of Mennonite churches in Africa, and inter-Mennonite consultations.

The 1994 genocide in Rwanda provoked a flood of refugees in the Eastern part of the Congo. In response, Mennonites from Africa, North America and Europe mobilized to provide humanitarian aid. An international and inter-Mennonite team called Inter-Mennonite Volunteers (VIM) including three Congolese Mennonites—Ngolo, Clément, and Mukambu—participated in the distribution of aid with the logistical support of MCC. Following the emergency relief work, they began to provide spiritual care to the refugees, centred on peace education.

This Mennonite contribution was so appreciated that after about six months the ECC in South Kivu asked the VIM team to plant Mennonite churches in order to continue the work of peace education among this population traumatized by the violence of genocide. Fidèle Lumeya and his spouse Krista, an MCC couple, went to Bukavu to work for several years to continue the work of VIM. Together with a Mennonite Brethren lay person, Dr. Kalumuna, they started a small Mennonite church. Dr. Kalumuna and his family were members of a small CEFMC church in Kinshasa that supported them spiritually and financially in their vision of going to Bukavu to be a part of this emerging church ministry. In the meantime, the request of the South Kivu ECC was passed on to CONIM and the members of the three Congolese Mennonite churches agreed to start mission work in South Kivu along with their partners, that is MCC, AIMM, and MBMSI. The first Congolese missionary family, the Begelas, were sent to Bukavu in 1997. Today there is another Mennonite family, the Mayoto family, that is working in Kivu in the name of all Congolese Mennonites. Five churches have been planted thanks to the peace witness of VIM volunteers and the missionaries sent by Congolese Mennonites. This work is called the Mission Project in the Great Lakes.

In 1997, Mennonites in Kinshasa initiated yet another mission outreach when thousands of refugees from Brazzaville, the capital of the other Congo, crossed the river to find refuge in Kinshasa. Julie Majiya, a woman who had obtained her degree from the University Center of Missiology, participated in distributing food aid and providing spiritual care to the refugees. When political conditions in Congo-Brazzaville improved, the refugees returned to their country and sent a request for Majiya to come and work among them. Today she is planting a Mennonite church in Brazzaville.

Several members of CMCo also started providing spiritual and material care to a group of Brazzaville refugees who were temporarily housed close to CMCo property at Kintambo-Magasin. After those refugees returned to Brazzaville they made one visit to see them, but this project did not continue. However, members of CMCo, like members of CEFMC, have since started church planting work among the Teke people not far from Kinshasa. Since this work started, more than 40 persons have been baptized and 600 persons have been reached by the Gospel.

It should also be mentioned that the CEFMC has started mission work among the Batwa people of the equatorial rain forest as well as among Muslims in Kinshasa. Currently CEFMC is involved in several partnership projects with MBMSI. The CEFMC and MBMSI have sent a Congolese Mennonite family to Angola to work under the international program of MBMSI. The Masolo family is assisting the Angolan churches in evangelism and church planting as well as leadership training. As a result of another partnership project, CEFMC and MBMSI have sent a Congolese missionary to work under AIMM in Burkina Faso. A third type of partnership is represented by a team made up of Congolese and North Americans working among Congolese refugees in South Africa under CEFMC, MBMSI and MCC. In all of these projects, Congolese churches contribute human and spiritual resources, whereas the North American churches contribute primarily financial and material resources.

Another recent development is the establishment of contacts between Congolese Mennonite churches and Francophone churches in Europe and Canada with the idea of creating a Francophone Mennonite network. This idea is supported by Mennonite World Conference and several meetings have taken place. A Francophone delegation from Europe and Canada visited the Congo, and Congolese Mennonites have also visited Europe.

Congolese Mennonites are playing a leading role in the process of peace education and conflict transformation. The Great Lakes project is the best known and most visible of these efforts, along with the program of CONIM. In addition, at the end of the 1980s, Pastor Erik Kumedisa created a theological study center for peace (CETP or Centre d'Etudes Théologiques pour la Paix). In 1994 this center became the African Institute of Conciliation (INAC or Institut Africain de Conciliation) with the purpose of developing information on the use of nonviolent approaches to resolve conflict.

When Mzée Laurent Desiré Kabila came to power in 1997, a time when violence and the recruitment of child soldiers into the armed forces were beginning to take root, a group of Congolese Mennonites began a public awareness peace education campaign through posters at the initiative of Dr. Pakisa Tshimika. Posters saying "No to violence, Yes to peace" were placed in Kinshasa and other cities. After working under VIM in South Kivu among the refugees from Rwanda, Pastor Mukambu created what was called the Program for Peace Education and Conflict Resolution (PEPR or Programme d'Education à la Paix et Résolution des conflits) in order to organize educational seminars for the public. Other Mennonites such as Kumakamba Mimboro and Felo attended training seminars in Nairobi, Kenya. After the training, Felo founded an ecumenical peace association (AJPR) in Kikwit. Finally, at the conclusion of a seminar held in Kinshasa in December of 1998, the participants created a Council for Peace and Reconciliation in the Congo (CPRC). In a country at war since

1996, Congolese Mennonites are actively engaged in peace education and nonviolent conflict resolution.

In the field of university education, the Superior Theological Institute of Kinshasa (ISTK) was created to train pastors from six participating member denominations including CEFMC and CMCo. This institution was created with overseas personnel and funds, so when the number of missionary professors diminished and subsidies were reduced in the late '70s and '80s, ISTK entered a period of financial and management crisis. This crisis pushed the board of directors to transform the institution into the Christian University of Kinshasa (UCKin or Université Chrétienne de Kinshasa) by adding the two year "license" program to the already existing three year "graduat" program in theology, as well as by adding other departments to the department of theology. With the participation of the CEFMC and CMCo, the Christian University of Kinshasa opened its doors to new students in January of 1996 with the vision of contributing to the education of Christian leaders in various fields and, through these leaders, to the development of the churches and the nation. The first rector of this new Christian university was Dr. Kidinda Shandungu, the son of a Mennonite pastor. Today there is another rector, but Mennonites continue to participate actively in the management of UCKin and a significant number of Mennonite students are enrolled there.

UCKin is not the only university with Mennonite students, however. There are hundreds of Mennonite students in state-run universities and colleges as well as in the many private universities that came into being in the 1990s. During the 1997-98 academic year, Noel Kuka initiated a Mennonite student organization called "Fraternité des Etudiants Mennonites" or FEM. The objectives of FEM are to facilitate gatherings of Mennonite students so that they can get to know each other better and address their concerns to the Mennonite churches as a group.

Conclusion

Fusion between local church and North American mission structures was followed by a period during which Congolese Mennonite churches confronted the legacy of the missionary past. The process of redefining church-mission relations in the post-missionary era continues to this day. The problems posed by dependency, however, need to be qualified. First, dependency affected CMCo and CEFMC—the two churches that inherited the work of CIM/AIMM and AMBM/MBMSI— but dependency was not a factor for CEM, a Mennonite church born almost exclusively of Congolese initiative and resources. Secondly, even within CMCo and CEFMC, the problem has been exaggerated. While different centrally- administered programs and institutions do indeed struggle to survive with insufficient resources in extremely difficult economic and political conditions, local congregations, church districts, and many regional programs have been and continue to be entirely self-sustaining.

In addition to the legacy of the past, Mennonite churches have struggled with internal divisions due to leadership styles as well as the centralization of decision-making powers. This has been followed by increasing ethnic competition and a push for decentralization in face of ever diminishing material and financial resources. These divisions have at times required government or ECC intervention and have resulted in the birth of unrecognized churches led by former Mennonite church leaders.

At the same time, many exciting positive changes have taken place in the life of the churches. Thanks to urban migration, the influence of the government's "authenticity" programme, and renewal movements, the styles and to some extent the content of preaching, prayer, and worship have changed significantly, reflecting a more authentically African expression. Women have always been active participants in the life of the church, but in recent decades they have organized themselves into a dynamic movement, encouraging young women to pursue their studies in all fields, including theological education. Lay members have also organized themselves in order to better contribute their spiritual, intellectual and material gifts to building the church through evangelism, public health, community development and higher education.

Finally, all three Mennonite churches have crossed traditional ethnic and national boundaries individually and in joint mission with each other and Mennonites around the world. The churches are experimenting with a variety of new paradigms in cross-cultural evangelism and church planting, as well as in peace education and conflict transformation. One of the results of this new vision is the birth and development of Mennonite churches in Eastern Africa, as will be noted later in this volume.

Notes

[1] G. Kajiga, *Untu et son apport universel* (Kinshasa: Edition Diocésaine, 1968), 35.

[2] Jan Vansina, *Kingdoms of the Savanna* (Madison: University of Wisconsin Press, 1966), 52.

[3] Ngongo Leteta facilitated the Arab conquest of the Kasai. The name "Ngongo" came from a Tetela chief and the name "Letela" from the verb meaning to travel.

[4] Leopold II's regime divided the land in Congo into three categories: indigenous land for the subsistence of the indigenous people; vacant land that belonged to him; and land that he would grant as concessions to third parties.

[5] Basil Davidson, *Africa in Modern History* (Editions françaises J.A., 1979), 74.

[6] *Ibid.*, 14.

[7] For a fascinating account of the role of American Presbyterians in this campaign, read Stanley Shaloff's *Reform in Leopold's Congo* (John Knox Press, 1970). For a more comprehensive account of Leopold's atrocities, see Adam Hochschild, *King Leopold's Ghost: A Story of Greed, Terror, and Heroism in Colonial Africa* (New York: Houghton Mifflin Co., 1998).

[8] Much of this information comes from Peter Falk's *The Growth of the Church in Africa* (Grand Rapids, MI: Zondervan, 1979), 366-73. For the revised and edited French version, see *La croissance de l'Eglise en Afrique* (Grand Rapids, MI: Zondervan, 1985), 331-40. Also in French, see *"Le Rôle de l'Eglise Chrétienne en Afrique Noire. Les Missions Protestantes,"* in *Le Monde Non Chrétien* No. 5 (janvier-mars, 1948): 582-613.

[9] Emile Vandervelde, a member of the Belgian Parliament, vigorously criticized this method of evangelization during the 1911-1912 session, saying that missionaries captured by force those who fled.

[10] Makanzu Mavumilusa, *The Power of the Cross in Zaire [Congo]* (Kinshasa: Editions JAPEMAK, 1978), 54.

[11] Reported by Fimbo Gavunze in " L'impact du christianisme au Zaïre à travers l'oeuvre de la Communauté Mennonite (1911–1987)," *Mémoire (non-publié) de maîtrise présenté à la Faculté de Théologie Evangélique de Bangui*, Bangui, juillet 1989, ix –140.

[12] Melvin Loewen, *Threescore: The Story of an Emerging Mennonite Church in Central Africa* (Elkhart, IN: CIM, 1972), 42, 62.

[13] Rev. Mayambi Diakande, from an interview at Nyanga in January 2001.

[14] From a conversation with Pastors Mukoso, Giwoma, Mabaya, Shindanyi, Kusangila, and Ndunda in Kikwit in February 2001.

[15] Dr. Keta Mbinze, Interview at Kalonda hospital in January 2001.

[16] Conversation with Pastors Mukoso, Giwoma, Mabaya, Shindanyi, Kusangila, and Ndunda in Kikwit in February 2001.

[17] Lamin Sanneh, *Translating the Message: The Missionary Impact on Culture* (Maryknoll, NY: Orbis, 1989), 160-161.

[18] Jim Bertsche, interview in Elkhart, Indiana, June 2001.

[19] In transferring the stations, UTM included four stipulations: 1) take care of their cattle, 2) access to the Ecole Belle Vue mission school near Kajiji, 3) ability to continue their work with AMBM and CIM on these mission stations, and 4) the right to stay in the mission cottages at Ecole Belle Vue during their vacation periods. (Kajiji

is high in elevation and much cooler than surrounding areas.) Garry Prieb, AIMM, email, June 2, 2003.

[20] E. M. Braekman, *Histoire du protestantisme au Congo* (Brussels: Librairie des Eclaireurs, 1961), 339-48.

[21] Crawford Young, *Politics in the Congo* (Princeton: Princeton University Press, 1965), 149-50.

[22] Peter Buller, interview at Elkhart, Indiana, June 2001.

[23] Jim Bertsche, quoting Harvey Driver, CIM Executive Secretary at the time, interview at Elkhart, Indiana, June, 2001.

[24] Jim Bertsche, interview at Elkhart, Indiana, June 2001.

[25] George W. Carpenter, *Les chemins du Seigneur au Congo (1878–1953)* (Leopoldville: LECO, 1953), 59-78.

[26] Rev. David Ngongo, interview at Nyanga, January 2001.

[27] Jim Bertsche, interview at Elkhart, Indiana, June 2001.

[28] Jim Bertsche, interview at Elkhart, Indiana, June 2001.

[29] Young, *Politics in the Congo*, 209.

[30] Excerpt from an unclassified document in the archives of the headquarters of the CEFMC in Kikwit.

[31] Rev. Mayambi Diakande, interview at Nyanga, December, 2000.

[32] Rev. Ntumba Kafunda, interview at Tshikapa, December, 2000.

[33] It was reported that Pastor Nkumbi viewed Old Testament patterns of polygamy sympathetically. Counsel failed, and Pastor Nkumbi was excommunicated. See Jim Bertsche, *CIM/AIMM: A Story of Vision, Commitment, and Grace* (Elkhart: AIMM, 1998), 407.

[34] Mary Anne Isaak, "A description of the theology expressed in song of the Mennonite Brethren Church of Zaïre (Congo Démocratique)," Thesis for the degree Master of Arts, Fresno, Mennonite Brethren Biblical Seminary, April 1993.

[35] Lamba-a-Gindamba, "L'instabilité: base de confusion et d'incompréhension dans la Communauté Mennonite au Congo," Open letter to the members of the church written around 1987.

[36] Excerpt from a memorandum addressed by Kinshasa pastors to the General Assembly of the CEFMC held in Kikwit from August 25 to 31, 1993, 22.

[37] Lutondo Matulanda, Final thesis, ISTK, July 1990, 32-33.

[38] Rev. Mukanza served for a number of years as a member of the International Peace Commission of Mennonite World Conference.

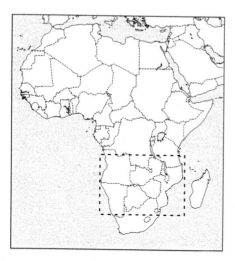

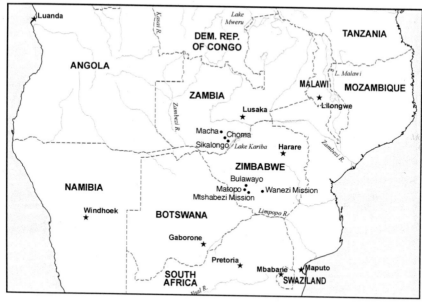

Southern Africa

Brethren in Christ Churches in Southern Africa

by Bekithemba Dube, Doris Dube and Barbara Nkala

Introduction

Zimbabwe occupies 390,757 square kilometers between the Zambezi and Limpopo rivers, and is situated in a tropical climate zone with a population of about eleven million people. These eleven million are made up of a ninety-eight percent black majority, a small Asian population and people of European stock (still referred to as Europeans), who make up 1% of the population. The majority of the peasant population is engaged in subsistence farming. Maize (corn) is the staple food and the main agricultural product, along with ground nuts and beans. Maize is also grown commercially by some black farmers and the mainly white commercial farming sector. Other agricultural activities include cattle, goat and sheep rearing. Zimbabwe produces her own milk, poultry and pork. Cattle are still a symbol of wealth among the black population.

The first known occupants of Zimbabwe were Stone Age people who lived off game and fruit of the wild. These cave dwellers left behind an array of paintings found in caves across the country. The Matopo hills have a fair share of these cave paintings. Inside some of these caves archaeologists also found chips of quartzite that were used as knives and arrow heads. The Bantu people from East Africa then occupied Zimbabwe, over 1000 years ago, pushing the San people further south and west to the desert. Those that were at the forefront, like the Xhosa of South Africa and to a lesser extent the rest of the Nguni, adopted clicks into their languages. The Nguni are a group of languages such as Zulu, SiSwati and the Sindebele language in Zimbabwe.

Zimbabwe is a name derived from *Dzimbadzemabwe* (Shona) meaning "houses of stones." The Great Zimbabwe is the largest of about

119

five hundred mortarless stone structures found in many places around Zimbabwe. One such ruin was found to the northwest of the Brethren in Christ (BIC) Wanezi Mission. A remaining wall was identified as *"imithangala kaMambo"* – the stone walls of Mambo – which was the royal name given to rulers of the Rozvi. Also in the vicinity is a former iron smelting plant, of which many can be found throughout Zimbabwe, attributed to the Rozvi people. The Rozvi (The Destroyers), a Bantu group led by the Mambo dynasty, occupied western Zimbabwe centuries before the coming of the AmaNdebele to western Zimbabwe. Other groups that preceded were the Birwa of Sotho descent, the Venda and the Mbire, ancestors to the present day Karanga. The Rozvi rule was broken by the wandering Swazi groups that came into the country from the south during the *Lifaqane/Mfecane* disturbances of the eighteenth to the nineteenth centuries.[1]

The AmaNdebele people originated in the place now called Kwazulu-Natal in South Africa under the leadership of Mzilikazi the son of Matshobana. They left Zululand at the beginning of the nineteenth century after their leader Mzilikazi quarrelled with Tshaka, founder of the Zulu nation under whom Mzilikazi was a general. He settled for a time at Mosega in the area now occupied by the city of Pretoria. While in this area he had to fight the Boers, a group of farmers of Dutch descent who were moving to the African hinterland to escape subjugation by the British who controlled the Cape. In addition to the Boers, Mzilikazi had to ward off attacks from Zulus sent by Dingani, the brother successor of Tshaka. It was here that Mzilikazi was visited by Robert Moffat, a London Missionary Society missionary to Kuruman in Botswana whom the AmaNdebele had named "Mtshede." The two were friendly. For the first time the AmaNdebele were exposed to the Gospel of Jesus Christ. Moffat told Mzilikazi about the open savannah lands across the Limpopo where he would be able to live in peace without harassment by either the Boers or the Zulus.[2] Mzilikazi then moved to the area which the AmaNdebele called *Budlanondo*—the place where the people eat worms—a reference to *amacimbi,* the Mophane/ Mnondo worms that are a delicacy of the area.[3]

As Mzilikazi advanced, he added more people to his group. Those who left Zululand with him were the *abeNguni* or *abeZansi* (those of the South), the *Abenhla* (those of the North) who were composed mainly of the Sotho-Tswana, and the *amaHole,* the Kalanga-Rozvi and other people

120

of Shona descent. Such people were scattered across Zimbabwe, particularly the south from Masvingo to Plumtree. However, those who were mainly in the Matopo hills became part of the AmaNdebele nation state. Mzilikazi died in 1868 and was succeeded as king by his son Lobengula in 1870.

The First and Second Uprisings

Prior to 1890, European hunters and prospectors had made incursions into the territory of AmaNdebele and the neighbouring Mashona. Neither Mzilikazi or his son Lobengula who reigned after him were keen on having the white man settle in their land. The final occupation of the area came in 1890 when a group calling itself the pioneers passed through the south of Matabeleland to settle in Salisbury (Harare). Two wars were fought against the settlers. The first was the *Imfazo 1* of 1893 (Matabele Uprising). At the end of this war, the second king Lobengula, "disappeared like a ground worm," as the AmaNdebele would say, "and was never seen again." The second war of resistance to White occupation, *Imfazo 2* (Matabele and Mashona Rebellion) was fought towards the end of 1896. It was after this *Imfazo 2* that the BIC missionaries came to preach the Gospel of Jesus Christ. At this time, most of the AmaNdebele were in the Matopo hills where they had taken refuge from the war.

Because of the war, the AmaNdebele mistrusted the white man. At a national level, there never was integration between the black people and the Whites. The Whites ended up occupying the better lands, mainly on the plateau. Even lands in the Matopo Hills were affected by the forced relocation of the AmaNdebele from their lands. This situation of racial tension would affect the life of the BIC church in Zimbabwe for many decades after the arrival of the missionaries.

Enter the BIC Church

The BIC originated in the United States of America in the state of Pennsylvania among the German-speaking community of Anabaptist/ Mennonite background. After expanding westward further into the U.S. hinterland and northward into Canada, the BIC began considering missions to foreign lands in the 1890s.

The BIC were not the first missionary agency to come to Zimbabwe. The very first missionary to the country of Zimbabwe had been a Jesuit missionary, Gonzalo da Silveira, who came to the kingdom of Mwenemutapa in 1560. He was martyred by Mwenemutapa at the instigation of Muslim traders who told the king that Silveira practiced witchcraft. They were supported by the traditional religious leaders, the *ngangas* (African doctors) and *mhondoros* (territorial spirit mediums).[4]

The next missionaries came some centuries later, when the London Missionary Society arrived in 1859 under the leadership of Robert Moffat who was then based at Kuruman in "Bechuanaland" (now Botswana). The Dutch Reformed came to Morgenster near Masvingo in 1872. The Society of Jesuits opened their mission near Old Bulawayo in 1880; the Salvation Army came in 1882; the Anglicans arrived in 1888. By 1906 Methodists, Adventists, Swedish Lutherans, the Church of Christ, Scottish Prebyterians and others had entered what had come to be called Rhodesia. Cecil Rhodes (1853-1902), the diamond magnate of South Africa, had arranged the annexation of Bechuanaland (Botswana) to the British Empire and in 1888 negotiated mining rights with Lobengula, ruler of Matabeleland (Zimbabwe). His British South Africa Company increasingly controlled what is now Zimbabwe and Zambia, named Southern and Northern Rhodesia in 1894.

Most churches that came after the colonial occupation worked among the people, aggressively preaching the gospel and opening institutions of learning and health to serve the needs of the nationals. This included the Brethren in Christ church. In the period after the Second World War, Pentecostal churches came, and after the independence of Zimbabwe in 1980 there was a proliferation of independent churches established by nationals.

The Church Planting Years, 1898-1920

The first group of BIC missionaries—four women and one man—left New York for Africa on the 24th of November 1897. They were Jesse Engle and his wife, Hannah Frances Davidson and Alice Heisey. A fifth member of the team, Barbara Hershey, ended up working in Johannesburg with another mission, having felt the call to move in that direction after reaching

Cape Town. When the missionaries left the United States they did not know exactly where they were going, except that they were going somewhere in Africa. At sea they heard about the land north of the Limpopo occupied by the AmaNdebele which did not have any missionaries working among them. Hannah Frances Davidson recalled her feeling for the African people: "A spark of Divine love for them had entered before we even set foot on the African shores."[5] On arrival in Cape Town the BIC missionaries found out about the AmaNdebele with whom they fell in love. On the advice of a Mrs. Stekesby Lewis, their host in Cape Town, the missionaries talked to Cecil John Rhodes who granted them 3000 acres of land in the Matopo Hills, south of Bulawayo. This is the land on which Matopo Mission stands today. Rhodes, who was bent on colonizing the area north of the Limpopo (which later bore his name) was enthused to see missionaries going into the land of the AmaNdebele. He saw missionaries as part of his strategy of taming the AmaNdebele, but at a cheaper cost than policemen.[6]

The arrival of the BIC missionaries at Matopo on July 7, 1898 came two years after the end of the second war of resistance to White colonial rule in Zimbabwe. These servants of the Lord had left home, family and relatives to bring the Good News of the Lord to this country, but they came to Africa at the same time as colonialism. The British South Africa Company had raised the British flag in Rhodesia (Zimbabwe) less than ten years earlier. The missionaries came to proclaim the Gospel of salvation, but they were viewed by nationals as having the same culture as the colonialists with whom the AmaNdebele had been at war only two years earlier. They were therefore regarded with suspicion. Cecil John Rhodes, who gave them land and permission to work among the AmaNdebele, obviously did not have the same motive as the missionaries. He was out to amass power and land; they were out to win souls.

The message of the missionaries was that people of whatever race were sinners who needed Christ, God's Son, who had shed his blood to save sinners. Intertwined with the message of salvation, the missionaries felt they had the obligation to bring the benefits of education and western civilisation to their converts.

In setting up home, the missionaries soon established a routine. Elder Engle spent the first few months occupied with building and growing an

Jesse Engle sets out with the donkey train.

orchard and a garden to supplement their food. Mother Engle was the homemaker. Hannah Frances Davidson and Alice Heisey were involved in village visitation and school teaching. After finishing their morning chores at the mission, they would go on village visitation, taking with them the young men they had allowed to settle at the mission. Some of these youth included Mlobeki Moyo, Matshuba Ndlovu and Siyaya. They would walk up and down across the hills and rocks to reach the neighbouring villages. On arriving at a village, they would sit and talk to the people, read the word from the Bible, take time to explain the Gospel, and then request permission to pray. The Sindebele language was new to them, yet they needed it to explain the Gospel. Distances to the villages were long, and they soon learned to ride on donkeys to enable them to move with more ease. Jesse Engle also used donkeys to travel to Bulawayo where he went to buy their supplies.

Mlobeki Moyo, one of the first ten to be baptised in 1899, said "As soon as the missionaries arrived, they started preaching to the people. We would visit the people as they were involved in communal labour (*ilima*). The missionaries would join in the work as well." At the end of the work session, the missionaries would request permission to preach. Everywhere they sang the song in Sindebele:

Nang' uJesu, nang' uJesu,	Here comes Jesus, here comes Jesus
Nang' uJesu manje,	Here comes Jesus, right now
Manje, nang' uJesu	Right now, here comes Jesus
Yiza kuye manje.	Come to Jesus right now.

The missionaries were quick to identify the social needs of the people they had come to reach. Disease was rampant, so often it was necessary to treat both body and soul. There had recently been war, hence there was little food. Sometimes the people were faced with starvation. Farming implements were poor, leading to low production. In this country which was in latter times troubled with poor race relations, relations between the missionary and the converts were warm and brotherly. Correspondence from early converts like Sitshokuphi Sibanda to Hanna Frances Davidson shows how those who grasped the Good News saw the missionaries as joint heirs in a kingdom not of this world. Part of relationship-building between the missionaries and their national converts happened as they worked together at the mission, where the nationals learned better farming methods.

The missionaries also faced setbacks, particularly in health matters. Within two years of arrival, Mrs. Cress, who had arrived after the first group of missionaries, and the leader of the group, Jesse Engle, had both died of malaria, in February and April of 1900 respectively. It would seem from the accounts of the early missionaries that Engle could have been saved from that premature death, had the missionaries taken greater care in health matters. There was delay in seeking the assistance of a doctor from Bulawayo, given that travel and communication was not as easy as it is today. Nevertheless, greater care could have been taken.

The Ndebele Response to the Gospel

As the Ndebele came to terms with the Gospel, cultural issues relating to Ndebele beliefs and customs had to be dealt with. Traditional Ndebele religion responded to the problems of disease, death, drought and fertility, by witchcraft and social cohesion. The missionaries (and later the church as a whole) also had to address these issues. How far did the BIC succeed, and how far has it succeeded in incarnating itself in the Ndebele society?

Matopo Mission church, built in 1905

Food and Drink

The conference minutes of 1914 show that traditional food was an issue. Were the new converts allowed to take such drinks as *Utshwala, umhiqo, amahewu, umkumbi* and the like? *Utshwala* was the traditional opaque beer made of corn meal. *Umhiqo* was the non-alcoholic thin porridge used in the manufacture of *Utshwala.* It was non-intoxicating. *Amahewu* was a non-alcoholic drink made by fermenting soft corn porridge in a specified water-to-porridge proportion. *Umkumbi* was a drink made of marula fruit juice which, if left for too long, fermented and became alcoholic. These drinks were used in every day life of the AmaNdebele people. *Utshwala* (beer) was used for traditional ceremonies such as ancestor worship, rain making ceremonies and for entertainment. It, along with other traditional drinks, was given to people who assisted in communal labour *(ilima),* as they tilled their land. It was therefore important that the Christian position be clarified. *Imbeka* was another drink about which the new Christians had to decide in later years. The fundamental question was, can Christians drink alcohol? The missionary answer was simply NO. Among the BIC the answer is still "no" to any intoxicating drink, even today.

Entertainment

Singing and dancing for entertainment also arose as an issue to be dealt with. Singing with dance was, and is, the traditional way of expressing joy and celebrating. According to the conference minutes of 1916, traditional singing and dancing was prohibited. The decision was "The songs sometimes are such as are improper to sing at a Christian gathering." Qedabakwabo, an early convert, published her testimony in *The Evangelical Visitor* of August, 1921. She told how the dancing both she and the people liked so much had to be overcome for her to become a Christian. She could not be a Christian and dance.

Dancing of all kinds continued to be prohibited for a long time among members of the BIC. This was so even at weddings where the Ndebele people would normally dance for joy. At the wedding of Bishop Henry Hershey Brubaker in June 1926 at Mtshabezi Mission, great care had to be taken to make sure that girls were stopped from rejoicing to the point of dancing. Neither was dancing accepted for worship by the missionaries. When Dr. Kaufman played the accordion in the Gwayi in the 1960s, she was was joined by the San people who played their own instruments. Bishop Climenhaga stopped the singing for fear that the San might end up dancing. Today, BIC members are starting to sway to the music during worship, and they now dance without any inhibitions at weddings. They also play musical instruments in worship, both modern and traditional.

Soil Fertility, Farming And Rain-Making

Traditional religion was concerned with farming practices. Should a Christian eat crops where the farmer had mixed his seed with seed obtained from an *inyanga* (African doctor)? This seed could either be obtained from an inyanga or obtained from the Ngwali shrines at the Matopo caves. People would bring a handful of seed to the Ngwali fertility shrine at the

> **Missionaries meet traditional religion.**
> Hannah Frances Davidson is said to have visited the Ngwali shrine at Njelele in the company of Sitshokuphi Sibanda, an early convert and later an active church planter and evangelist who dedicated her whole life to the service of the Lord. Oral history actually has it that Sitshokuphi cut a "sacred" reed that was growing at the shrine. When about two years later there was a drought in the area, she and other Christians were accused of being responsible for the drought. Tradition has it that the Ngwali cursed her and said she would never conceive. Sitshokuphi actually never married.

> **Esta Ndlovu (MaDube) of Maphane, baptized at Dula in 1949, describes her late mother-in-law:**
> My mother-in-law was a prayer warrior. She taught me that if you pray with all your heart God answers. She used to give testimonies of how God was the pillar of her life (*Insika yakhe*). She prayed about the crop production in her field and the education of her children. She prayed virtually about every aspect of her life. At some point, one of her daughters was so sick we thought she would die. Mother-in-law prayed for her healing. She was healed and lived to be a helpful member of the family.
>
> Before sowing in the fields she would pray over the seed. She prayed over the manure before it was carried and scattered in the field. As a result, we always produced a good crop. She was a hard worker as well.
>
> To me all this was a great surprise because I had known my own father to mix his seed with *muthi* (medicines) to ensure a good harvest. This was a completely new approach to living, which saw God at the center of every thing. I had never had an experience like that before.

Matopos, where it would be put together with seed brought by other people and "blessed" by the Ngwali priest. The people would then take a handful of this seed home to mix with their own seed before planting. The purpose of using the "doctored" seed was to ensure a good crop. This was an important ritual in the lives of the AmaNdebele and their neighbours since their land was prone to drought. The church decided that while a Christian could eat food prepared from the resultant crops, the Christian farmer could not follow the customary practice with his own seed.

The question of the fertility of the land is linked to concern about rainfall. In Southern Zimbabwe the rainfall is erratic and cannot be relied upon from season to season. The Ngwali cult found in the area of the Matopo hills is a fertility cult concerned with the issues of human fertility, animal reproduction, crop production and rainfall.

The historian Terrance Ranger quotes an old myth that Musikavanhu (Creator of humans) fell from the heavens landing on the Matopos. This fall led to the Matopos becoming wet and swampy.[7] This was seen to represent the reproductive capacity of the land. The Ngwali shrines at Dula and Zhilo lie within the area in which the Brethren in Christ operate. The other shrine at Njelele is close to the Brethren in Christ community at Dewe, and former BIC stations at Bundule and Sibali were also close to Njelele.[8] Various communities in southern Zimbabwe have officials of the Ngwali system known as *amahosana, imbonga, imondolo* and *abanyayi.*

All these are types of priestly officers related to the Ngwali cult of the Matopos. These act as emissaries between the "Voice at the Rocks" and the various communities. They are responsible for the mobilization of people for the ceremonies related to rainmaking, soil fertility and farming.

Early converts learned to pray to God about every aspect of their lives. Today it is common practice for Christians to lead the community in prayers for rain if the onset of rains has been delayed or if there has been an unusually dry spell, particularly in January. These meetings are held under trees, near a rock or in a Church building. In the case of Mtshabezi, such meetings are sometimes held near the Mtshabezi River. In the towns like Gwanda and Bulawayo, BIC members join other churches to pray for rains in football arenas or in open parks. At Matopo mission, they meet under a *Mkhuna* tree (a local evergreen broad leaf) to the southeast of the mission, or in the church building at the mission. At such times, denominational differences do not matter.

Observing Wednesday as Sacred

Another challenge was observing a day of rest during the week. Wednesday is observed as a day when those who believe in *Ngwali* should not work in the fields. In the past, all this was voluntary. These days, this observance seems to be enforced with great vehemence by those who believe in it. All members of the community, including Christians, are pressured by the local community who suggest that it is against the law of the country to work in one's fields on Wednesdays. Many Christians who have tried to challenge this have been harassed for doing their work on Wednesdays. One interviewee concurred by saying, "In the past people were not forced to observe this day, but now, since independence, they want to force everybody." In effect, it means that rural Christians cannot work on their fields on Sundays which is their Sabbath, or on Wednesdays which is the "traditionalist" day of rest (*Chisi*).[9] This leads to lower productivity.

The question of observing Wednesdays has been a hot issue at many meetings of rural pastors and church leaders, and it has been the subject of discussion at leadership training sessions. Legal experts have been invited to explain the law to people, so that they can defend themselves using the law of the land. To make good use of this traditional day, mid-week prayer meetings are now a characteristic of the BIC in Zimbabwe.

Early converts to the BIC church in Zimbabwe.

Polygamy

Polygamy was a common practice among the AmaNdebele, where many wives were a symbol of status. A well-to-do man with many cattle could marry additional wives if he could pay *lobola* in cattle to the family of his intended wife or wives. A man would also marry a second wife if his first wife was childless. His first wife's family was obliged to give him his wife's brother's daughter to bear children on her behalf. Another reason for polygamy was the taking over of a brother or cousin's wife (or wives) if he died. A woman could also invite her close relations to be junior wives for her husband if she felt they could be guaranteed food security. Thus polygamy was, from the start, a well-established social custom that posed a problem for the BIC church. Over a number of years, the question was debated back and forth between the nationals, the missionaries and the American church.

In the 1970s the question of polygamy came up again when the church reached out to the San people in Tsholotsho. In the 1980s, it came up once again when Maria Tshuma, the veteran evangelist/church planter, was working among the Batonga of the Binga area in Matabeleland North. The position of the BIC church has always been that a polygamist cannot be a full member of the church. Acceptance of polygamists has been opposed particularly by the women because they feel their men would use it as an excuse to take other wives. In all cases, the first wife in a polygamous marriage is not bound by church restrictions. She may be baptised and can be a member of the church. The argument is that she was wronged by her husband and subsequent wife or wives.

Belief in Ancestral Spirits

One of the beliefs that affected the AmaNdebele reception of the Gospel of Christ was their belief in ancestral spirits. First, the concept of ancestors as intercessors made it easy for them to accept Christ as the mediator between humanity and God. On the other hand, the AmaNdebele were preoccupied with the ancestors because to avoid harm by death or disease, the people had to appease the ancestors. Some reasoned with the early missionaries that it was not necessary for them to spend time worshipping Christ since he was a "good spirit" who would do them no harm. They did not need to appease him since he was already on their side. Instead they felt they needed to worry about the demands of the ancestral spirits, who could do them harm.

Fighting

Asked to comment on the changes that the Gospel brought to the AmaNdebele, Timothy Ndlovu, born before the First World War, responded, *"Sasisilwa"* (we used to fight). The AmaNdebele had a culture of fighting. The herd boys, for example, were organised into groups like military regiments for the purpose of fighting boys from other areas, even if the other boys were also Ndebele or even relatives. It was said of the late Rev. Joel Ncube that when he grew up, he would not engage in these fights because he was different. At the head of the group was an *ingqwele* (a type of war lord). An *ingqwele* was one who could out-do all the rest in a bout. Any boy or man had to prove his manhood by out-doing others in a fight to gain the respect of his peers and even the women. This practice came to an end as a result of the impact of the Gospel.

Witchcraft

The fear of witches and practices related to them is as alive today as it was when the missionaries came. In African traditional religion, the *Sangoma* (diviner) is called upon to identify the witch if there is a death or an illness in the home, or if there are problems in the community.[10] From time to time an itinerant prophet appears who, in collaboration with community leadership, conducts activities aimed at exposing witches and wizards. Through supernatural means the prophet identifies these witches and other people who are alleged to possess such items as human parts or "familiars," which assist them in getting rich. These familiars include *Tikolotshes* (believed to be half human and half spirit) said to be obtained from South Africa. Once identified, those who possess these familiars are accused of being responsible for droughts or other misfortunes in the community. Some are accused of causing the deaths of their own relatives and neighbours to attain wealth through supernatural means. This is more the case with those who are apparently well to do. Those who refuse to take part in these witchcraft investigations are accused of hiding the truth about themselves. Some church members believe that there is nothing wrong with the whole practice and rejoice to the point of giving testimonies if they have been found innocent.

Members of the church who are well grounded in their faith and who know their rights have been able to stand against these prophets. The answer to this problem seems to be more Christian education in the Word and in one's legal rights. Another major reason why people are victimized is the problem of fear. With greater confidence in the Lord Jesus Christ, the church members will be able to withstand the test.

Death

The time of death is another period in the life of the Ndebele that still causes problems for the Christian, because in African culture the family unit is wider than the nuclear circle, and even Christians sometimes get caught up in unchristian activities. Death is believed to have a human cause. This is so whether death was caused by an accident or an illness. Whenever there is an illness or death in the family, the head of the family is supposed to inquire about the cause from *Izangoma* or *izanuse* (people engaged in divination through possession by ancestral spirits).

The funeral of Maphendla Moyo.

During the funeral, there are traditional rites that are supposed to be performed, such as informing the corpse about the progress in digging the grave. The deceased is requested to soften his heart if digging up the grave is slowed down by rocks or hard ground. The deceased is supposed to be informed when the coffin is to be moved to the grave: *Sesisiya kulalisa endlini yakho yokucina* (we are now going to lay you in your final resting house). This causes conflict for the Christian who believes that once dead, the person is beyond the reach of those on this earth.

At the gravesite, close relatives, beginning with the wife or husband throw some soil into the grave and say the words *Hamba kuhle* (go well). This is said by some to be an act of dealing with death and not necessarily an act of communicating with the dead. Those family members who are not able to attend the funeral place a small stone at the grave and repeat the words, *Hamba kuhle zibanibani* (go well so and so). This is done during the time when they visit the grave for the first time.

After the funeral, there are cleansing rites. *Ingcotho* (a wild onion-like bulb) is scattered along the path from the gravesite to the homestead and around the gate of the cattle kraal.[11] This rite is believed to prevent the cattle of the community from becoming unproductive. The community nature of this belief is a difficult one for the Christian, since the one who rejects the customary act may be accused of the causing infertility of the community's cattle.

Those who will have attended the funeral go through ceremonial cleansing at the gate of the homestead, using water mixed with herbs. This is done again a week or two after the funeral during the *Ngcekeza* ceremony, when the tools used in the funeral are cleansed. Those who are Christian are usually offered water only. Members of the close family take a sip of water mixed with a concoction of herbs, then spit a part and swallow a part of the water. Pregnant women or their husbands do not take part in this ceremony for fear that it might disturb not just the pregnancy but the woman's fertility as well. With the coming of Christianity, some people did not observe these rites and proved that they are harmless, since no harm has befallen those who chose to ignore them.

The church has been more categorical on the *umbuyiso* (bringing back home of the dead) ceremony. This ceremony is usually done at least a year after the death of a family head or his spouse where his spirit is invited to act as custodian of the family. Subsequent to that, there is a ceremony held if there have been problems in the family, called *ukuthethela* (the appeasement of ancestors, or ancestor veneration). This particular ceremony has been a subject of discussion particularly in relation to a now-popular practice of a memorial service, or *Isikhumbuzo.* The memorial service is a problem because it is seen by many to have the potential for syncretism. It is suggested that the night before the memorial service some families perform a bringing home or ancestor veneration ceremony. The church is then asked to bless these activities the following morning. This is usually linked with the tombstone unveiling ceremony and is usually an occasion of feasting and sometimes drinking by those members of the family and neighbours.

The question of a memorial service has been discussed at several church council meetings. Some members take it to be an occasion they can engage in without any problems, while there is a group who believes it is syncretistic and should be avoided. This has remained an area of tension for the past twenty years, and all the more so because the advent of political independence in 1980 saw the ushering in of a cultural revival, which has included a revival of traditional religious ceremonies.

There is still no unity on this issue. Some church members, particularly the young, oppose this practice as a new form of ancestor worship, but BIC ministers have been involved in officiating at some services, and members of the church have conducted memorial services for their deceased relatives. The church still needs to go back to the Bible to come up with a unified position.

Traditionally, children were not told when a member of the family died, no matter who it was. They were not supposed to even see a corpse. This has become a problem because children today are more inquisitive. Furthermore they spend more time with their parents than children did thirty years ago. Because of the Christian answer to death, they have an easier way of dealing with this problem. Parents are even able to show their children their loved ones when they die. It is easier to stand against some of the traditional practices when members become more independent of the extended family.

Missionary Attitudes

Mpofu and Shenk in *Izithelo* (the Ndebele publication prepared for the 75th anniversary in 1973) referred to the testimonies of those who had known the first missionaries. They were impressed by the transparency of the missionaries: the missionaries allowed them to peep into their dwelling tents, since they had nothing to hide. This "transparency" fostered trust between them and the people to whom they had come to minister.

It is interesting to note that the later missionaries seem to have adopted the culture of colonialist separation from the African people. While they would mix and share African food when they visited African homes, in later decades they did not reciprocate this hospitality when

Cultural misunderstandings. African dance is sometimes accompanied by facial expressions, which a person from another culture may not quite appreciate or understand. H. Frances Davidson gave this account:

"Once when we were out kraal visiting we happened to come upon some of these worshiping at Fusi's kraal. We stopped only a few minutes to see what they were doing and were greatly shocked by the hideousness of their looks and actions. The very stamp of the bottomless pit seemed imprinted upon their features."[12]

nationals visited them. They were not able to share their own table with the Africans in their homes, as was also the case among the colonial Whites of the day.

While the missionary hearts overflowed with thankfulness to God at the reception they got when they settled in the Matopo hills, it is also clear that they perceived themselves as better than the Africans they came to save from hellfire. This is derived from the language they sometimes used to describe the natives of their mission field, often using words like "savages" and "pagans."

The missionaries left their homeland and came to serve in Africa. They determined to learn the language and tried to understand and appreciate the culture and the customs of the people among whom they served. Generally they gained the love and respect of their converts. Even if their accent could never be perfect they were respected for the effort they put into learning. But there was also a kind of missionary who lived in the country for five, ten, fifteen years or more and could only say a basic greeting, and then needed an interpreter for the rest of his communication. Though no one would challenge such people directly, some of the Africans seriously questioned their presence on the mission field.

Often missionaries had domestic help from among the many students who came to study in the mission stations. Stories are told of how they sometimes set traps for these helpers. Two former Mtshabezi girls talk about how coins would be left on the floor or under the bed to see whether or not they would be picked up and returned to the missionaries. Perhaps this was better than the establishment of monitoring systems, but it showed a lack of trust nonetheless.

BIC Missions in Zimbabwe

Therefore go and make disciples of all nations, baptising them in the name of the Father, and the Son and the Holy Spirit, and teaching them to obey everything I have commanded you. And surely I am with you always, to the very end of the age (Matt 28:19).
The "Great Commission" could never be fulfilled by one person, or one church, or one mission. Jesus himself had twelve chosen people that he trained and sent out to influence the world. The work did not stop with

The First Students at the Matopo Mission School.

the twelve. When Rev. Jesse Engle and his team first settled at the Matopo Hills, they had no idea how widely the work they had started would expand. First, it was Matopo Mission, then Mtshabezi, then Wanezi, Phumula, and Nono missions. Those missions in turn had numerous outstations. This is probably not the end of the work either. As these missions nurture individuals, many of them are are determined in turn to "go and make disciples..." Others are giving back to the church in kind. For example, Hlengiwe Mlotshwa, who although far away overseas, bought Bibles for people back home in Zimbabwe. Such people are making a difference to the lives of others.

The major thrust of the BIC ministry in the missions was preaching and teaching, which seemed to go hand in hand. Many mission stations became well known particularly for the education they offered. Parents who did not know much about the Gospel that was preached did know that Matopo, Mtshabezi and Wanezi offered a good education. They had seen products of these missions who were doing fine in society.

The BIC in Zimbabwe established three major missions: Matopo, Mtshabezi and Wanezi, with schools that have offered both primary and secondary education that now goes up to 'A' Level. There are seven years of primary education and six years of secondary education. Many students go as far as the 'O' Level standard (four years of secondary school) then move into training for various professions and occupations. Those who attain 'A' Level courses (six years of secondary school education) can pursue university education. There are many graduates from Matopo, Mtshabezi and Wanezi who have proceeded with their education to university level, carving out excellent careers for themselves that have enabled them to impact their communities positively.

In the early years of mission work, the teachers and all those in administration were full members of the BIC church. As time went on, and particularly after the running of the schools was nationalised, staff was recruited from outside the church. Most times, a concerted effort was made to look for qualified personnel from within the church in vain, especially for the science subjects. All of the schools need to have excellent laboratory facilities and good science teachers to produce good science students who would then pursue those courses in colleges and universities in order to come back and teach the same. There were years at the University of Zimbabwe when the bulk of students from BIC schools pursued courses in the Humanities department, which resulted in certain skills being recruited from outside the BIC church.

Matopo Mission

The Matopo Mission Statement:
To strive to build a complete character by providing quality academic, technical, moral and physical education through a conscientious discharge of quality instructions to produce individuals who are equipped with relevant skills to ensure that they are fit for cultural, social and economic development of the country while endeavouring to uphold the moral tone of the school and society...

The very first BIC missionaries made their settlement at Matopo Hills about forty kilometers south of Bulawayo on July, 6 1898. The mission site covered 3,000 acres, adequate for the development that has been taking place for over a century now. First a dwelling place was built for the missionaries, then a school, a church, a clinic, and more buildings for teachers' houses. The latest dream is a university, which is still in the planning stages.

The missionaries quickly realised that if their mission work was to have a meaningful impact for years to come, the people needed to learn how to read and write. Rev. Jesse Engle delegated the task of starting a school to sister H. Francis Davidson and sister Alice Heise. The school opened its doors on October 11, 1898. The two lady missionaries taught reading and writing, which was a great marvel for people in the area—that a person could talk on a paper. Classes quickly came to average between twenty and thirty pupils per day. Pupils started by learning the alphabet printed on charts, after which the Gospel of John was given to them as a text book. Students were taught to memorise certain portions in connection with daily worship, and there also was hymn singing.

Not many pupils attended school on a regular basis. To most of them, school was something to pass time when there was nothing better to do. Some people professed skepticism about school activities, where people seemingly wasted time grouped in a room with no offer of food or meat or money. It seemed a futile exercise. Such people felt it was more beneficial to spend time herding cattle, discussing worthwhile issues with other men. Nevertheless, progress was made. Some of the first converts in 1899 were Matshuba, Mlobeki Moyo, Kelenke and Siyaya.

As teaching and preaching expanded, work was taken to Ntabeni Mission by Rev. and Mrs Cress who arrived in 1898. Other out-stations that developed after Matopo were Mahlabathini, Silobi, Maphane, Gale (presently Nyumbane) and then Mtshabezi. Starting more and more mission stations was possible because those who had completed three to four years of education were mature enough to also go out and teach others. Such people were well-respected, godly people who not only taught others how to read or write but also preached the Gospel with the desire of winning more souls to Christ. More people began to appreciate the value of education, and children began to fill the classes. Those who had gone to school lived better. Men had been trained in building and agriculture. These practical subjects enabled them to improve their homes, their buildings and agricultural methods, rendering them more enterprising people. The girls attended home craft classes that enabled them to sew clothes for their families and also to take good care of their homes.

Whereas previously, learners had to be persuaded to come to school, by the 1930s more people had recognized the benefits of education and were keen to enroll their children. Many satellite schools were started in Matebeleland. These BIC schools looked to Matopo for teachers and

---

Maroma Nkomo, a second year teacher trainee in 1937 writes:
When I was thinking about the education which we are getting here at Matopo Mission, so many things come in mind. The first thing is that the education we get here is better education because we put God first. The second is that education which does not have God inside is useless because it gains nothing in the world.
—*The Matopian*, 1937.

Carpentry Class

preachers. A teacher training school was opened in 1932 at Matopo to equip those who would go out to teach.

Many parents steeped in traditional culture were selective in sending children to school. They tended to send more boys than girls to school, in the belief that the male children would care for them in their old age, while the female children would marry into other families. Some seemed to think that educating girls was a waste of time. What is amazing, however, is that the first year teacher training class in 1942 was comprised of seven young men and seven young women. This seemed to negate the theory that school was the prerogative of male students. There also were champions of education for girls. One such was Stephen Ndlovu, son of Zwanizwani, who wrote in *The Matopian* (Matopo school magazine) of 1941:

I have heard many people say educating girls is a waste of money.
We must not censure these people for they are simply blind.

Girls should be educated because they are the ones who are helping their people by teaching the children. Most of the girls are more patient with children than we boys. If a girl is educated, she wants to send her young brothers and sisters to school. We must not say they are useless.

—Stephen Ndlovu, 1st Year, T.T.

Matopo established itself by offering good quality education in Matebeleland South. Many students came from all over the country to advance their education at Matopo—some even came from Zambia for teacher training. The syllabus was rich in practical subjects. For young men, there were subjects such as agriculture, animal husbandry, forestry, woodworking, woodcarving, basketry, building, clay modeling and leather work. The young women's industrial classes consisted of needlework, laundry, housewifery, gardening and pottery. Matopo mission in the 1940s had become a place for spiritual and intellectual growth, as well as a place that nurtured service for humanity as Christ did.

James Stewart, the inspector of the Matebeleland Circuit School gave high praise in the foreword of *The Matopian* in 1941: "Matopo School is regarded as a centre where the educational and spiritual needs of the African are catered for with thoroughness and consciousness which is difficult to surpass in any part of the colony."

Memories of a former Matopian:

I'll never forget the experience during my first year at Matopo in 1966. It was during the dark hours of Easter morning that I was awakened by the most beautiful singing I had ever heard. Other girls in my dormitory had heard it too. We all crept out of our beds in wonderment and peered out through the windows where we saw beings in white. The sight of this spectacle and the sound was too beautiful to be true. I thought they were angelic hosts declaring:

Namhla uvukile, Haleluya	He is risen today, Hallelluia
Namhla unqobile, Haleluya	He has conquered today, Hallelluia
Umkhululi wethu, Haleluya	He is our Redeemer, Hallelluia

The melodious proclamation filled me with awe and joy concerning the risen Lord. I thought I was in heaven, and was disappointed to see the figures drift away into the dark. It took me days to be convinced that those were some of the school girls singing. The following year, I was in the group that donned white sheets and moved from spot to spot in the mission compound singing the wonderment of Easter day to the new Matopians.

Matopo Secondary School

The teacher training school moved to Mtshabezi in 1955 and a secondary school opened at Matopo in 1951. The intake of students grew and more school and dormitory buildings were added. The running of the school was interrupted in the late 1970s when the war of liberation was raging country-wide. The school had to close in September 1978 for the safety and security of the students and staff. This was a critical time of the year as examinations were close at hand. Different churches in the city of Bulawayo came forward and accommodated the students enabling some classes to continue and exams to be written. Matopo became one of the refugee schools for almost two years and only re-opened at the mission in 1980 as the independence of Zimbabwe was celebrated.

In the early 1980s, the secondary school had an enrollment of about 500 students. By 1985, steady expansion made it possible for the school to be accorded the status of 'A' Level. These classes were started in 1988, and students have been performing well in comparison with other schools in the region. As the school grew, measures were put in place to improve the quality of food in line with ministerial regulations. The school undertook intensive cultivation of vegetables under irrigation, a very successful project that was only disrupted by the drought of the early 1990s.

Mtshabezi Mission

Mtshabezi Mission was started in 1906, eight years after the establishment of the first BIC mission at Matopo. Rev. Harvey J. and Mrs. Emma Frey were its pioneers. They had arrived in Africa in 1905, and first helped with work at Matopo Mission. They had a three-year-old son, Ernest. Their aim was to start the work of God in this mission and to preach the Gospel that would transform the lives of the inhabitants of that area. Mlobeki Moyo, one of the first Matopo graduates, along with other young men and Rev. Steigerwald, accompanied the Freys on the trek to Mtshabezi. Rev. Frey immediately set about visiting villages and inviting the people to come to worship. Many heeded the invitation and about forty came to hear the Gospel, many of them for the first time. Rev. Frey also started a garden of maize and vegetables and a poultry project so they could have home-grown food.

The families of Nyamazana Dube and Bhunu Ncube.

The grass shelter that was used for services on Sundays was used as a classroom during week days, with Mrs. Frey teaching. The learners were very eager and their ages ranged from about ten years to those over twenty years. By 1908, a brick church building had been completed and dedicated. Sunday school attendance was about seventy-five people and the Mtshabezi Day School had enrolled fifty-four pupils. One of the early pupils in the day school was Bhunu Ncube. Missionaries had noticed that he was alert and outstandingly bright, and they courted his life for Christ. They prayed fervently for him. Bhunu offered to stay at the mission, applying himself to study, and shortly opened his heart to Christ. He married one of the admirable girls from the Girls School and became a trustworthy worker, a pastor-teacher for a time and later the foreman at the mission. Bhunu's heritage spans children, grandchildren and great-grandchildren. They maintain a close association with the BIC church that their kinsman faithfully served for many years.

The Girls School was opened in 1908 and most of the first pupils came to the school to find refuge from parents who wanted to give them away in marriage, against their wishes. Mrs. Katie Anna Myers had visited Africa and been impressed by the African girls and also was concerned at their fate in forced marriages. When she returned to America, she solicited funds for a rescue home for these unlucky girls. That is how Mtshabezi Girls School, a haven for girls, was born. One such girl was Kelina, who had run away from home to escape marriage to a man older than she, who also already had a wife. The man had tried to way-lay her at the train station without any success. Kelina did not return home. Though she longed for her mother and wanted to get money for school fees, she dared not go home. The man made many unsuccessful attempts to get her.

Melina Tshuma's story.

Melina's father did not believe in educating girls. Once they could read and write, that was considered adequate. Most of her brothers, who were more privileged, were not really interested in pursuing higher learning. Her pretty sister, Felani, had already been married off to an older man, Phathi Moyo. ... Melina was not going to be married off to any man old enough to be her father or grandfather when there were so many eligible bachelors about. She had already heard about this Rescue Home, Mtshabezi, from Sithembile Moyo, a friend and former classmate at Lubuze. She stealthily left home at night, with a chicken that she would sell in order to raise the train fare from Mbalabala to Stanmore. Her father did not pursue her. During the holidays, she would remain at Mtshabezi working for the Wingers to raise school fees. She was fetched home after her father's death in the mid-1940s.

This famous lot of girls at Mtshabezi were often referred to as *Izintombi Zegedini*—the girls of the gate—which is still used as an example of a high level of chastity. Most of these women became very strong leaders. Those who married became good wives and mothers because they revered the Bible teachings. There still is a sprinkling of these ladies walking strong in the church today. It is hoped that Mrs. Myers lived to realise the blessing from her efforts.

Girls who completed standard VI at the Central Primary school became house-wives, teachers, student nurses and teacher training enrolees. By 1953, there were 270 girls in the morning school, making a total of 548 pupils at Mtsabezi. It was a simple life then, when people used grass mats for a bed rolled out at night and a couple of blankets.

By 1956, there were over 700 pupils at the Central Primary School. Altogether Mtsabezi had eighty-eight teachers. It was a big challenge to minister to each of them for Christ. In 1956 Mtshabezi celebrated fifty years of service to Africa and her daughters. By that year, 2,342 girls had gone through the Home Craft School. During the same year, a building course was started at Mtsabezi for boys who were unable to go on with academic education. This proved to be a valuable asset to the college and for those particular individuals.

In 1956 a Primary Teachers Training Course was transferred from Matopo to Mtshabezi Mission. The first lot of graduates for the PTL School (Primary Teachers Lower Certificate) graduated in December 1957, and in January 1960 the Primary Teachers Higher course was also transferred from Matopo to Mtshabezi. Many teachers graduated before the school was moved to the United College of Education in Bulawayo in 1978, because of the escalating liberation war. After the war the teacher training courses were not re-established.

Mtshabezi Secondary School

The secondary school at Mtshabezi began in 1971 with a strong emphasis on industrial and technical subjects. Mtshabezi Secondary School closed in 1978 due to the escalation of the war of liberation in Zimbabwe, and students were absorbed by various schools in Bulawayo. Great property losses occurred during the time the mission was vacated, although some materials were salvaged and hauled to Bulawayo for safe-keeping, and some was entrusted to local people until the situation improved.

When the school re-opened in 1980 the new democratic government abolished all programmes started by the previous regime because they seemed to be racially biased. None of the white schools had been offering the technical programme, and it was perceived as something created to undermine black people and to keep them from pursuing the academic line and then university. Any good that might have existed in the programme was overshadowed by the possibly negative motives that prompted it, and so it was eliminated from the education system. All schools then offered a strictly academic education, though many schools were ill-equipped both with human and material resources, especially after the government decided to nationalise all schools.

Ekuphileni Bible Institute

Ekuphileni Bible Institute (EBI) is the BIC Bible institute that began originally as Wanezi Bible Institute at Wanezi Mission in Filabusi. As the school grew and facilities became inadequate for the needs of the expanded programme, leadership agreed to relocate it on a newly-developed site at Mtshabezi Mission in 1968. The change of place necessitated a change of name. Mr. Sampson Ndimande, a long-standing member of the church, suggested the name which was chosen: Ekuphileni Bible Institute. *Ekuphileni* means "where there is life." The bulk of BIC church leaders in Zimbabwe have passed through the doors of EBI since its establishment and over 1000 people in total have obtained leadership training from this institution.

Curriculum development at EBI from the mid-1990s has come to include social sciences such as anthropology, psychology, sociology, and philosophy, to better equip leaders for their demanding work. Also included are practical courses like carpentry, drip irrigation, cutting and designing, building, and typing. From time to time, the school offers and conducts seminars for those already involved in ministry.

Wanezi Mission

S'thandazel' eNtshonalanga, lihambe	We pray for the North, let it go
S'thandazel' eMpumalanga. Lihambe	We pray for the East, let it go
Liyahamba, hamba	It is going, spreading
Liyahamb' iVangeli	The Gospel is spreading

This chorus was sung in the BIC church congregations and schools for many years. It was a heart-warming song sung with actions to show the Gospel moving and spreading everywhere. The Gospel had been taken from Matopo to Mtshabezi and many out-stations towards the east. The fields were white, but the reapers few. Manhlenhle Kumalo had been transferred from the Matopo area in 1923 to Shamba, a place very near to where the mission was established the following year. He worked as a teacher and pastor in that area. Bishop and Mrs. H. P. Steigerwald established the new mission, Wanezi in 1924. Wanezi quickly developed as the feeder point for the many outstations in the Insiza area.

Rev. R. H. Mann arrived in 1926 to assist with the work in the area. When Bishop Steigerwald went to be with the Lord in December of 1928,

Bishop Steigerwald, second bishop of BIC church, Zimbabwe.

Rev. H. J. Frey was chosen to be in charge of Wanezi mission, in 1931. Manhlenhle Kumalo and other nationals worked hard with all these missionaries to establish and encourage preaching in the out-stations in the Insiza area, such as Gwabhila, Dekezi, Gwatemba, Mazhabazha, Bungwe, Siwaze, Nsedlu, Shamba, Mpopothi, Nyathishazha, Mbawulo, Sabhabha, Filabusi, Fulunye, Zilwane, Mleja, Gumbalo, Ntunte, Mtshezuki, Mtoba, Mtshingwe, Elangeni, Phumula, Mwele, Malole, Doro, Lufuse, Gumbalo, Mkwabeni and Hlatshwayo. All these preaching points also became schools, a wonderful heritage for the various places nurtured by the BIC church. Wanezi Mission continued to grow. In 1945, the boys boarding school started at Wanezi Mission, and people like Mapendla Moyo and others assisted in the work.

Secondary School

The secondary school at Wanezi was opened in January 1962, and the first Junior Certificate examination was written in 1963. That same year a circulating library did its rounds in the area. One hundred and fifty books on prayer, Christian life and Bible studies were taken into many homes. Expressions of appreciation for these books were received with words such as "I received much power in my spiritual life from your book." Those who completed their Junior Certificate exams successfully applied to continue with their schooling at Matopo Secondary School. Others went to Mtshabezi to pursue teacher training. 'A' Level classes were introduced in 2000 at Wanezi Mission, and Miss Dorcas Kumalo was chosen to head the school from May 2001, after a brief stint as Deputy Head at Mtshabezi.

Though she had been Head of Mawabeni Secondary School from 1989–2000, Miss Kumalo said it was frightening to accept the task of heading Wanezi. She took headship of such a big school during a very challenging period in the history of Zimbabwe, when the whole country was under siege politically and economically. She said,

> We urgently need a well-equipped laboratory if our children are to excel in their efforts. But, that has taken a back-stage position as we battle with hunting for the scarce commodities, and queuing for fuel. The activities are time consuming and not productive at all to the academic well being of our students. When there are no food supplies and other daily consumables, the students do not understand. Nor do their parents, most of whom are in Botswana, South Africa and the United Kingdom. These parents send them adequate money, but the commodities are just not available.
>
> Our dam which is the main water supplier for the mission dried up in February 2003. It was a frantic period, but, in God's mysterious ways, the heavens opened recently. Cyclone Japhet came to our rescue. Our dam is full and overflowing with the much needed water and we thank God even as the winds seem to be a curse that is wreaking havoc in other parts of the country. Another challenge is that there is no easy transport to the school. The main highway is about 12 km from Wanezi. Unless parents drive, it is not easy for them to visit their children. All the same, we do thank God that we are surviving. I am particularly joyous about our results too. Our school does not have the cream in terms of intake, but if you look at our results, for 'A' Level, they have been good and they are improving all the time.[13]

Miss Dorcas Kumalo is the first indigenous woman to head a BIC Secondary School in the three big missions. She is the granddaughter of Rev. Manhlenhle Kumalo, confidently walking in the footsteps of her grandfather, her father Mr. Iddo Kumalo, and her uncle Mr. Leslie Kumalo, who headed Mtshabezi Teacher Training School. Rev. Manhlenhle Kumalo worked hard to transform the many lives he impacted to his work. He left a proud legacy to the BIC church in Zimbabwe.

BIC church hierarchy in Zimbabwe
Bishop
Overseers
Pastors
Deacons
Evangelists
Lay People

Church Administration

The administration of the Zimbabwe Church has not changed much from the structures which were established by the founders. From the time of inception, the top leader was always the Bishop. For some years he was also called the Superintendent and was appointed by the Board for Missions. To help the Bishop with the decisions on the field, an executive board was composed of missionaries.

The year 1906 could be considered a landmark for the start of special meetings. In October of that year, a general meeting was held at Mapane attended by thirty-five nationals and eight missionaries. There was Bible teaching, worship and a communion service; there was no business session. In later years, general conferences were set up for the purposes of worship and also for transacting church business. They included missionaries from both Zimbabwe and Zambia (then Southern and Northern Rhodesia respectively), but the Africans were not involved in any decision-making. This situation went on for quite some time.

As the church developed, it was recognized that nationals needed to be more involved in the decision-making of the church if the church was to have an impact in the future. The first council meeting which involved both nationals and missionaries was held in 1919 at Mtshabezi Mission. In later years, such meetings were given the name General Conference of Zimbabwe. At the second council meeting in 1920, the nationals sent a request to the Executive Board that one of them be appointed as a church leader, to be a go-between the Africans and the all-white Board. The Executive Board discussed this and recommended that three rather than one be appointed. The three chosen were Manhlenhle Kumalo, Nyamazana Dube and Mawogelana Kumalo. Only the first two actually served in this capacity. The church was then divided into two districts. In 1921, Kumalo became the first Overseer for the churches east of Mzingwane river, while Dube covered all those west of the river.

The first three national leaders: (L to R) Overseers
Manhlenhle Khumalo, Nyamazana Dube, Ndabenduku Dlodlo.

In 1930 it was decided to form three districts, each with a mission school as a center. It was therefore necessary to choose a third Overseer. Ndebenduku Dlodlo was chosen to serve as Overseer for Matopo District. In 1944 the three overseers were ordained. By this time, more and more nationals had taken up positions of responsibility. In 1930, a decision had been made to choose Evangelists who would spend two weeks at a time evangelizing at each congregation, and would then move on. Mlobeki Moyo was one such evangelist, and there were many others who travelled extensively doing the work of evangelism.

Two great events took place at the conference held in May 1964 at Wanezi Mission. The Board for Missions sent their Chairman, Rev. Samuel Wolgemuth and Rev. H. H. Brubaker to bestow independence and autonomy on the church in Zimbabwe. The document granting independence to the church was handed to Rev. Mangisi Sibanda who received it and responded on behalf of the church in Zimbabwe. This coincided with the time to choose a Bishop for Zimbabwe. Up to this time, the Board for Missions had been doing the choosing. Rev. Alvin J. Book was the first nationally-chosen Bishop for the Zimbabwe Church. The year that Bishop Book was chosen, Rev. Ira M. Stern became the

Zimbabwean BIC Bishops through History	
Jesse M. Engle	1898 – 1900
Henry P. Steigerwald	1901 – 1928
Henry H. Brubaker	1929 – 1950
Arthur M. Climenhaga	1950 – 1959
David E. Climenhaga	1960 – 1964
Alvin J. Book	1965 – 1969
Philemon M. Khumalo	1970 – 1979
Stephen N. Ndlovu	1980 – 1989
Martin S. Senda	1990 – 1994
Jacob R. Shenk	1994 – 1999
Danisa Ndlovu	2000 –

first Field Secretary to look after the concerns and needs of the missionaries, while Bishop Book concentrated on the church.

After considerable discussion and some agitation by local pastors, the first non-missionary church leader, P. M. Khumalo, was elected Bishop of the Brethren in Christ Church in Zimbabwe in 1969. This was a well regarded move with an esteemed leader in office. At the end of a ten year term, however, Bishop Khumalo did not automatically step down, thus precipitating a conflict in the church. Stephen Ndlovu, another well regarded church leader, was elected Bishop in 1979. The conflicts of the church were in part the failure of conference leadership to address issues of deep concern to the church. In 1982 the Annual Conference was cancelled because of several conflicts.

The pattern of conflict finally forced out Bishop Martin Senda in 1994. His successor, missionary J. R. Shenk, was in turn succeeded by Danisa Ndlovu in 2001. Transitional difficulties reflected the inherent honour of the office, strong personalities with their supporting groups and not-so-subtle interference by missionaries still in the country. Current

Ordination of four couples as Oversseers, 1970: (L to R)
Rev. Stephen and Ottilia Ndlovu, Rev. Joel and Rebecca Ncube, Rev.
Jonathan and Neddie Dlodlo, Rev. Mangisi and Hannah Sibanda.

Bishop Danisa Ndlovu says the church requires "ground rules with no regard" to the incumbents, as well as defined term limits. The church is maturing in handling transitions with less tension and conflict.

Independence from the mother church meant greater responsibility for the church in Zimbabwe. In 1965, the church chose Jack D. Ndlovu, Henry K. Ncube and Samuel Mlotshwa as the first Trustees to look after all the church property. More nationals were added to the administration as the different programmes in each mission were separated and a person was appointed to head each. With more and more work falling into the hands of the nationals, the number of missionaries in the field decreased. Coupled with this, the war of liberation from the colonial regime had intensified. In Zimbabwe, the final exodus of the missionaries occurred in 1978.

National independence came to Zimbabwe in 1980. The church experienced considerable growth numerically, but not financially. The church had not been nurtured well in the habits of giving and stewardship. The mother church in the United States had done too much for the daughter, and had not taught the baby how to become financially independent. It became increasingly difficult to care for church workers and also to finance church projects.

In 1989 it was decided to decentralize administration by setting up District Committees responsible for each district. The districts were also expected to be financially autonomous. At the 1995 General Conference, the church boldly formed a Finance Board to deal with all financial matters in the church. The Finance Board was responsible directly to the General Conference. It was this board which led the church out of the financial difficulties which had seen the church almost go bankrupt. In 1998, at the time of its centennial, the church had cause to celebrate. It had become financially stable. Many new churches had been planted, and many church leaders had been ordained to ministry.

Other Arms of the Church

Church Planting and Growth

In August 1899, Siyaya Moyo, Jani Moyo, Mzeze Dube, Masikwa Mlotshwa, Matshuba Ndlovu, Hanyana Mpofu, Mlobeki Moyo, Ndalimani Moyo, Kelenki and Sibongamanzi Ndiweni were baptized in the river Ginqa. Together with the missionary pioneer team of Jesse and his wife Elizabeth Engle, as well as H. Frances Davidson and Alice Heise, they formed the whole of the Brethren in Christ church in Africa. The ten new converts represented the planting of the seed which over the years has borne much fruit. Today, just over a hundred years later, the BIC church membership has spread to Zambia, Malawi, Botswana, South Africa and Mozambique. In Zimbabwe alone there are 29,000 people scattered in over 272 congregations and preaching points in the year 2000.

Church planting and growth have always been at the heart of the BIC church ministry. Many strategies have been employed to reach this end. When the first school was opened its core reader was the Gospel of John. Old people who were students in that era could cite passages from the Gospel from memory even after many years. They taught the same to their children and grandchildren. All the students who learned to read and graduated to the Gospel of John were doubly equipped to go out and win souls.

The students were taught so that they too could go out and teach. This method of spreading the Gospel was repeated at Matapo, Mtshabezi, Wanezi and Pumula Missions. Those who heard the Gospel message and believed, took the news to others who were still in darkness. More and more nationals were equipped to go and teach others.

Part of the spread of the Gospel was due to the method of teacher deployment the missionaries used. In the very early years the teachers were sent out to the schools to be teachers as well as preachers. They reached out to the people who came to the schools as well as to those who lived in the surrounding villages. From Matopo, the work first expanded to Mapane, Ntabeni and eventually Mtshabezi, which was opened in 1906. Church growth was achieved through home visitations, one-to-one discussions and invitations to church services.

In 1906, H. Frances Davidson and Miss Adda Engle together with Ndabambi Moyo and Gono Sibanda crossed the Zambezi to open the BIC work in Zambia. In 1911, Rev. Levi Doner in the company of Mawogelana Kumalo, his sister Lomapholisa Kumalo, Sitshokuphi Sibanda, Mahutsha Mafu, Mantshi Moyo and Mafa Baloyi took the work to Chibi. This was the first in-road to Mashonaland, although this early effort failed to take root.

In the 1970s, a church was established in Salisbury (now Harare), at Glen Norah. Glen Norah supported the establishment of the Mount Pleasant congregation and nurtured it and also the church at Mutoko. Congregations have since started at Chitungwiza, and Budiriro. Efforts to encourage growth at Chegutu and Kadoma were hampered by the volatile political situation in 2001–2002. The efforts will be revived once the political climate improves. Church growth in this region has led to development of a new District, Mashonaland.

As the work spread it was necessary to deploy evangelists to follow-up and hold evangelistic services to strengthen or revive young churches. Some of the evangelists who gave years of notable service to the church were Rev. Sandi Vundla, who worked extensively to plant the church in the city of Bulawayo, Mtshazo Nkala, Mahutsha Mafu, Delelani Moyo and Bafanya Mlilo, who later became overseer for Gwayi.

In the 1950s, lady missionaries Dorothy Martin and Mary Breneman made it a habit to visit former Matopo Students who had moved to Bulawayo, and this led to the planting of work in the city, with active congregations by the 1960s. In the 1970s, congregations took root in Victoria Falls and Harare.

Evangelists and church planters:
Maria Tshuma (L) and Qedabakwabo Nkala (R).

In 1980 Rev. and Mrs. Fred Holland came to Zimbabwe to help establish a church planting team. The team worked in Bulawayo, Filabusi, Esigodini, Victoria Falls, Hwange, Kamativi, Binga, Plumtree and Harare. The first team was composed of Rev. Ortson Moyo (co-ordinator), his wife Janet, Getrude Ncube, Taddious and Busi Moyo, Zibusiso Moyo and Maria Tshuma. Maria Tshuma has planted the highest number of churches in the Zimbabwean Church. Over the years, members of the team have changed, but the focus remains the same: they look for opportunities to begin new churches. Sometimes they are invited by BIC members who, because of employment opportunities, find themselves in areas where there is no BIC church. After a careful survey of the area and its potential, the team is sent to the place for a determined length of time, anywhere from four weeks to two months. When the team arrives in a new place, they do door-to-door visitations where the members introduce themselves to the people of the area and get to know them. In the following days, they hand out tracts and follow up to answer questions which may arise. People are given a chance to make commitments. They are invited to attend evangelistic services in the evening. When a number of people have responded to the Gospel some afternoons are spent in teaching on repentance, the new birth, faith, Matthew 18, the BIC church doctrine, and any other aspects of church life on which the new converts may have questions. Before leaving the area the team helps the group choose someone who can serve as the leader of the new congregation. The Overseer for that district is responsible to see to the nurturing of that congregation.

The BIC church in Zimbabwe now boasts a high membership. Lobengula church, led by Rev. Albert Ndlovu since its inception, is believed to be the largest BIC congregation in the world. When people make a commitment, they join the inquirer's class where they undergo Bible study and an understanding of church doctrine before going on to baptism. In the early years of church planting this period lasted two years; later it was reduced to one. Now some pastors even allow new converts to go into the inquirer's class after baptism. Church growth in Zimbabwe is linked to wider congregational activities which do not just meet on Sundays but also have midweek cell or Bible study meetings. This encourages spiritual growth as members study and discuss the Bible together.

Each church planting effort has a story behind it. The movement of the people from the South to the Gwaai led to the opening of Pumula Mission. The movement to the cities was due to people seeking employment in the cities in the 1970s. They were fleeing the ravages of the liberation war. Bulawayo Central is a result of people moving from the high-density suburbs of Bulawayo to the low-density centre after independence, when former White residential areas were opened to native African people. As new suburbs spring up in Bulawayo, congregations have arisen at Nketa, Mganwini, Cowdry Park and Mahatshula. The Lord is indeed at work.

Medical Work

The Missionaries who came to Africa to win souls often found themselves facing challenging medical needs. Often the missionaries were ill-equipped to respond. When some of the early converts heard the stories of miraculous healing, they believed. When sickness threatened their lives or those of their families, they felt free to request prayers of healing from the missionaries. The early missionaries record a number of such stories of healing through prayer and how these situations encouraged the faith of the nationals. Later, when missionaries with a medical background came

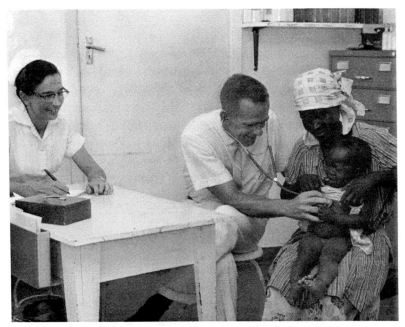

Dr. Stern with a small patient, Mtshabezi Hospital.

to the field, they found health care to be a very helpful way of making contact, leading to discussion on matters of the soul.

In 1916, the missionaries wrote to the Foreign Mission Board requesting the recruiting of a well-equipped medical missionary for the African field. Martha Kaufman and Grace Book were the first qualified missionary nurses who were stationed at Wanezi and Mtshabezi respectively in 1924. Wanezi had no clinic, but medical work was still carried out. Martha was assisted by Seni Jubane, a graduate of the Home Craft school. Dr. Thuma was the first qualified doctor to serve in the BIC hospital in Southern Rhodesia (Zimbabwe). He came into the country in 1950 and was stationed at Mtshabezi Hospital. Immediately he started monthly visits to Wanezi. When a telephone line was installed in 1953, it was possible for him to contact the doctor at the Filabusi hospital when there was need to transfer a patient there, or even just for consultation.

Dr. Thuma did not remain long in Zimbabwe. In 1954 he moved from Mtshabezi to Macha in Zambia where he was to start a new hospital. Dr. R. Virginia Kaufman came to relieve him in the same year. At that time, the hospital at Mtshabezi was made up of only three buildings. Dr. Kaufman remained at Mtshabezi until 1959. She continued monthly visits to the other mission stations, Wanezi and Matopo, which by that time also had functioning clinics. A special feature of her work was the establishment of baby and ante-natal clinics.

In 1960 Dr. J. Myron Stern arrived at Mtshabezi hospital to be the doctor in charge. He worked very hard to upgrade the facilities and so contacted many donor agencies to request funding. The Women's Missionary Prayer Committee gave money for the construction of a new doctor's house. Bread for the World gave $41,000 which was used to build a 35-bed pediatrics ward and a 27-bed tuberculosis ward. This grant also connected Mtshabezi Mission and hospital to the main electric line. With more buildings in place, Mtshabezi hospital was finally dedicated on January 23, 1965.

When Dr. R. V. Kaufman returned from furlough, she was stationed at Phumula Mission to start a hospital there. On arrival, she found one three-roomed building with patients housed in five thatched huts. George Bundy did a lot of construction work to add more needed buildings. Dr. Kaufman spent two terms at Phumula, finishing in 1973. Again, she expanded medical services to the neighbouring community where she did immunizations and treated less serious illnesses.

When the War of Liberation errupted, it became necessary to move all missionaries to Bulawayo for their own safety. The national nurses carried on working under very difficult conditions. As the war intensified, many rural health centers were forced to close. Mtshabezi was the last to do so in 1978. With the mission stations deserted, a lot of damage was done to mission properties, and at independence in 1980, much reconstruction was needed. The new government had coined the slogan "Health for All," and there was a directive that most health services had to be free or very low fees were to be paid. This strained most institutions. Loraine Buckwalter came into the country at that time. Her role was to be the link between the Ministry of Health and the church. She took charge of all the administrative work in the BIC health centers. To help ease her work, she employed hospital administrators. Others who held the position after Loraine were Mrs. Flora Dlodlo, Sister Zwane, Sister Nomuhle Ncube and Sister Sithabile Ncube.

Dr. Ralph Devee Boyd also contributed much to the rebuilding of the health institutions, particularly Mtshabezi. In addition to visiting clinics, he sought funding and re-equipped and re-stocked the hospital. Two ambulances were purchased and a hospital chaplain was hired to care for the spiritual needs of the sick. As the work load increased, more staff was employed and better housing was built for them. A training school for village health workers also was started. Dr. Boyd made Mtshabezi hospital the envy of many. People travelled from as far away as Harare and other parts of Zimbabwe to be treated there. Mthabezi attained a reputation for unprecedented professional and spiritual care. Other doctors have also come and done their part, such as Dr. Arthur Dick, Dr. Dennis Barlow, Dr. Swinton, and Dr. Moyo.

At the time of this writing, one of the greatest challenges facing the nation is the fight against the HIV/AIDS scourge, which has had devastating consequences for the country. It has torn families apart and has brought untold suffering to the relatives of those who have died. A direct result of the HIV/AIDS battle is the increase in the number of orphans countrywide. The BIC have joined the rest of the nation in caring for both the sick and the orphans.

The first AIDS case to be diagnosed in Zimbabwe was recorded in 1985. Because of the stigma attached to this sickness, it was not easy for the general public or the government to come to terms with it. Denial led to its quick spread so that by 1993, the health institutions in the country were overstretched and could not take care of all the patients needing hospitalization. Many were simply sent home to die. It was then that the BIC set in place an AIDS programme at Mtshabezi Hospital, with assistance from the Mennonite Central Committee (MCC). This was the initiative of Sister Elizabeth Brandt Edwards. HIV patients were counseled, those HIV positive were helped, and the families of the sick were taught how to care for them.

At present the programme has components of home-based care, orphan care, and prevention and counselling through funding from CIDA. The programme launched the "care kit" which contains materials to assist in the care of the sick. Energy is now being given to prevention as well as helping the affected set up income generation programmes. This BIC-run programme gives hope and respite to patients and to those who care for

The present Matopo Book Centre, Bulawayo.

them, thanks to a Christ-centred approach that provides peace of mind as well as physical care.

Matopo Book Centre

When the first Mission school and out-stations were opened, emphasis was placed on arithmetic and reading. At the height of BIC activity in the country, the church was responsible for both teaching and preaching. The people needed school books, Bibles as well as other supplies. To meet the need, these materials were bought from the book suppliers of the day who were found in Bulawayo.

The idea of establishing a BIC bookroom started at Matopo Mission, which was the headquarters of all early church activity. By 1934 the church was purchasing most of their books from the government bookshops. It was decided that the BIC church should buy and stock its own supplies to be able to cater to the needs of the people in its schools. The first Matopo Bookroom was operated from a storage room near what was known as the Mission house at Matopo Mission. There were educational materials for the schools and religious ones for the church. In 1960 the Executive Board passed a resolution to start a bookshop in Bulawayo, since such services were required by other communities beyond the BIC church. The first trading place in Bulawayo was rented space at Corner House.

Initially the Bookroom operated with a minimal staff, but this rose to sixty people by the end of the year 2000. Most of the employees were BIC church people, so in a way the Bookroom provided the church with finances as well as employment to the members. A significant development was the move from Corner House to the present site. In 1970 the doors of the newly-built Bookroom were opened to the public. As this was built with plenty of storage as well as office space, some of the rooms were given over to be used as church offices. As Matopo Bookroom became better known in Bulawayo, the volume of trade increased tremendously. In December 1976, Matopo Book Centre dedicated a new shop in the town of Gwanda. This shop, like the main one in Bulawayo and the one in Beitbridge, were built by the BIC church.

Since its inception, Matopo Book Centre has endeavoured to complement the church's mission of evangelism and discipleship. In earlier years, its staff took time off to conduct evangelistic meetings. Some taught Bible classes in government schools. Others participated in a reading room ministry. People were invited off the streets into the reading room at Matopo Book Centre and given ample opportunity to read tracts, ask questions and get answers from the Bookroom staff. Some were counselled according to their needs. In 1936, the first literature booth was set up at the African Conference. This enabled church people to make purchases while at Conferences. Matopo Book Center has been an important part of General Conference since that time.

Serious challenges have been faced. Immediately after the completion of the Bulawayo shop most of the Brethren in Christ schools—which formed a core market base—were taken over by the government to be managed by rural authorities. For many years Matopo Bookroom had enjoyed the privilege of being able to purchase from an overseas market, and also was the local distributor for Zondervan publishers. In 1970, import regulations were tightened and many supplies bought outside the country could no longer be imported, negatively affecting sales revenue. To make things worse, the war of liberation led to the closure of many rural schools toward the end of the seventies. After independence, many new bookshops appeared and competition intensified.

The 1980s marked the start of a turbulent period in the life of the church administration which also had a negative impact on all aspects of church life. The Matopo Book Centre chain of stores did not escape the trials. When the church found itself facing a great overdraft in the 1990s, many members could not understand why the milk-cow could not continue supplying the needs of the church.

Matopo Book Centre has become more of an educational supplier than a religious one. Many church people lament the shift. The Bookroom Administrative Committee was set up in 1965 to face the challenge of taking the Bookroom back to the glory days of the sixties, when it enjoyed huge profits—but those days have yet to return. In the early 2000s, staff were given the option of taking early retirement packages. At the time of this writing, the chain has closed some of it branches, leaving only seven.

The Literature Committee and Good Words

In the late 1950s, BIC church members felt the need for a church paper. The paper was born in June 1957 and became *Good Words—Church Newsletter*. *Good Words* was published on eight pages. It contained church announcements, Bible lessons and items of prayer and appeared in English, Ndebele and Tonga. The paper was published twice a year until 1964 when it was published on a quarterly basis. In June of 1967 the last trilingual *Good Words* was published. Thereafter, it appeared in English and Ndebele, on four pages, published bi-monthly. The format and contents have constantly been reviewed since this time. Sometimes selected themes are followed issue by issue; at other times a variety of topics are found in one issue.

When Mr. Jacob D. Moyo, the full-time editor, passed away in 1989, a full-time replacement was not appointed. Because of their passion to keep producing *Good Words* for the churches—the only literature some of the rural people ever received—Doris Dube and Bekithemba Dube worked hard in their spare time to produce the paper, until responsibility for its publication was given to the Literature Committee. Their efforts were greatly appreciated. In addition to continuing with *Good Words*, the literature committee produced the centennial book, *Celebrating the Vision: A Century of Sowing and Reaping* in 1998,[14] and spearheaded ongoing work on a museum at Matopo Mission.

Trans World Radio (TWR) operated a Christian radio station in Swaziland to broadcast Christian programmes in English as well as in numerous African languages. When the BIC church was offered a chance to produce Ndebele programmes in the mid 1970s, the church embraced the challenge. A workshop conducted by David L. Carlson of TWR in Bulawayo prepared participants to embark on this new way of taking the Gospel to the people. Mr. Robert T. Mann was programme director with the overall executive responsibility for production, promotion and administration of the Ndebele radio broadcast over TWR. His assistant was Mr. Edgar Ndlovu.

The first programme was broadcast July 4, 1975, followed by broadcasts every Tuesday and Friday evenings with repeats in the mornings. The Tuesday programmes aimed especially to encourage Christian listeners. They contained Bible studies done by Donald Vundla and others; readings from a continued story such as *Izithelo, Uhambo Lwesihambi* (Pilgrims' Progress), read by Mr. I. N. Mpofu; and a panel that answered questions sent in by listeners. The panel consisted of the late Rev. N. S. Moyo, with Mrs. Martha Mpofu, and the late Agripa Masiye, who took turns answering questions dealing with practical Christian living.

A survey in 1976 and 1977 revealed that the majority of the *Amagugu Evangeli* listeners were rural people. Bulawayo, Harare and other towns had access to FM and MW broadcasts from Rhodesia Broadcasting Corporation. The urban dwellers hardly listened to short wave broadcasts. It may also have been the case that listeners in rural places were more likely to respond to the survey than those in the urban areas.

What impact has this arm of the BIC church had on people's lives? *Amagugu Evangeli* continues to reach the unreached for Christ. Fellowships have begun when people came together around a radio to listen to a particular programme. Some of these prayer groups have written requesting help in starting a church when they are five, ten or fifteen interested persons. *Amagugu Evangeli* then passes on that information to the Church Growth Committee. Such requests have come from Plumtree, Tsholotsho and Nyamayendlovu. Many lives have been transformed by Christ through some of these radio programmes. Broken relationships have been mended and those with HIV/AIDS and others confronted by various crises in their lives have attained hope in Christ. The potential for *Amagugu Evangeli* is great.

The BIC Church and the Peace Stand

The Shona and Ndebele are the two major tribes in Zimbabwe. In the early 1880s, long before the arrival of the BIC missionaries, the warring Ndebele tribe subjugated the Shona people and drove them further East. The BIC missionaries worked mainly among the Ndebele people. A missionary effort that went to Chibi to reach out to the Shona people lost its missionary leader, Rev. Doner. In the 1970s, another church planting effort bore fruit in the establishment of the first BIC church in Harare. Relations between the Shona and Ndebele people, though not hostile, have generally been cool.

The doctrinal statement of the BIC describes it as a peace church. At baptism all the candidates are made aware of this stand. For many, that is as far as they have to think about the meaning of this peace witness. It is to be noted that during the war of liberation of the country of Rhodesia, many young men and women—products of the BIC mission schools—went off to war with or without the blessing of their BIC parents. There are very few like Themba Nkau, who with his well-known words "I will not kill a man. I am a Christian," held the BIC stand of non-violence and refused to participate in war.

Murder Forgiven.
Abednico Moyo, the son of one of the early BIC converts Mantshi Moyo, was was abducted from his home one dark night and was never seen alive again. His remains, identified by some of the clothing he was wearing at the time he was taken, were identified more than 10 years after he went missing. Abednico was a well-to-do member of his community. When abducted, he was a headmaster with prospects of rising in the education field. Today his family continues to believe in God. None of them display any bitterness. None are continually asking "Why?" None desire revenge.

The joy of independence from colonial rule was short-lived for many people in Matebeleland, including church members. Soon they found themselves hunted—and some even killed—for no reason other than that they were Ndebele. Hundreds suffered horrifying deaths after being tortured before crowds of forced spectators. Many were buried in shallow graves. The perpetrators of these ruthless killings were a government-sponsored army called Gukurahundi, which was deployed to wreak havoc in Matebeland North and South, as well as in the Midlands region.

In October 2000, President Robert Mugabe was a guest of the Brethren in Christ Church at a service held at the Bulawayo Central Church. At that service he apologised for the pain and suffering which was caused to the people of Matebeleland and the Midlands by the Gukurahundi. He invited all those present to inform all the victims who could still be traced to report the extent of their injuries and material losses to the District Administrators' offices. He promised that all would be compensated. To this day none of the victims has been compensated. Many are still hurting, many others died from their wounds, and others were traumatised. One may ask where the BIC people stand as a peace church. How have they handled this provocation? How have they dealt with the pain of loss? Have they forgiven? Have they let go of the anger bred by this attack on them, as a people? There are stories and incidents that illustrate faithful responses to our call as a peace church.

Bishop Danisa Ndlovu recalls the death of his father.
The late Baba Ndlovu, the bishop's father, was a storekeeper in the Beit Bridge area. Though he was not a Christian, he was well loved and respected in the community. He cared about the people. As a kraal head, people often came to him to help settle their disputes. He presided over community gatherings and was a father to all. He was not a politician, and yet he died a politically-related death.

One day eight soldiers in uniform came to his store and demanded beer. He had none to give to them, and so they began beating him. They filled his mouth with bottle tops and hammered his full mouth with the butts of their guns. They left him half dead. He could get no medical help for two weeks because the area was completely sealed off, with no traffic allowed either in or out. When he finally was taken to hospital, his jaw had become cancerous.

About one month after the beating, Bishop Danisa got to see his father again. His dad's face was completely disfigured. Bishop Ndlovu struggled with the desire for revenge, the wish to punish those who had brought such pain to his loved one. His father brought him peace with the simple words, "Son don't! Don't, son!"

When his father died a few months later, it was Scripture that comforted him. When God called Danisa Ndlovu to ministry, the war of liberation in Zimbabwe was at its climax. The loss of a beloved father was part of his Christian walk, and prepared him for his present task.

The late Bishop Stephen S. Ndlovu tells stories of his encounter with the squatters who had invaded Wanezi Mission farm in the early eighties. When he, as head of the BIC church, asked them to move off of the Mission farm, they called for his blood. He could have resorted to violence, but true to the BIC peace stand, he sought dialogue. At the end of this encounter which lasted many months, the squatters moved out. Some of them had started attending services while on the Mission farm and made up part of a core group that formed a congregation.

Bishop Stephen Ndlovu's courage was also witnessed during the time when the Gukurahundi were deployed to parts of Matebeleland North. He courageously went to Phumula Mission to encourage the Christians there. Though he could have been killed on the spot, he did not hesitate to preach the love of Christ to units of the Fifth Brigade.

Living the peace testimony calls for the ability to forgive and let go of the pain one has experienced. These are the teachings the church has called us to preach and to live. In times of conflict, BIC members have upheld the teaching that they should not take each other to a court of law. This has been tested on many occasions. From time to time, the church has had to deal with the dismissal of workers who have erred. In cases of theft, they have been quietly dismissed, whether or not they are able to refund or replace misappropriated goods or money. The business sessions of General Conference are sometimes prolonged, as individuals exchange heated arguments over specific administrative issues. Often, the elders of the church are asked to intervene and bring an end to the arguments by giving counsel. The teaching found in Matthew 18—humility, forgiveness and love—continues to be the ideal of behaviour in settling disputes.

Individual Portraits

When the first BIC missionaries came to Africa and started their evangelistic ministry, they had no idea how much their work would impact the lives of the local people. Their agenda was to win souls, but the end result also contributed significantly to the building of the nation. A notable number of national leaders were products of the Matopo, Mtshabezi and Wanezi mission schools. These men and women came to the mission schools, drank from the cup of knowledge and went out to share what they had learned. They contributed to the social fabric of the country, determined policies and gave significant leadership. Now, more than a hundred years since the arrival of the first church planters, we can look back and appreciate the changes that came about because of those who obeyed the "Go ye" command.

The years 1931-1964 were years of transformation, when many leaders were raised to serve the nation in various fields. The bulk of these people were teachers, but others went into the professions. Some broke into the traditional domain of white people. For example, Lot Senda's practice as a black lawyer brought pride to the church. Nurses, social workers, lawyers, school managers, builders, business people, literary people and many others were nurtured by the BIC, and many maintained their relationship with the BIC church. Many who maintained their roots in other denominations went back to their congregations and shared what they had gained. What follows are some brief portraits.[15]

Msindo Moyo of the San (AmaSili) People

During the time of the Zimbabwe BIC's 75th aniversary a young man called Msindo Moyo stood up to give his testimony. He represented the BIC reaching the Bushmen, also known as the San. The Ndebele called them AmaSili.

*Msindo Moyo and his wife were the first among the San
people to be baptized and to have a Christian wedding.*

In the early 1950s many people who had come under the influence of the BIC church in the Matopo, Mtshabezi and Wanezi areas were moved by the government from their homes in areas which were designated for Europeans, into a new area called West Gwaai (Gwayi). For both the people and their animals, coming as they did from a higher altitude, the mosquito- and tsetse-infested climate of the low veldt presented a problem. Many lost their lives in the process of re-settling. This was not the only depressing factor. There were no churches or schools for these new settlers.

Two evangelists went to do a follow-up with these re-settled people. The evangelists also helped to build schools, started preaching points, and ministered to the spiritual needs of the people. While they were doing this, they heard of a group of people referred to as Bushmen. These people lived in an area close to the border with Botswana. They were nomads living from food found in the bush and the animals they could kill. The AmaSili had been untouched by the Gospel. Msindo Moyo was one of them. When he became a Christian his stand influenced many others.

The first seed of contact was made the day the two evangelists found a group of AmaSili near a river about fifteen miles from one of the new schools. Some were spearing fish and others had guns. When they saw the evangelists, they aimed their guns at them. One evangelist called out in Kalanga, a dialect of some of the people in the Gwayi area. He raised his Bible and said, "We are not policemen. We preach the Gospel of Jesus Christ." The inhabitants put their guns down and gathered for a service. The Word was preached and seven gave themselves to the Lord that day.

More Christian workers moved into the Gwayi permanently, and more contact was made with the AmaSili. It was not always successful, for they kept moving in search of food. The coming of resettled people meant that there was less and less space for them to wander. They began staying longer in each of the places where they made temporary settlements. Though they were very skilled in treating a whole range of ailments with wild herbs, roots and barks, they started visiting Phumula Mission hospital for further treatment. Some were even beginning to make huts similar to those of the AmaNdebele with whom they were having regular contact.

Msindo Moyo was among the AmaSili who came to work at the Mission. Having made a commitment in 1966/67, this young man was able to enroll at Wanezi Bible Institute to take a vernacular course in Bible. When he returned to work at the hospital he was a witness to many. Another sign of growth on his part, was when he and another San person came to the resident doctor at the mission and asked if a certain sum could be taken from their wages every month in order to support the work of the church. This action showed more than he could possibly do with his mouth how deeply the Gospel had been instilled in him.

Msindo Moyo participated in the first Christian wedding among his people. When he first went to Wanezi Bible School he already had a wife and two children. They had been married in the African customary law. This union prevented him from being granted church membership when he desired it. After re-marrying in a Christian ceremony in 1972, he could become a full church member. In July 1973, after an appropriate time of preparation, Msindo Moyo and his wife followed the Lord in baptism and church membership. They were the first AmaSili to have taken that step, but more would follow.

In later years, more outreach was done among the Bushmen and some converted to Christianity. Unfortunately, the follow-up was not as constant as it should have been. One church leader has expressed disappointment that the BIC missed a chance to make disciples of the AmaSili because they did not intensify their ministry among them. One notable result of the contact with the San was that the first missionary outreach to Botswana was made in an attempt to follow some of the converts who had wandered across the border into that country. Again, full advantage was not taken of that move.

Amon Dube Nyamambi

Amon Dube Nyamambi (15 March, 1931) was born of a polygamist father with seven wives. His mother, Anne Ntengo Moyo was wife number four, but ranked second traditionally because her aunt was the most senior wife and her progeny was heir. Nyamambi Dube kaMehlwamnyama, Amon's father, yearned for the white man's education, which he had seen elevate his peers to clerical positions in the mines and other industries. As a result, Nyamambi's family policy was that all members of his homestead should strive for this education. No one was to be seen at his homestead during worship hours. Everyone had to attend Sunday school. At Sunday school, family members benefitted educationally as well as spiritually.

Nyamambi first came into contact with the white people at Fred Mine where he was a wood vendor. Later he was often occupied with building pole and dagga huts for the mineworkers. Contact with the white people and observing their ways provided him the chance to learn and appreciate the value of education. His village was about 300 meters from Shamba Primary School. Nyamambi took advantage of this chance to have members of his family learn. In 1945, Amon was among the pioneer boys who became the first boarders when Wanezi Upper Primary was opened. This was the first boarding school in the Filabusi District. All those boys became beacons of light back in their villages. The New Testament was used as a reader and so all learned to read it and memorize passages from it.

For young Amon Nyamambi, it was not only the impact of the missionary contact that made him choose the life of a believer. His maternal uncle, Poly Sayi Moyo, a devout Christian who was among the pioneer teacher-preachers, became his role model. In later years Amon could look back and thank the Almighty God for this background, which led to his recognizing fully that God had a mission for him. He is one of the people whose lives have shaped the nation.

Asked about what stands out for him in all that he learned, Amon says that BIC teaching during his time stressed the need for knowing God, adhering to the truth, fellowshipping with other believers, loving unreservedly, not coveting other people's property, and faithful attendance in church and school. For him, education became the foundation and ladder to God. Armed with these tools, he went out and changed the lives of those who crossed his path.

Like many people who studied in BIC mission schools, Amon Dube Nyamambi became a teacher. After teaching in Matebeleland, the adventure bug drove him to Harare. At that time, there was no BIC church, so he attended services at the Methodist church. In 1953 another avenue of service opened when he was invited by the broadcasting corporation to do a number of programmes. He covered educational topics like health and hygiene. In 1956, an opportunity presented itself to launch the first recording studio of the then Central African Broadcasting Station (CABS). Live broadcasts emanated from Lusaka and Northern Rhodesia (now Zambia)—a novelty at that time, as very few people even owned radios. Later, he introduced the first English Language record Hit Parade called "Top of the List." This was again beamed from Lusaka under the new Federal Broadcasting Corporation's African Services (FBC). The radio ministry took him to Lusaka, Zambia, and finally back to Salisbury (Harare). One of his greatest achievements was the overwhelmingly successful launch of the primarily Ndebele Language broadcast Studio, Radio Mthwakazi. This popular service became the envy of other language broadcasts. This station was closed, to the disappointment of the SiNdebele speaking people during the infamous Gukurahundi era, for reasons that still are not clear.

In the years that Amon Nyamambi lived and worked in Harare, Zambia and then again in Harare, there were no Brethren in Christ churches with which he could affiliate. He therefore fellowshipped with the Methodists, Anglicans and later Church of Christ brethren. It was during his second stay in Harare that he became instrumental in building the Harare BIC church.

The BIC were well-established in rural Matabeleland and had been present a few years in the city of Bulawayo. It seemed an insurmountable task to have to penetrate the Shona territory. There were a few Shona people who had been educated at Matopo mission. There were also some from Matabeleland who worked in Harare. With the help of his cousin, Ruth Dube, Amon carried out a survey to find those who had been to the BIC mission schools, with positive results. A group of interested persons approached the mother church at Bulawayo headquarters for permission to assemble a congregational meeting. The late Bishop Philemon Mtsholi Khumalo enthusiastically gave his blessing to this notion. Amon convened the first meeting at his house. The first church committee was comprised of Daniel Nyamazana Dube as Chairman, Amon Nyamambi as Vice Chairman, Agritty Ndodana Gumede as Secretary. Mr Canaan Moyo and his wife Lister became the moving spirit in mobilizing the first BIC house of worship in Harare.

Veteran Evangelist, Maria Tshuma, was immediately deployed to Harare to teach new converts and gather in the lost sheep. When the chairman, Mr. Daniel Nyamazana Dube was called home to the Lord, it fell upon Amon Nyamambi to complete all the official paperwork that needed to be done before a site could be located and a church built. Today, Amon looks back and thanks God for the vision and the strength to accomplish the construction of the place of worship at Glen Norah. Nostalgically, he reminisces and marvels at the expansion that has led to the expansion to Chitungwiza, Mt. Pleasant, Mtoko and Budiriro.

Amon Nyamambi has given his whole life to service. Apart from serving as a member of the Radio Committee of the BIC church and the Book Room Administrative Committee, he was a strong mover for the establishment of the Finance Board. It was this Board that went on to pull the church out of a financial crisis which threatened to swallow all the church assets. Nyamambi served on the Lobengula congregation church committee for many years. This congregation is reputed to hold the largest BIC membership and attendance worldwide and has been pastored by Rev. Albert Ndlovu since its inception. Initially, the opinion was that the upheaval of the 1980s was the catalyst to the large numbers of people filling the pews on Sundays, but twenty years down the line, growth continues.

A look at this man's life reveals a person who has impacted the church, the community and the nation. For the soccer lovers, Amon Nyamambi is appreciated for helping found the Supporters' Club for the Highlanders football club. When the Bulawayo boys went to play in Harare, there always was a welcome team to host them. For budding and established writers, appreciation is shown for the poetry he has published in the various anthologies as well as the Ndebele book of proverbs—*Izaga*. For the young members of the church, he is now the elder counselor who at a conference is asked to give a word of wisdom when the younger generations have argued to their heart's content.

Stephen N. Ndlovu

On 12 June 2000, the Rev. Stephen N. Ndlovu went to be with the Lord after a long and painful battle with cancer. He was 69 years old. He lived five years beyond what doctors had predicted could happen with the type of liver cancer he had. When the news of his death became public knowledge, the people of Zimbabwe mourned deeply. With heavy hearts, they went about shaking their heads and murmuring "*Asazi*," meaning "We don't know." This is a lament for the loss of a departed one and an acknowledgement that we can never understand the mystery of death, when the living review the impact made on people's lives by the departed.

The late Rev. Stephen N. Ndlovu had a profound influence on those with whom he had contact. Stephen was the son of Ndlalambi, former cook to the second Bishop of the Rhodesian BIC Church, Steigerwald. As a young school teacher Ndlovu, like the biblical Jonah, tried to resist the call to ministry, but once committed he never looked back. He began teaching in 1951. In 1960 he came to serve the BIC church as a teacher at Mtshabezi Primary School and as Boarding Master at the Teacher Training College. In 1970 he and his wife Ottilia were invited to serve as Overseers for Mtshabezi District. Ten years later, on February 3, 1980, he was consecrated as the second national Bishop of the Zimbabwe Church.

Ndlovu earned an undergraduate degree at Messiah College, Grantham, Pennyslvania in the mid 1970s. On his return to Zimbabwe, he taught at and became principal of Ekuphileni Bible Institute. After serving as Bishop he once again went to the United States where in 1992 he graduated from the Associated Mennonite Biblical Seminary in Elkhart, Indiana. Back home in Zimbabwe, he taught at the Theological College of Zimbabwe (TCZ). At TCZ's graduation in December 1999, the Faculty and Trustees of the College created the "S. N. Ndlovu Award for Servant Leadership," to be given to TCZ students who demonstrate servant leadership. His funeral was attended by over 900 people.

> **Bishop S. N. Ndlovu remembered.**
> Bishop Ndlovu was not just the Bishop of Zimbabwe only, but of the whole of Africa. He travelled to Ethiopia when the Communist government closed the church, imprisoned its leaders and confiscated church property. His warmth, love and care has comforted many in Bulawayo, Zimbabwe, Africa and around the world. MCC Africa has benefitted from his endless wisdom and counsel in many forums, one of which was his committed service on the Advisory Committee of MCC Zimbabwe.
> —Tesfatsion Dalellew,
> MCC Coordinator for Africa

Ndlovu was a man of prayer. He brought home to many young people the realization that God talks to people in their prayer times. Even up to the time of his death, he and his wife MaNkala woke up at 5:30 a.m. to intercede in prayer for other people. As a member of the BIC Home and Family Committee, he not only counselled those he joined in holy matrimony, but also helped to mend and heal strained relationships.

Ndlovu travelled extensively internationally as a preacher and as a representative of the many church-related bodies on which he served, including the Africa Mennonite and Brethren in Christ Fellowship (AMBCF) and Mennonite World Conference. That is why it was possible for him to approach the Ethiopian government on behalf of the suffering church. He was known and held in high esteem as an African leader. The

Western Church had its eyes opened to vast and available human resources in the African continent through him. His wisdom and counsel were needed more in his old age than they ever were in his earlier years of service. Even when his health was declining, he continued serving right up to the end. He visited the sick, comforted the mourning, taught, and resolved conflicts. He was a man of God and

> **Bishop S. N. Ndlovu remembered.**
> We saw for ourselves.
> When you attempted
>   to straighten the crooked
> When you held straight the plow
> When you brought back those
>   who like oxen had gone astray,
> We saw, we heard
> Those with ears have heard.
> —Barbara Nkala, Director
> International Bible Society,
> Zimbabwe and Malawi

also a man of the people. His life was an example to many.

In the unstable economic climate of Africa, one of the greatest challenges for the church has been to have adequate resources to meet the material needs of church workers. Ndlovu enjoyed working on the land. From his grain field, vegetable patch, chicken run and rabbit hutch, he raised enough to feed his family and cover the cost of other needs. When the church could not supply his needs sufficiently, he was still able to live off the land, so that the Lord's work did not suffer because of lack. He was a powerful example of those who have answered the call to serve the church in Africa.

Mabel Louise Sigola

Reference has been made elsewhere to Rev. Manhlenhle Kumalo, who died at an estimated 112 years of age. He was one of the first three Overseers ordained by the BIC church in Africa. The testimony of his love, faithfulness and commitment to the Creator does not end with him, but lives on in his children and grandchildren. From this family have come many great teachers. The last girl born of this family was Mabel Louise, whose married name is Sigola. She, like all the Kumalo children, was nurtured with much Scripture teaching. At the time of writing, Mabel tells her story with the pillar of Proverbs 16:1-3. "We may make our plans, but God has the final word."

Mabel learned this truth at an early age. She wanted to be a nurse, and so from an early age she committed her plans to the Lord who not only fulfilled them, but took her to greater heights than she had ever imagined. Her nurse's training was in a mission hospital in Durban, South

Africa. She went there because that is where she felt the Lord wanted her to be. Furthermore, she felt a deep desire to be a nurse with a difference. Because of the high standard of performance she attained, she was invited to remain at the Mission Hospital as a staff-nurse. This gave her experience in both administration and management.

Back home in Rhodesia in early 1961, she joined the Ministry of Health as a staff-nurse where she worked in several different wards and departments, and so gained more experience to prepare her for major challenges ahead. After marrying Jerry Sigola and raising two children, she pursued further education. This time she enrolled for a diploma in Industrial Nursing at Birmingham Accident Hospital in the United Kingdom. The industrial component included one month in a mine, a factory and a burn unit. On completion of this study, Mabel dashed to Scotland to do a Diploma in Administration. Armed with a deep faith, educational experience and wider exposure, Mabel then headed home to Zimbabwe where she rejoined the Ministry of Health as a Clinical Instructor. As such, Mabel has participated in training nurses who today are serving Zimbabwe in various departments of the Ministry of Health. She is loved and admired for her high standard of professionalism.

The year 1976 saw her at the University of Zimbabwe doing a course in Hospital Administration in conjunction with a Diploma in Nursing Education. She graduated with a Master's Degree in 1978. In 1986, a Certificate in Family Planning was added to her many qualifications. Mabel has served the country faithfully in her chosen field. Promotion has come through merit and hard work. She has worked through the ranks of Clinical Instructor, Tutor, Senior Tutor and Principal Nursing Officer (Principal Matron). She has been a consultant for the World Health Organization (WHO), and part-time counselor for HIV/AIDS for the Population Service International.

In 1995 she was awarded the Certificate of Excellency by the International Nursing Council (ICN) and received three medals for outstanding professional work. In 1998 she was awarded the "Woman of the Year" certificate based on her outstanding leadership, accomplishments and noble example to her peers and the entire community. In 1997 the Western University, USA awarded her the certificate for Curriculum Development.

Mabel is grateful to her parents for giving her a Christian base which formed a solid foundation for her life. The BIC church has benefitted from her guidance on its Medical Administrative Committee. She is among the founders of Bulawayo Central Church, and she served on the first church committee. Like all God's children, she has not been spared pain and suffering. Her firstborn son died in a shooting accident in South Africa. Her surviving daughter has brought joy to the Sigola family. She is a medical doctor and her husband is a lawyer. The Sigolas have been blessed with four grandchildren. They have walked bravely through life's challenges because as Mabel says "The Lord is my shepherd, I shall not want." Psalm 23:1. "Where He leads me I will follow."

Isaac N. Mpofu

Isaac was born on April 2, 1932 at Malole near Wanezi Mission. All schools in the country at that time were church schools and the BIC was one of the churches that ran schools. Isaac attended Malole school and then went on to Wanezi Mission, which was a boarding school for boys. He graduated to gain a Standard Six Certificate in 1948 and the following year enrolled at Matopo Mission to train as a teacher. At the end of 1950, Isaac graduated with a Primary Teachers' Lower certificate (PTL) and straightaway became Head Teacher at Filabusi School.

In 1952-53 Isaac Mpofu, not satisfied to remain at the level of education he had, and being wise to the possibility of greater service when equipped with a higher certificate in education, moved on to Goromonzi Secondary School where he did his 'O' level (Cambridge School Certificate). It was a special feat to be accepted at Goromonzi because it was the only government school in the country and one of the only three Secondary Schools in the whole country.

On graduation, Isaac Mpofu found himself Headmaster at Mzinyathi Primary School, a Methodist school with eighteen teachers. It was considered an unusually large rural school. This was followed by years of service as Headmaster, Teacher/Lecturer at both Musume and Mtshabezi Teacher Training Colleges, Teacher at Matopo Secondary, and Headmaster at Mzinyathini Secondary. In between, Mpofu continued to seek further education. In 1966 he majored in languages and theology at the University of Zululand. In 1972 he obtained a Graduate Certificate in Education at the University of Zimbabwe.

After a stint as Inspector of Primary Schools, Mpofu became Deputy Regional Director of Secondary Education, followed quickly by the post of Regional Director of Education. By 1985 Mpofu was the Chief Education Officer, Standards Control at the national head office. Though at this position he was doing a great service to the nation, the position kept him away from his family. In 1987, he became Regional Director of Education for Matabeleland South Region, but because of his high level of professionalism and experience, he again was promoted to head office as Deputy Secretary of Education for Finance, Administration and Planning.

Many stories are told of how the high standard Mr. Mpofu set and expected of his subordinates totally revamped and improved the performance of both staff and pupils. As an inspector of schools, he is appreciated for bringing to an end the attitude of some rural teachers who had developed a tendency to leave school on Friday morning to head for town, leaving students without teachers. Some even went further and missed school on Mondays as well. After putting corrective steps into place to deal with such behaviour, Mr. Mpofu enjoyed a well-coordinated teaching team that produced good results. Today he is honoured by many who have benefitted from his oversight.

Mpofu is also a renowned Ndebele writer and has published a number of books, some of which have been set as texts in schools. As an educator and a writer, Mpofu has had a tremendous impact in shaping minds and preserving culture. He held many administrative roles in the Teachers' Association at both district and national level and travelled widely internationally to recruit teachers and attend international conferences.

Mr. Mpofu has also served the BIC church in various capacities and is a member of Bulawayo Central Church where he has served as chairman of the church committee and also conducts the church choir. He is the Chairman of International Bible Society, Zimbabwe, and is currently part of the team that is translating the Bible into SiNdebele. Because of his wide experience, the church recently invited him to assume the position of Matopo Book Centre Manager. There is no doubt that with God's help, he will use his administrative skills to get the BIC chain of bookshops to improve in performance.

BIC Churches in Zambia (Northern Rhodesia)

*"Whom shall I send? And who will go for us?" And I said, "Here
am I. Send me!"* (Isaiah 5:8)

The very first person in the BIC church to submit an application to the call
for foreign mission work was Miss Hannah Frances Davidson of Kansas,
in March 1897, followed by three others that same year. Miss Frances
Davidson worked in Zimbabwe for about eight years before setting out to
the interior, northwards, across the Zambezi River where it was believed
no missionary had penetrated. She was accompanied by Miss Adda Engle,
Ndabambi Moyo (later called David) and Gomo Sibanda. Many people,
including the District Commissioner of Livingstone, the Administrator of
Kalomo, and the Secretary of the Lands Department in Northern Rhodesia
tried to discourage and block the venture, especially since it was led by
two women. But nobody was going to stand in the way of these women of
resilience. Their tenacity earned them respect and reluctant assistance.
They had chosen to make their destination the Macha area in the Mapanza
District. Sister Davidson and her team travelled for six weeks to cover a
distance of about 780 kilometres from Matopo to Macha, where they set
up the first Brethren in Christ Mission station on 3,200 hectares of land.
This was an area populated by the Batonga people, known to be loving
and peaceful.

Sister Davidson, her team, and some local people set up a hut for the
helpers and a building for the missionaries, with make-do simple furniture.
They had to protect themselves against malaria-causing mosquitoes as well
as against ants that were very destructive to property. The missionaries
had to learn a new language, Tonga, in order to communicate the Gospel
they had come to share. They did not waste any time in their quest, but
immediately embarked on evangelising the people they had hired to help
them put up buildings and work the garden. They visited kraals. A service
was organised for Christmas where people met to hear the Word and to
feast together.

In the new year, 1907, word was sent out that a school was starting at
Macha, but no pupil showed up for the first six weeks. The missionaries
discovered that children feared the strange white faces as well as wild
animals such as lions that prowled the surrounding area. The breakthrough

came when Chief Macha himself brought his own son to the missionaries and asked that he be taught to read and work. Other people soon followed, and soon there were about seventeen boys coming to school. The youngest were about ten years old. They learned reading, writing, arithmetic and industrial education such as carpentry, building and gardening. An important component of the lessons was Bible knowledge. This was the beginning of evangelism, church services and schools at Macha, which soon grew with more buildings and more missionaries

Frances Davidson, *Nkosazana Debison* as she was fondly called, did a lot of village visitation. She would dwell in temporary straw huts doing evangelistic work in and around a particular area, up to two weeks at a time. The people in those areas were fascinated by a white woman who could communicate with them in their own language. In 1910, she opened the first out-school, and many more followed. Many young men who had been trained at the mission taught in these out-schools. Education was important if nationals were to evangelise their own people effectively in the future. Sister Davidson found a lot of satisfaction in seeing both males and females come to the schools, keen to learn. Some of the women came along with their suckling babies, eager to get book learning. Sister Davidson was also involved in the translation of the Scriptures to the Tonga language. Other missionaries from other denominations in the area relied on her skill in Greek to help them in their translation work.

Some of the out-schools that Sister Davidson helped to found were Simambi, Muyanda, Kabanze, Kabwe, Mabwe, Aluba, Haabunkulu, Chisikili and Halumba. All these were sub-stations to Macha Mission. She visited them as frequently as possible on donkey-drawn carts or ox-drawn wagons. Sister Davidson lived a very simple life, and true to a disciple of Jesus, her food was provided by the villagers who gave her eggs, chickens, pumpkins, melons, *busala, chimbwali* and *mawa*. She also gave oranges from the Macha orchard to the people

> **R. M. Sichala remembers Sister Davidson.**
> She put her feet on Chief Macha's soil
> And she offered thanks to the Lord.
> The faithful one of God prayed,
> For God to give her strength she needed.
>
> She would not cease from spiritual fight,
> Nor could her sword sleep in her hand
> Till she had a perfect Mission Station.
> That is today's Chief Macha's pleasant fountain
> Where God is worshipped by all
> The students, patients and villagers.[16]

she visited. Sichala records that people spoke of her as *Mutumwa Wa Laza*, the "Sent One of God."

Though at that time women were not recommended for leadership positions, Sister Davidson was a strong, hard-working, devoted person to the cause of spreading the Gospel, as the early development of Macha Mission and the out-stations demonstrates. Though somewhat overbearing and intimidating—several people remembered that she had the appearance of a man—it is noted that those who got to know her well appreciated and loved her. She was an undisputed leader who planned, organised and controlled activities, despite difficulties. There is no doubt concerning her dedication to the winning of souls and educating in service to God. Sister Davidson was a woman of the people who served them in their time of need.

Stories are told that provide examples of her heart for the people. She made several visits to the home of Semani, one of the schoolboys who had returned home because he was sick and slowly dying. She was there to comfort him and his relatives, and was joyful that he was dying in the Lord. One day during her village visitation, she had to go behind a bush to remove her petticoat and bring it to the house to wrap a child who was very sick and cold. Another time she walked at night with schoolboys to comfort the family of one of her schoolboys, Apuleni, whose father had died.

Sister Davidson also served as a nurse and there were times when queues of fifteen to twenty people could be seen at Macha awaiting treatment. In due course, one of the huts was made into a makeshift hospital. Sister Davidson is also known to have carried some medications on her visits to the out-stations, so that she could offer treatment where required. E. Morris Sider writes that Sister Davidson brought typical Brethren in Christ approaches to her spiritual contacts with the Africans which included fasting and prayer for the entire mission, modified revivals, confessions, and testimonies. She also delighted in reporting occasions of spiritual renewals.[17] Her diary entry for May 3, 1913 describes a fascinating event which inspired several young men to take the Gospel to their own people:

> The Lord descended to give us a real Pentecostal shower. Three
> spoke in tongues, others had revelations and visions of the Lord
> and the place was shaken in general. Some of the girls were

blest. And there was a very lively time for a while and yet no one got [out] of order. The testimonies that followed were good and I believe everyone was blessed in soul. . .[18]

The spiritual manifestation of speaking in tongues is unusual in the BIC records, as speaking in tongues is not a thing encouraged. There have been heated debates on the subject during the last part of the century, creating rifts among the young and the elderly in both Zimbabwe and Zambia.

Church Structure

The highest institution of the BIC church in Zambia is the General Conference that meets annually at a designated place, usually at Macha or at Choma. The Executive Board reports to General Conference, then District Councils, followed by the congregations. The Bishop is the head of the BIC conference in Zambia, supported by Overseers. There has only been one Overseer so far in charge of all the ordained ministers. A resolution has been approved to have five Overseers in 2003 to oversee the work in five areas that will be divided for easier management. At the end of 2002, there were sixteen ordained Ministers, and 58 recognised Pastors in the church in Zambia. There are many more church leaders in the rural areas that hold pastoral roles without the necessary qualifications. There are to date about 162 congregations in BIC in Zambia. The smallest congregations have about thirty-five members, and the biggest at Macha Church has 800 members.

Longest-serving Zambian Overseer Mwaalu and his family

Macha Mission

Macha Mission is situated in the Southern province of Zambia, mainly populated by the Tonga speaking people. The Macha Mission of the 1940s is described by R. M. Sichala as a mission station with villages dotted around it. The villagers formed the majority of the Macha congregation. Worshippers who were ardent believers kept inviting other people and the church filled up most Sundays. Sichala says those were days that had purpose. The common purpose was that people are saved to serve others, which is one of Jesus' principles. He came to save and to serve. His was a servant leadership. This was seen in Zambia from Miss Frances Davidson, and the leaders who followed. So it was that the many villagers who were saved through the Gospel preached at Macha Mission served the Lord God in their different ways, according to their gifts. Some preached, others spoke the Gospel in the way they lived, which the young aspired to emulate. Sichala says the strength of Macha Mission congregation in the 1930s and 1940s resulted from men and women of God whose lives "did more preaching than what they were able to say about their love for God and His saving grace."[19]

> **Chief Macha.**
> If you were fortunate enough to meet Chief Macha away from his palace, it was either on the road to the church or on the way to his maize field. He often chose to walk though he was a very good cyclist. He associated with the churchgoers, his court officials and men who loved manual work. Chief Macha (Kaiba) was influential. Very few men of his type of authority knelt down before God in that humility and simplicity. On Sunday, young ones walked with him to church to sit with him there. One can imagine that it was nice to sit with the Chief in the presence of God in the church.

Girls from villages and from the Mission Station School never lacked examples of women who lived in obedience to the Holy Scriptures. Bina Mukalambe, often called Bina Nkeete, and Bina Jacobe (Mrs. Mwendo) were sources of spiritual strength. They never missed a single church service unless they were unwell or they were attending to extended family matters away from Macha. They were described as preaching in "loud silence."[20] As Sichala notes, the depth of the Scriptures read in any service was aided by the presence of respected local people who sought spiritual nourishment, not social advancement.

Beulah Mungamba of Zambia with her youth Bible quiz team.

Macha Mission has grown to become a large institution with three schools: Macha Primary School, Macha (Girls) High School, and Francis Davidson Basic School. The latter is a co-educational day school requested by the BIC community, named after the founder of Macha. Macha High School is a boarding institute. There is also the Hospital and the Nurse Training Institute. The medical part of the mission is a large sector in its own right.

Macha Mission Hospital

Macha Mission Hospital, founded in 1954, has become a large referral hospital that has contributed immensely to the health delivery system in Zambia. The first missionary, H. Frances Davidson performed the super-human task of being teacher, preacher and medical officer all in one. Macha Hospital started from humble beginnings as a room used by Sister Davidson to treat patients; today it is a hospital that has a capacity for 208 beds for admitted patients.

There is no better person to tell about Macha Mission Hospital than Mukuwa Kalambo who has worked in various capacities as Treasurer, Administrator and Executive Director of Macha Hospital for about deighteen years. Mr. Kalambo started working at Macha Hospital in 1984, as an administrator who looked after everything but the medical side of things. He co-ordinated all activities, including the maintenance of hospital buildings, equipment and vehicles, procurement of all medical facilities and other equipment; he also recruited staff.

The hospital was originally managed by the BIC church, but now is managed by the government. There is a local board that sees to the day-to-day administration. Various departments have been added to the hospital as the years go by. The Primary Health Care Department actively dealt with immunisation health education in the 1960s and 1970s. A paediatric ward was dedicated in 1969, and Chief Macha graced the occasion and had the honour of cutting the ribbon. A chapel was built in 1970. In 1985, the Eye Unit was added to the hospital, and in 1988, the Water and Sanitation programme began with the sinking of boreholes to provide water for the neighbouring community. Villagers were helped in the construction of toilets to engender a cleaner and healthier environment. They were provided with cement and iron sheet for this purpose. While the church provided spiritual grounding, and the school provided knowledge, the hospital generated a health delivery system that enhanced wholesome family life.

Mr. Kalambo became the CEO of the hospital in 1989. He had attained a BA degree in Industrial Arts from Shoreditch College in UK in 1974. At this time, Messiah College offered places for two Zambians to go for further training. All they needed was to sponsor themselves with tickets. The BIC church in Zambia encouraged Kalambo to apply for that position so he could be equipped as Financial Secretary. He was preparing to go and do the BSc course in accounting when the church decided he should become Hospital Administrator at Macha Mission Hospital. He went to Messiah College and completed a Human Resources Management course instead. From Messiah he was sent to Ireland for Hospital Administration studies which he undertook at the Irish Institute of Public Administration from June 1984 to December 1986. Kalambo attained a Masters in Health Management at the University of Birmingham in 1991.

At Macha, one of the resident doctors is the Medical Officer in charge of all clinical matters. There is also a chaplain. Rev. Joseph M. Sikalima has worked as chaplain at Macha Hospital from 1986 to the present, though he pastors one of the churches in Chikanta area and he also holds a full time job as the Maintenance Manager of the hospital with duties ranging

Esther and Mukuwa Kalambo.

from supervising any building projects, electricals, carpentry, and mechanics for the mission fleet.

In discussing the challenges and achievements at Macha Hospital, Mr. Kalambo had positive things to say about the committed workers at the Hospital: "We have all managed to keep the hospital going in spite of the tough financial and human resource constraints." There were serious financial limitations before 1992 as non-government hospitals such as Macha did not receive any support from the state. Even after 1992, when there was supposed to be parity, no assistance was forthcoming. The BIC church had to source funds from donors to keep the hospital operating. Kalambo found it a challenge to continually and creatively write project proposals. He bemusedly said, "I became the Chief Beggar at Macha."[21]

Another challenge is staffing. It is not easy to keep highly qualified medical people in the rural areas. Many people love the comfort and glitter of city life. The Rural Hardship Allowance of 20% over one's salary is not enough to attract large numbers of medical people to rural areas.

The Churches Health Association of Zambia which Mr. Kalambo served as Treasurer from 1985 to 1990 is an association that brings together church related hospitals so that any lobbying with government or any contact with Ministry of Health personnel is done through this organisation. There is strength in numbers and unity. It has helped for the BIC church to be part of this Association.

In recent years Macha Mission Hospital has begun malaria research. Malaria has been a big problem for years in many tropical countries, including Zambia. Dr. Alvin Thuma spearheaded this project and his dream has been to eradicate malaria from Zambia. Even after he left Macha, he continued to visit every six months to check on progress made. The Macha Hospital Malaria Research Centre is affiliated with the Johns Hopkins School. Much has been done to understand malaria. People from the University Teaching Hospital (UTC) in Lusaka also visit the research centre often. This research has put Macha on the map not only in Zambia, but in the international arena.

On the hospital grounds is a beautiful centre which was created specifically to offer nutrition for children. A qualified nutritionist is needed as well as funds to keep the programme going. It is awesome to think that the vision of one or two people has culminated in such a big institute that keeps growing to save and serve. Surely, the Lord God's mercies endure forever.

Sikalongo Mission

Physically, he hunted and brought us meat.
Spiritually, he hunted and brought us to God.
Please God, receive him in our tradition
For he lived with us and loved us.[22]

These words are a eulogy for Rev. Myron Taylor who founded Sikalongo Mission Station about 1912. Sichala says he was nicknamed *Sikayasamuliso* because of his pinpoint accuracy in rifle shooting, but what mattered more to the people in Sikalongo area was his devotion to preaching the Gospel and winning souls for Christ.

Rev. Taylor was devoted to taking the Gospel to the people of Zambia, sometimes at the expense of his health. There are many times when he fell victim to malaria. Sister Frances Davidson records instances when she worried about him and when she had to nurse him back to health. When he was sick, he allowed the local people to visit him in his sick room, and he had prayers with each lot of people who visited. In this way he nurtured a strong bond with the inhabitants of Sikalongo. At his death, people mourned him as if he had been one of them. Rev. Taylor was laid to rest at Sikalongo Mission. Sichala mentions the main bell of the mission which was purchased for church services in honour of the late Rev. Taylor as a prominent item that used to ring in one's mind all the time.[24]

Sikalongo, situated on 180 hectares of land, became an important education centre as was the case with most other BIC educational institutions in Northern and Southern Rhodesia (Zambia and Zimbabwe). Religious education—Bible study—was a prominent subject in the curriculum. There are many students who received their first knowledge of God's saving grace through their scriptural studies. Sichala says they came face to face with Jesus in the classrooms.

> **Rev. Taylor, remembered by Arthur Kutywayo and Rev. Peter Munsaka.** He visited and he was visited. The missionary sat on the native stools or on the same bench with local people. He was among very few white people who prepared a "sit" for the local people inside his house. In most cases, natives were to be met outside the house and spoken to there. They must be seen to leave the place immediately after their business.[23]

Sikalongo had a record of good teaching to the extent that Standard IV examination results at Sikalongo were almost always better than those of other mission and government schools. Some of the teachers of excellence remembered at Sikalongo in the 1940s were Miss Eyster, Miss Anna Graybill and Mr. Jonathan Muleya. Sichala remembers Mr. Muleya's zeal:

> I still remember Mr. Jonathan Muleya's ability to teach and help boys almost up to midnight. He woke up at about 05.00 hours and shook boys off their floor beds and led them running towards Bukwemba Hills, cutting through the winter winds. Every boy came back sweating. It was easy for every boy to wash in the June cold water after running a course of about 6-8 kilometres every morning. This was only to prepare boys for hard work. . . Often I wonder what the BIC would do at Sikalongo Mission School without Jonathan. God be thanked for Jonathan's youthful and useful time at Sikalongo.[25]

Some of the out-schools that fed into Sikalongo were Mukukula, Nakempa, and Mbole. Today, there are many men in prominent positions in society who were nurtured at Sikalongo Mission. They are men who started well, who have served well, and are on the road to finishing well. It is with grateful nostalgia that the early Christian leaders are remembered. The poet Sichala sings praises to them by writing:

> Through your strong hands that carried the Bibles,
> Through your tough legs that climbed the hills,
>
> By your tireless mouths that preached the word,
> By your efforts, God's Kingdom has appeared.
>
> Through your kind and firm voices,
> By your soft and kind nature,
> Our souls have come face to face with God
> May we living take our part to praise God.[26]

Sikalongo Bible Institute

It is fitting that the BIC Bible Institute was set up at Sikalongo. Many BIC ministers in pastoral work both in urban and rural areas attained their training there. Sikalongo Bible Institute (SBI) in Zambia was established along the same lines as Ekuphileni Bible Institute (EBI) in Zimbabwe.

Sikalongo Rural Health Centre

Sikalongo Rural Health Centre (SRHC) is a large clinic serving the area around Sikalongo. When the Mission Station was first founded, it became necessary to develop a health facility to cater for physical ailments, while the church catered to spiritual needs. It is recorded that the many battles and feuds in the Zambezi Valley resulted in terrible injuries. Spear wounds, ugly skin diseases, and other ailments were treated successfully, making Sikalongo an important place of Christian influence. Today it serves as a national rural health centre. Most important still, the "Food for Work" programme during the years of drought in past years and in 2002 is directed from SRHC.

Choma

The BIC headquarters in Zambia is in Choma and it sits on 200 hectares of farmland. That is where the Bishop's residence is situated. The residence of the Overseer, the Financial Secretary, who manages the funds for missionaries, and the country representative for the Board of Missions are all found at this farm. There are five boreholes (wells). Choma

Secondary School is also found here, which takes students from grades 8-12 and had a total of about 1,500 students—of which 800–1000 were boarders—and a staff complement of 65 in 2002. The school produces some very good scholars and good athletes who earn awards both in the province and in the nation. The students do well in football, netball and basketball.

Choma Bookroom

Choma Bookroom was opened in 1965. It used to be well stocked with a variety of Christian and educational books that brought spiritual blessings to the community. Students in first and second years at university used to buy books there. It greatly supported various BIC Church programmes for many years. But of late the Bookroom is not functioning well because of the depressed financial situation.

Choma Bookroom, Zambia

Nahumba

Another BIC farm is at Nahumba; the Nahumba Basic School is located there, headed at present by Simon Mpasela. Nahumba started in 1958 and first went up to Grade 4. Now it is a fairly big school with Grades 1-9 for both boys and girls. Mr. Mpasela started heading the school in 1990. At the end of 2002, the school had a complement of thirty-three staff members and 1,642 pupils. The farm also keeps about 250-300 chickens at any one time; it also has a piggery and a herd of dairy and beef cattle. Since land is limited, the farm keeps only about 80 head of cattle. The farm supports various conferences by offering cows for slaughter. Vegetables are also grown at the farm, and there is an orchard as well.

Portraits of Church Leaders

Bishop Enoch Shamapani

Bishop Enoch Shamapani was born in 1949 at Mubulu village, under Chief Siyachitema in the Kalomo District. There were eleven children, and he was second in the family of five girls and six boys. His father was a fireman with the Rhodesian Railways during the Federation of Rhodesia and Nyasaland. Shamapani started his schooling in Southern Rhodesia at Sizindi Township in Bulawayo, where he completed the first three years of schooling. As a result he still speaks Ndebele perfectly. He completed his primary education in Lupata School in the Macha area, and Choma Secondary School where he completed grade twelve.

Shamapani was a bright boy and he longed to continue with schooling, but there was no money. His occupation became herding his uncle's cattle in the Macha bushes. He daydreamed a lot about what he wanted to be, but it all seemed like an impossible dream. It was then that he would recall Bible stories of those who prayed and their dreams were fulfilled. He also prayed:

> I said, "Lord give me a chance! If you give me one more chance to go to school, I will serve you." I also prayed that the Lord would take me to a good Christian School. I had noted that teachers were pastors and vice versa. I reckoned that I would become a teacher and serve God by preaching the Gospel as well. The prayer to continue with schooling was answered when I eventually landed a place at Choma Secondary School. I was delighted and determined to do well.

By the time Shamapani had completed his secondary schooling he had his heart set on joining the Zambian Air Force. Like the proverbial Jonah, that is where he applied, but the doors remained firmly closed. Instead he was accepted at David Livingstone Teacher Training College. It was as if that was a reminder to go to Nineveh and not Tarshish.

It was at David Livingstone College that Shamapani's call to ministry became distinct. He recalls, "I desired to touch the hearts of people with the Gospel as they had touched my own heart. The books I read at that time also strengthened my resolve. Some of the stories that impacted me greatly were those of David Wilkerson in *The Cross and the Switchblade*, and also Nicky Cruz in *Run, Baby Run.* I prayed to become a preacher."

Bishop Enoch and Lastinah Namoomba Shamapani.

After completing teacher training Shamapani did not forget his home area. He went to teach at Macha Girls Primary School. It was at Macha that Shamapani met the beautiful and serene Lastinah Namoomba, who was doing nursing at Macha hospital. The sweet romance culminated in a big wedding on November 11, 1977. This same year BIC offered him a scholarship to go and study outside the country. Though this was a chance for exposure and new ventures, some of the decisions were not easy to make. Shamapani was besieged with doubts about becoming a pastor. Enoch and Lastinah sat down and carefully considered the way forward. Lastinah had wanted to pursue a course in mid-wifery at Chinkankata. They agreed that she should do just that while he pursued applications to do the theological course in Kenya, after their wedding.

Shamapani embarked on his training at Scott Theological College run by Africa Inland Mission in Nairobi, Kenya in May 1979. Lastinah joined him in May 1980 and she also did a full year of the evangelism course. All the learning was done in good faith, but the call to ministry was not part of the big picture at this time. It was only in 1982 during the third year that Shamapani was impacted afresh for ministry. The studies were on the book of Isaiah Chapter 6. "Though I had previously desired to serve the Lord by preaching the word, the first time I was hit hard by the call made to the prophet Isaiah was when the voice of the Lord said to him, 'Whom shall I send and who will go for us?' It was as if that was a personal challenge directed specifically at me for Zambia. My reaction was, 'No Lord, No! I am a teacher, not a pastor. I have to teach and earn a salary to take care of my family. There is no salary in pastoral work.' That did not give me peace in my heart or in my mind. I could not read well in my studies. I broke down before the Lord and cried. My dear wife did not help matters at this instance. When I broached the matter of going into full time ministry she said, 'Enoch, I want to remind you that I married a teacher, not a pastor. Don't be infatuated with new things. Please pray over that issue.'

We talked back and forth, prayed, and I tried to listen to the Lord. The Scripture in Isaiah 6 did not give me rest. The more I said, 'No Lord!' the more I encountered fear. I prayed for Lastinah to understand my position. I had conceded just as Isaiah had done, by saying 'Yes, here am I, send me!' Yet I felt uneasy because my wife and I were not in harmony on such a crucial decision. It was a long year of battling spiritually and mentally before Lastinah consented that my strong feelings were coming from God, and agreed to support me. I was overjoyed when she said the Lord will be our provider. I shed tears of happiness, and I was overjoyed that she was prepared to stand by me, which she has done these past twenty-five years. I wrote home wondering whether I would go back home to be a pastor, to teach at Bible School or to teach in school. The response was that I should come back and teach at Macha Primary School, which I did in 1984. On weekends, I went to preach. My efforts in the teaching field were recognised as I was given a promotion, but my heart yearned for full-time ministry as a pastor. I resigned from the teaching profession in 1985 to become a full-time pastor. I became a pastor at Macha Mission Church. It was a thrill to encourage people in the Lord, to see them accepting Christ, praying and growing in the Lord."

As time went on, Shamapani held two full-time jobs, as a pastor and a teacher. There was a third job when he became mission coordinator. He was later transferred to Lusaka when he was pastor at Chilenje Church where he served God for two years. In 1987, he was chosen as Principal of

Sikalongo Bible Institute where he remained for four months before he was elected Bishop of BIC church in Zambia. He and his family moved to Choma where he remained Bishop, a position he held for three terms from 1988 to 2002. He is the longest-serving Bishop in Zambia and for more than a decade was a member of the Mennonite World Conference general council.

Bishop Shamapani faced many challenges that during his term of office as leader of BIC church in Zambia. When he first came to office as bishop, he asked God to help him lead the church to strengthen evangelism and discipleship, in Bible study, in developing leadership training, in expanding even beyond the borders of Zambia. He was keen also to work towards improving the salaries of pastors. The Board for Missions in the United States was very supportive in all these objectives, and many pastors were trained, sent into the field and advanced the work of the church.

Poverty in the region is a central problem. Agriculture is not thriving due to lack of rains and poor farming implements. Micro finance programmes intended to alleviate poverty have not functioned well. In this context meaningful pastoral support remains a big challenge. Related to the economic stress is the scourge of HIV and AIDS that is ravaging the nation. Resources are needed to fight this pandemic.

One of the biggest challenges for Bishop Shamapani came at the end of his two-year term as he was going into the third term. There were accusations by a group of five pastors who agitated against his leadership.

I must say, that hurt deeply. That sort of thing almost paralyses the soul. I am truly indebted to those who stood by me then, and prayed for and with me. Lastinah and I would get up at 2:00 a.m. to seek the Lord's face and to listen to his counsel. There were many church members who came to pray with us and who stood by us, and we even received encouragement from members of denominations who were not BIC. My golden scriptural verse was, "If God be for us, who can be against us." (Rom 8:31-35) I determined that nothing would separate me from the love of God. Leadership demands patience and perseverance. It can be a lonely road to travel, but one draws strength from knowing God is in control.

It was not all smooth sailing, but Shamapani is grateful for the hand of the Lord that kept the church ministry on track. He is very grateful to

God for a praying wife and partner. "Lastinah had said she would stand by me through thick and thin; and God has been faithful to us these last twenty-five years. Lastinah is a prayer warrior. She gets up at 4 a.m. to pray. Without a partner like that, it would have been very difficult to face some of the challenges that came our way. Prayer and God's faithfulness have shown us the love of God and that of people, so overwhelming. We have had some wonderful relationships and are gratefully humbled by that."[27]

Bishop Shamapani said he is very happy to hand over the baton. He looked content and relaxed during the consecration of the new bishop in October 2002, and said he looked forward to continued service for the Lord in a different capacity.

Rev. Moses Munsaka

Rev. Moses Munsaka has worked for the BIC church in Zambia as Evangelist, Pastor, Translator and Overseer for over twenty years. He has been a dedicated, determined, hardworking and gifted evangelist. Few have travelled the road he has journeyed and remained committed.

Munsaka was born in 1954 of a father who was an African doctor who did not subscribe to church activities. His mother was not a believer either at that time. Moses' early beliefs were influenced by the Pilgrim Wesleyan church where he lived in Gwembe. He later moved to Choma, and taught at Chisanja Primary School, where he was greatly influenced by one of his teachers, Mr. Davidson Mweetwa, whom he admired greatly. He wanted to grow up to be like Mweetwa. Munsaka loved singing at church and was challenged by the messages. It was at Choma that he gave his life to the Lord and was baptized in 1968. His father had died in 1966, and so, he had to leave school in 1974, at grade seven as a mature student. There was nobody to pay fees for him for further education.

Munsaka sang a lot in church and helped teach Sunday school. The church noted his gifts and urged him to go to Sikalongo Bible School in 1976. He was not keen to go to Bible school. Like Jonah of the Bible, he decided to go to Mazabuka instead, to work in a sugar company, but he could find no peace of mind or satisfaction there. After nine months, he resigned and applied to Sikalongo. He experienced more peace in his heart as he pursued education at the Bible school. He also taught Sunday school there.

Munsaka graduated from Bible School in 1980. He was assigned to go and pastor a rural church at Siyamuleya, but did not go as his services were required to work with the Christian Service Department as a translator of Sunday School books, as well as the Theological Education by Extension (TEE) materials. These were translated from English to Tonga and were used by the church all over the country. Moses enjoyed doing this work, happy to serve the Lord this way.

Munsaka has travelled to North America twice for enrichment and study, first to the United States on the International Visitor Exchange Programme (1981-82) and then to Emmanuel Bible College, Kitchener in Canada where he attained the Bachelor of Theology course after two years (1987-89). Munsaka is an eloquent speaker and can hold his own in many places. He communicates fluently in a number of languages.

In 1982 Munsaka married his love, Elisa Munsaka. From 1977 to 1999, Rev. Munsaka was actively involved in evangelism and church planting, and was the sole overseer of BIC churches from 1992-1996. This was a heavy responsibility for one person to carry, but Munsaka took it as a challenge, which he knew he could not manage on his own. He says, "I have found it to be a blessing to have the assurance of knowing that my Lord and my God is in charge and in control. I don't panic. I know I am not alone."

Rev. Munsaka was transferred to the Copperbelt in the North where he has been since September 1999. He is responsible for three congregations. One is at the Theological College of Central Africa (TCCA) at Ndola, where attendance averages about 100 each Sunday. The full membership is seventy in the congregation. The second congregation is in Kitwe, where there is a membership of fifty to sixty people, and the third congregation is at Mufulira where there is a membership similar to that at Kitwe. There is no stable leadership at Kitwe and Mufulira, so Rev. Munsaka stays two Sundays in a month at each congregation. The congregations Rev. Munsaka pastors are far away from the other BIC congregations in the south of the country and life there can be lonely. Rev. Munsaka attends the Interdenominational Pastors' Fellowship there, which he has found to be encouraging, and he does enjoy networking with others church leaders.

One of the toughest times in his work was during the period of 1995 to 1998, when there were leadership issues within the church. It was a solitary period with feelings of isolation. He looks back to that period with gratitude, as the Lord gave him peace of mind and eventually sorted out the conflicts. One passage that has sustained him in his pastoral work is found in 2 Corinthians 3:2-3: "You yourselves are our letter, written on our hearts, known and read by everybody. You show that you are a letter from Christ . . . written not with ink but with the Spirit of the living God." Rev. Munsaka says this Scripture passage helps him live an open and exemplary life. "It gives me the confidence to live what I teach," he said.

Rev. Munsaka has found God to be faithful in every respect. The income pastors get is very little. It cannot sustain pastors' families. And yet God has shown his faithfulness by providing for the Munsaka's basic needs through the generosity of various people. The Munsakas have four children who still have to be supported in schooling and in various other needs. God's faithfulness has even conquered in Rev. Munsaka that fear of the unknown, of what the future holds. He has put all his faith in the one who holds the future. Rev. Munsaka also thanks the Lord for a lovely Christian wife who is very supportive in his work and who has stood by him in good and bad times.

Asked about the future of the BIC church in Zambia during the consecration of the new bishop at Macha in October 2002, Rev. Munsaka said, "I hope we shall refocus our vision as a church and revisit how we can make schools, farms and the book store function productively. There also needs to be an arm of evangelism geared at hospital and school staff. They also need to be evangelised and discipled, even as patients and students are reached with the word."[28]

Rev. Howard Sikwela

Rev. Howard Sikwela, like the missionaries of old who brought the Gospel to Africa, holds two major professions. He is a fully ordained minister of religion in the Brethren In Christ church, and is also the principal of David Livingstone College. Rev. Sikwela converted to faith in Christ and became a member of the BIC church when he was a student at Choma Secondary School in the 1970s. Following theological studies at the Theological College of Central Africa and several teaching posts, in 1988 he was named the Head of Choma Secondary School; his wife held the position of Head of the Home Economics Department at the same school.

After having been led through prayer, Rev. Sikwela accepted an appointment to David Livingstone Teachers' College first as Chaplin, then as Vice Principal, and then as Principal in 2001. David Livingstone trains about 450 students per year. Livingstone Town has two BIC congregations at Dambwa North and Maramba. At Maramba the services are conducted in Tonga, the dominant language in the area. At Dambwa the sermons are conducted in English to cater to a congregation that is made up of a variety of people who speak different languages. Rev. Sikwela and his family fellowship there and he preaches there on occasion.

David Livingstone trains male as well as female teachers. The quest for gender balance, which has been one of the focal developmental issues of the last decade in Pan African countries, is well looked after. Asked about women in leadership roles in church and in politics, Sikwela said that he believes leadership roles should be open to any person.

> At the BIC church, we have not yet ordained women evangelists or pastors, but I believe strongly that God can use any person to preach his word. Edith Miller used to preach during the main sermons at Macha/Sikalongo. A lot of women here preach at the grassroots level. Things are changing, and change is inevitable.

The inevitability of change is seen in the various occupations and professions now open to women, some of which were occupied exclusively by men prior to the 1980s and 1990s. Mrs. Sikwela now teaches at Mulwani Basic School in Livingstone where she also is Acting Head of the school.

Esther Kalambo

Esther Kalambo is a graceful lady, with a ready smile. She is the Macha Hospital Assistant Chaplain, a role she has held since 1987. Esther married Mukuwa Kalambo in July 1976 and they have been blessed with four children. Esther's challenge to work for the Lord came as a resolution made in 1982 when she was accompanying her husband who was studying in the United States. Their second son was born with a heart murmur, a life-threatening condition. Doctors did not seem to allow much hope for complete healing. Esther began to pray. She says,

I had read many testimonies by people who had gone through similar or even tougher experiences, whose prayers the Lord had answered. These testimonies blessed my heart and gave me hope, that if I prayed the Lord would show me mercy and my son would be cured. I began to pray hard. Actually, I told God that I would serve Him for the rest of my life if he showed mercy and healed my son. I prayed from the bottom of my heart. Three months later, when we visited the heart specialist for a review, the doctor looked a little perplexed and asked what had happened? The results were perfect. I knew what had happened. God had healed my son. I was overjoyed. When we arrived back home in 1984, I asked to help with pastoral work at the hospital. I was filled with joy when my request was answered positively.

Esther receives a blessing when those who are suffering and in pain are cheered up. She can identify with their pain because of her own experiences when her child's life was under threat. Some patients ask to hear more about God and also ask for prayer, and there are those who return after their discharge to say thank you. Esther says,

They often think I am a nurse who helped heal them, and I have to tell them in some detail about Jesus Christ our Lord and Saviour, who died to give us life.

One of Esther's favourite verses is found in Joshua 1:8: "Do not let this book of the Law depart from your mouth, meditate on it day and night so that you may be careful to do everything written in it. Then you will be prosperous and successful." Esther says, "I find encouragement in knowing that if I abide by the laws of God, I will be blessed. This verse is a light that spurs me on in my service. I feel God has been blessing me already as I have a husband who cares and is good to me, and our children are doing all right. I cannot take these blessings for granted."

Esther sometimes worries about preaching the right message to the people she serves but, she says, "as I note the responses to the words of God, my own faith is strengthened. I strive to practice the golden rule and to identify with the needs of the people, growing my own faith in the process."

Mrs. Elisa Munkombwe

Mrs. Elisa B. Munkombwe is the first BIC woman to become Head of a Basic School, and is still the only one to date. She has been the Head of Batoka Basic School since 1996. In 2002 she had a staff complement of twenty-six teachers and nearly a thousand pupils. Elisa's path to this position of responsibility led through a Secondary School Teacher's Diploma and more than twenty years of teaching experience at various schools. In 1996 she got the chance to be Head of Batoka Basic School, the BIC Basic School in Choma which offers classes in grades one to nine. "I enjoy working with children. I get satisfaction when I see them work hard and succeed in their school work," Elisa says. She frequently talks to girls in particular, encouraging them to study hard and to aim high. She is not only an administrator and educator at this school, she is also heavily involved in church work as a Church Deaconess, a position to which she was ordained in 2001.

Elisa says there are times when she feels tired and wishes to retire, but she must carry on for a few more years. Life has not been a comfortable bed of downy feathers for Elisa. She lost her husband in 2000, yet she still had a number of children (from a total of eleven) to put through school. It is not easy being a single parent. She has tried to be a role model not only to her own children, but also to pupils and staff at the school she heads. Elisa is also pursuing a Primary School Diploma by private distance learning. It is true that learning does not end. Her lifestyle is a challenge for young people to follow. Years to come will tell the impact of her influence, especially among girls who may wish to walk in her steps, the steps that try to follow Christ.

Mr. Frey Mweetwa

Many BIC nationals who were born in the era of the early missionaries in Zambia were named after one or another of the missionaries. Frey Mweetwa was named after Harvey Frey. The recently installed bishop, Thuma Hamukang'andu was named after Dr. Alvin Thuma, who worked at Macha hospital for many years.

Mr. Frey Mweetwa is one of the respected, retired educators in the BIC churches. After training, he taught for many years, was promoted to headmaster, then to manager of the BIC schools for seven years, before he got a post as an education officer in government, a post he held for ten years. Later, he became education secretary for BIC from 1982 to 2001 when he retired. Mr. Mweetwa has been in the BIC Board for Macha Mission for many years, offering invaluable wisdom and counsel.

Veronica and Thuma Hamukang'andu

On the 5th of August 1955 a baby boy was born to Anderson Mudenda, a Zambian teacher who had trained at Matopo Mission under former bishop Philemon Khumalo. Dr. Alvin Thuma, a missionary serving on his second year at Macha hospital, delivered the baby. As so often happens in African culture, when the family sat down to decide on a name for the baby it was agreed that his name should mark something significant at the time of birth. The logical conclusion was that he should be named after the doctor. So Thuma Hamukang'andu started his life. He grew up in Chikanta village, about thirty kilometres from Macha Mission.

Thuma began his schooling at Haamonde Primary school, eventually graduating from Sikalongo Bible Institute (SBI), after which he pastored churches in Haamonde and the city church of Chilenje in the Zambian capital Lusaka. By that time, he was married to his sweetheart of many years, Veronica Malake. Veronica had wanted to be a nun but was discouraged by her parents. Because she had always wanted to work for God, she was happy to marry a pastor so that she could serve beside her husband. Veronica and Thuma's union was blessed by the additional gift of two sons and two daughters who have brought much joy to their lives.

Thuma was well prepared for church leadership by other positions he has held. In 1993 he was elected to the Executive Committee of the Zambia Council of Churches. He held this position until 2000, when he was named Chairman. Growing up in the BIC Church and observing the older generation deliberating and making decisions, he has often wondered if there was no better way of handling certain decisions. Among the areas of greatest concern to him is the way some preachers go out to preach without adequate preparation. The messages are not always appropriate, with some out of context and season. His other concern is the church's stand as a peace church. During the struggle for independence, Thuma had wanted to be a soldier but his father discouraged him. It was only when he was at Bible school that he learned the pacifist doctrine. He believes the church should address this stand more aggressively than it does. As a coordinator of Christian Education since 1995, one of his passions has been to disciple those who have been baptised. Many are baptised but not enough is done to disciple them. Much needs to be done to improve the quality of church leadership.

Asked about his call to the position of Bishop, Thuma and his wife feel they are where God would have them be. They know there will be lonely times ahead. They quote words from the late Rev. Stephen Ndlovu who said, "In times of decision-making, kneel, pray and fast. Look to God because sometimes people tell you what they think you want to hear and not what should be." Thuma is concerned that the church has remained poor though there are many well-paid people in its pews. The missionary-sponsored projects are suffering. Church workers must realise that they are employed by God and he will look after them. There is a lot that needs to be done in the area of Leadership Training. Their prayer as they take up the position of Bishop is for guidance that God may show them where he would have them go as a church.

Women's Programmes

Women are the pillars of the home. Children are nurtured mainly through the hands of women, most of whom are homemakers. When women come to know Jesus as Lord and Saviour of their lives, you can rest assured that the children and the whole family will follow suit. The BIC church in Zambia initiated a women's programme in 1989. The women's programme committee consists of the Coordinator, the Bishop's wife, and the Overseer's wife. For many years, Mrs. Rachel Mushala coordinated the women's meetings. Mrs. Moono was Coordinator in 1997-1999, and the programme was supported by Tear Fund International (UK). The aim was to enhance the spiritual development of women and their families, and to empower them economically so they could become self-reliant and improve their families' health through lifestyle changes and balanced nutrition.

Spiritual development was fostered through Bible study. At the end of each meeting, the leader would assign the participants certain chapters of a book of the Bible to read at home. When they met again, they would discuss those chapters together. The process of group discussion fostered self-confidence among the women, helping them overcome reticence in asking questions or offering comments. It was hoped that this process would also help the women hold similar studies with their families at home, thus encouraging spiritual growth for each member of the family. Bible memorisation also was encouraged, and participants were encouraged to put into practice what they had learned. For example, if their Scripture reading or memory verse encouraged helping one another, they would put that into practice. They were encouraged to visit people in their communities, such as the sick, the old, the helpless, or someone with a new baby, to offer much-needed assistance. This truly was love in action and it encouraged many who did not know the Gospel to also want to come to know more about Christ and to become members of the church. The women's theme was "Serving Christ thorough serving Others."

Women were taught to make use of the God-given resources in their surroundings to create handicrafts that could be sold to generate income, or used in their own homes. Women engaged in moulding clay pottery, making floor mats, decorating mats and tablemats, knitting, crocheting, making household decorations using mealie-meal and fertiliser bags or sacks as well as sisal products. Some of the women became gainfully employed and brought home income through some of these handicrafts. Women were encouraged to use needle and thread to make or mend items for the family. They sewed and embroidered tablecloths, tray cloths, pillowcases, aprons, children's dresses and other such items. This has improved the way their families dressed, and neatness as a whole.

As part of the programme, women were taught how to prepare nourishing food for the family, how to preserve food for lean times, and how to make jam from available fruits. Awareness of food combinations that create a balanced diet improved the children's nutrition. Women were taught how to grow root vegetables and to construct chicken runs. In the midst of poverty, it is useful to know how to use the little that is available.

Each occasion was used to inculcate the values that edify the spirit, and to nurture a Proverbs 31 woman, with biblical principles and values at the centre. Many women became good preachers, as each was given a chance to share her testimony or some profound experience with God. Singing and musical skills improved for many women because they often learned new songs or sang together in their meetings. The BIC church Women's Programme has been a positive influence, bringing vibrancy to the local congregations that have active committees.

The fact that men always seem to lag behind women in spiritual matters is not unique to Zambia. Whereas great strides have been made in organising women to participate in their programmes, similar moves for men's meetings have been less successful. In the last two years, positive moves have been made to urge grass root level churches to develop their own men's fellowship programmes.

The young people are active in various activities that help them grow spiritually and gain confidence. There have been running battles in the past with some pastors and church leaders on ways of worshipping. Young people are more exposed to what is happening in other places, among other church denominations and the ways of tele-evangelists; the young usually are the first to embrace new ways. Church leaders have tried to show young people that one does not need to be Pentecostal to be a true worshipper, but the dialogue continues.

The Consecration of Bishop Hamukang'andu

Sunday, October 27, 2002

The church was completely packed full on all three sides, and filled with a serene and reverent atmosphere. The women looked beautiful in their church attire of black skirts, white tops and white headscarves. The Brethren in Christ church, Zambia Conference, had gathered for the consecration of Bishop Thuma Hamukang'andu at Macha Mission church.

The many women ushers led dignitaries and ordinary members to their designated seats. Beautiful and uplifting songs sprang up from all sides of the church; cameras flashed from every direction.

Call to Worship

At a few minutes after 10 a.m., the master of ceremonies, Mr. J. S. Muchimba, welcomed the congregants and asked Rev. Moses Munsaka to lead a call to worship by reading Psalm 100. This call to praise set the mood for worship of the Lord who is worthy of honour and praise. After the first congregational hymn of praise, Rev. Robinson Mudenda offered the opening prayer. Bishop Enoch Shamapani came forward to introduce the special guests, starting with three royal dignitaries: Chief Macha from the area, Chief Chikanta and Chief Singali. The Zambian church maintains a very good relationship with the traditional leaders and their representative, Chief Macha, welcomed all those who were present to grace the occasion. The Zambian Brethren in Christ church also has a very warm relationship with the government, and District Administrators and other civic leaders were also present for the special service.

Next came the General Secretary of the Christian Council of Zambia (CCZ), Rev. Japhet Ndlovu who brought greetings. The BIC church is a member of CCZ, and the Bishop designate, Thuma Hamukang'andu, was the current Chair of CCZ. Rev. L. Haamasele, the National Overseer was also introduced, and he brought BIC greetings to all present. Zimbabwe Conference had sent a delegation of eight people led by Rev. Joel D. Ndlovu. Esther Spurrier represented Mennonite World Conference (MWC), while Siegfried Holzhaeuer (Siggy) represented Mennonite Central Committee (MCC). Each guest was asked to stand and greet the church with a few words. Siggy Holzhaeuer brought greetings and talked a little about the relationship of MCC with the BIC church. MCC had recently shipped in maize, split beans and maize seed to alleviate the difficulties caused by drought in the country.

Outgoing Bishop Shamapani expressed his happiness that the Zambian Church was a growing church. Zimbabwean Bishop Danisa Ndlovu, who could not attend, sent greetings and best wishes to the church. He expressed the solidarity and prayer support of the Zimbabwean church, with a desire that the new Bishop would be a man of God. Esther Spurrier, representing the BIC World Missions brought greetings of joy as well as blessings from the BIC administration and the North American Church. She expressed the hope of the North American church for the annointing of the Bishop and for blessings of peace, joy, and hope for the Zambian church. The Salvation Army, the Pilgrim's Wesleyan Church, and the Roman Catholic church also were represented.

Last to be introduced was Miss Marian Buckwalter, who was fondly remembered by many, having worked in Zambia for many years beginning in 1985. She had fellowshipped at Chilenje South and had worked closely with Bishops Shamapani, Hamkang'andu, and Rev. Munsaka. Miss Buckwalter is currently the Secretary to the Africa Director for MCC. She brought personal greetings and also read a letter of congratulations from the MCC Africa desk which was written by Tesfassion Dalellew. Tesfa affirmed the good working relationship which MCC has always had with the BIC. He hoped this would continue. She also announced a consignment of food that was on the way to support the people with food aid. She encouraged the church in Zambia by saying, "May God's unfailing grace carry you through in your work, and may you be guided by God."

Bishop for Zambia Thuma Hamukang'andu and his wife Veronica.

Special Songs

After another uplifting song, "Guide Me O Thou Great Jehovah" sung in a most glorious harmony of hundreds of voices, Mrs. Esther Spurrier read relevant Scriptures from 1 Timothy 3:1-7 and 2 Timothy 1:3-9. There followed a presentation of special songs by the Sikalongo Boys, Mazabuka Church Choir, the Macha Women's Area Choir, the National Choir, Nahumba Choir and the Shampande Choir, all of which enriched the service.

The Sikalongo Boys' Choir was made up of some of the prominent senior citizens within the BIC, some of whom are Grey Mweetwa, Daniel Munkombwe, Gideon Munsaka, Jacob Muchimba, Deacon Mudenda, Johah Munganje and others. They are products of Sikalongo Boys School in the earlier years of development, groomed within the BIC, who served the church and society for many years afterwards. Some of them are still actively serving the church in various capacities. For instance, Mr. Grey Mweetwa is still a member of the BIC Board for Macha Mission; Mr. Daniel Munkombwe is a very successful farmer and former Member of Parliament during the President Kenneth Kaunda's reign. He farms 5000 acres in the Choma area. Mr. Munkombwe was educated at Sikalongo from 1952 to 1954.

Next to give a special song was a choir of about thirty ex-Macha girls. They were not recent Macha graduates, but the Senior Citizens, the present grandmothers, who believe music is the oil with which the Word of God is spread. Again, there were notable BIC church women of character who enchanted audiences with their songs. The Mazabuka Church sang a most beautiful song, which was a plea to God that just as God used Moses to lead the children of Israel to the Promised Land, may He use the new Bishop to be a guiding light. He is only human, but the plea was that God might imbue him with Godly wisdom, not earthly wisdom, so that he might be able to see and accept everyone: the rich, the poor, and the fallen, with the grace of the Lord. This choir was enchanting to watch because they not only sang with their voices, but with their eyes, their faces and their whole beings.

The Macha Women's Area Choir, about forty of them, sang a lovely song about the call of the Prophet Isaiah in Isaiah 6, where the angel touched his sinful mouth and made him clean, and he said to God, "Here am I, send me." The song was sung in the hope that the new Bishop was truly saying, "Here am I, send me." A quartet of four ladies from Nahumba sang a touching song reminding people that the Lord God is the true guide, leader and shepherd who is there for everyone. The Shampande Choir sang while the offering was taken. It was an alluring song that sought revival of God's vision that had been lost, for each member to get out and be a witness of the Gospel, as were the disciples that Jesus sent out. It was a song of commitment, that though the world might be full of danger and Christians are like sheep among wolves, children of God should be prepared to go forth for the sake of the Gospel.

Mazabuka delighted the congregation once more with a reminder that as Christians, the church has received a heavenly call which will need to be defended before the Lord who will be the judge. A vivid illustration was drawn from the careless and wicked way people lived during Noah's day. Noah and his family were the only obedient servants of God. Noah was mocked and called all sorts of names as he did his work. But when the rains flooded the land, the very same people who had mocked him were crying out to him to be saved. The song entreated present-day Christians to be serious about their call and realise that one day there would be an accounting before the Saviour.

The Consecration Sermon

Rev. Howard Sikwela, principal of Livingstone Teachers' College, delivered the consecration sermon. His sermon was titled "Divine Standards," which are God's standards. The main reading was taken from the story of David anointed by Samuel in 1 Samuel 16:4-13. Rev. Sikwela said that life is full of choices, and that many choices people make are sugar coated. Once the sugar is finished, a bitter pill is left. The choices people make determine their destiny. Persons are what they are because of the choices they have made at certain times in life. Leaders need to come into their office ceremoniously and also finish well. Leaders need a discerning heart not to move forward too fast, leaving others behind. Leadership demands more wisdom from God than it does education.

Rev. Sikwela also cautioned against judging any leader before he comes into office. The new Bishop should take office and do his work before people evaluate his work. To the outgoing Bishop, Rev. Sikwela said only God could justly assess how well he had performed, and only God alone could reward accordingly. The outgoing Bishop is still expected to be a good role model in the church.

In conclusion, Rev. Sikwela produced a lovely picture of a person and asked the congregation to say if there was anything wrong with the picture. The person was perfect in every way except that he had no ears. An ear is a good symbol for leadership. A good leader should be able to listen to what the people he leads have to say and act with wisdom. Rev. Sikwela closed his sermon with words of David to Solomon when he implored his son to acknowledge the God of his father and serve him with wholehearted devotion and with a willing mind, for the Lord searches every heart and understands every motive behind the thoughts. If you seek him he will be found by you; but if you forsake him, he will reject you forever (1 Chron 28:9).

Act of Consecration

The act of consecration was carried out by Bishop Shamapani with exhortations from 1 Timothy 3 which clearly lays out the duties of a church leader in directing the affairs of the church, to shepherd the flock of God and to guard the church from error. He also led the Bishop-designate and his wife, Mrs. Veronica Hamukang'andu, in the solemn consecration vows. Rev. J. C. Mwaalu gave the consecration prayer. Bishop Hamukang'andu was then declared the Bishop of Zambia. Congratulations were now open to various people and there was a lot of goodwill and love shown to the new Bishop and his wife, accompanied by a lot of hugs and material gifts. The closing prayer was offered by Rev. J. D. Ndlovu from Zimbabwe.

BIC Church and the Government of Zambia

The BIC church has made significant contributions to the nation of Zambia. This was acknowledged by the guest of honour, Honourable G. Mpambo, MP, in a speech delivered on his behalf by the District Administrator of Macha during the consecration of Bishop Thuma Hamukang'andu. He first congratulated the new Bishop and advised him to look to the Lord for wisdom. He then recounted the impressive things that BIC church has done in its long history of participation in the nation. They include:

1. Schools that educate the sons and daughters of Zambia.
2. Hospitals and clinics that give health to the citizens of Zambia.
3. A Nursing School at Macha.
4. HIV/AIDS campaigns and community-based care for sufferers.
5. Orphan care.
6. Assistance with food relief at Macha, Chikanta and Sikali. It was noted that the BIC church was one of the first churches to come forward to work with the government in food relief in the year 2002.
7. The role of Mennonite Central Committee in assisting in various ways was mentioned.

The BIC church was commended for producing persons of character who fear God, responsible citizens who will be instrumental in combatting corruption in the country.

A Retrospective Look at the Mission Legacy

Missionaries brought the Gospel to Africa and indeed, many renowned Zambian leaders hail from mission institutions. In their quest to civilize the "primitive" African, however, missionaries at times went overboard in inculcating values that seemed good to them.

Musical Instruments

In retrospect, one mistake the missionaries made was in not understanding the cultural basis for a particular value or activity. All cultural activities tended to be painted with one brush, and the stroke spelled barbarism and heathenism. All that was African therefore was heathen.

Whereas Africans usually respond to the rhythm of the drum, drumming was to be discarded when the missionaries came. Drums were associated with ancestral worship and were therefore taboo in Christian circles. In North America where the missionaries came from, and so in the African churches they founded, musical instruments were not considered suitable for use in church. Missionaries therefore translated their hymns into the local language (Tonga) or wrote their own tunes.

Robert M. Sichala's "Keep The Light Burning" contains the following interesting extract:

> I almost saw the devil in my first prayer meeting at David Livingstone Teacher Training College when I was sent there by the BIC to become a lecturer. I had to seek help from Miss Fanny Longenecker to establish my imaginations of the level of Christianity in the College. I later discovered that I was using the white man's spectacles to see the College. I was wrong. My faith was offended when students sat to the accompaniment of village drums, which musical instruments I associated with sin. This is the upbringing I had. . . . Judgement is personal but always based on social upbringing.[29]

Teaching on Giving

One of the problems which continues in the BIC church in Zambia is the lack of giving by members to advance the work of God. The missionaries did not adequately train the nationals to support the work of the church.

When the BIC missionaries first came to Zambia they did all they could to persuade the indigenous people to come to church. It is they who established good residential buildings, schools, churches, hospitals and clinics. They furnished these places and provided all that was necessary. Teachers and doctors were sent to work in Zambia and the church paid for their general upkeep. Parents were literally begged to allow their children to come to school when missionaries first came out. Whenever a need arose, missionaries sent an S.O.S to the mother country and whatever was requested would come.

When independence was attained in 1964, nationals had to take over running the church. The missionaries returned home, recalled by the home church in just the same way the colonial administrators were recalled by the British Overseas Office. R. M. Sichala has said,

Many organisations left all that they lived and worked for in the hands of men and women whose hands were least prepared for it. Many church supporting facilities were said to be either property of overseas churches or personal to the departing missionaries and those were therefore put on sale. Shops that served residents at the Mission Stations and facilities that made money to support church work lost their working capital a little before missionaries left. If in some denominational groups these were not done, at least funding was phased out.[30]

Those who took over did not have the expected support from the mother church, and meanwhile the national church did not realise how much it was expected to give towards supporting church leadership. Nationals were like dumped babies who continued to look to the West for sustenance. When the missionaries went home, the expectation remained that the mother church would continue to support all the local needs. People did not understand that they would need to give to the church in order for the church to be able to give back its work of ministry.

Training on giving and tithing has improved somewhat but it still needs to be encouraged in order to make people aware of the importance of giving. Poverty can never be an excuse. The apostle Paul wrote about the Macedonians who gave as much as they were able and even beyond their ability. Their overflowing joy and extreme poverty welled up in rich generosity. They excelled in the grace of giving, and God gave grace to their church (2 Corinthians 8:1-8).

Wrong Emphasis on Ideals

Because of cultural differences, some ideals were emphasized with a misplaced zeal, making people focus on the less important at the expense of true faith and spiritual maturity. Head covering at all times and the prohibition of jewellery have been issues for a long time, especially among the more enlightened women who did not see where morality and righteousness came into the picture. These contentions have been put forward to a General Conference which resolved that it is not a crime to go to church without a head covering. However, during baptism and other solemn occasions, women have been asked to cover their heads.

There is no doubt that the church will continue to open itself to the teachings of Christ, and in the process discard all that is not worthwhile.

Outreach to Other Countries

Brethren in Christ Church in Malawi

One night in Troas the Apostle Paul had a vision. A man of Macedonia stood and begged him saying, "Come over to Macedonia and help us" (Acts 16:9). The establishment of the BIC church in Malawi is reminiscent of this particular event in the Bible. A group of worshippers in Malawi who called themselves Brethren in Christ sent a message to the BIC in Zimbabwe in 1983, to come and help them. The call came from Pastor Sani Selemani Chibwana who had obtained the address of the BIC in Zimbabwe from a friend, and had felt a strong urge to make this invitation. The very first Brethren in Christ church in Malawi started in Ndirande township in Blantyre. Pastor Selemane Chibwana, his family and Christian friends had started by fellowshipping together and in the process had adopted the name Brethren In Christ.

The BIC church in Zimbabwe sent several teams to Malawi on fact finding missions. During the services that ensued, many repented and professed a new life in the Lord God. A number of people came forward to tell about their desire for the church in Malawi. Five out of fourteen of those men were chosen as a Board of Trustees, and their names were submitted to the relevant government body to register the church in Malawi. Mr. Mclawrie Fred Mbamera was chosen General Secretary, and Mr. Ephraim B. Disi was chosen Church Secretary. This committee had to seek legal advice on how to register the church in Malawi. Also discussed were other pertinent issues such as how to support the work of the church and how to handle banking and other administrative issues.

There are no proper statistical records for membership when the church first started, but Rev. Ephraim Disi remembers that when he joined the church in 1985, there were about forty-three members at Ndirande. There were branches of the church already at Kuphaya in Zomba, at Chinangwa in Chikwawa and at Chisitu in Mulanje. The total members in the whole of Malawi stood at around 460. Membership seemingly grew primarily through transfer from other denominations, but later through evangelistic outreaches.

Rev. Khumalo made another visit to Malawi in April 1986 to help organize the BIC church of Malawi, to baptise new converts, to receive those wanting to join the church from other fellowships, and to give instruction about BIC doctrine and church policies. The first baptismal services were conducted by the late Bishops Khumalo and Stephen Ndlovu, and Rev. Roy V. Sider of Sherkston BIC church in Canada.

It is worthwhile to tell a little more about Mr. Disi, the first Malawian to be ordained in the BIC. He was born in 1958, the middle child in a family of eleven children. He completed his primary education in Bulawayo, Zimbabwe, where his father worked. His knowledge of the Ndebele language enabled him to serve as an interpreter when the Brethren from Zimbabwe first came to help in Malawi. He became the Ndebele/Chewa interpreter. Disi was baptized in 1976, but did not adhere to strict Christian values; he continued to live a worldly lifestyle. In 1989, with the challenge of responsibility, Disi sought a deeper understanding and relationship with God, and he became determined to walk in the light and serve the Lord God in a more wholesome way. He experienced a spiritual revival and felt a deep commitment to service.

In many organizations, change upsets the status quo and begets conflict. The young church in Malawi was not spared in-house conflict but, with prayer and a willingness to build a strong church, the leaders were helped to come to an understanding and to be unified. Mr. Disi and Mr. Chauluka Gama were sponsored to attend the International Brethren in Christ Fellowship in Canada in 1990, a significant experience for both leaders. Mr. Gama was licenced to carry out various pastoral duties.

All those years, Mr Disi had been fully employed by the government, but in 1992 he resigned that job so that he could pursue further training for pastoral work which he completed in Nigeria, returning home in May, 1993. In 1995, Bishop J. R. Shenk of Zimbabwe Conference conducted the first ordination of a BIC minister in Malawi. This was on the request and recommendation of Rev. Jack Mclane, Executive Director of BIC World Missions.

The BIC church in Malawi has truly come a long way. During the early years of the 1980s, the church in Zimbabwe tried to support the church in Malawi financially, but the BIC church in Zimbabwe was itself struggling financially, and did not have adequate personnel to nurture the problems of an emerging church. There was a concerted effort to urge the church in Malawi to move toward becoming self-supporting. Bishop Shenk of the Zimbabwe Conference met with some of the pastoral leaders and taught them about stewardship. He says,

The leaders sent to Malawi to assist always came back with reports of how poor the church was and how disabling that was. But, when I had meetings at Mlanje and at Zomba, I was amazed at how much the people had. They had maize stacked on wooden storage platforms, they had goats, rice, bananas, some acres of tea, and cloth. They could sell some of these and get an income. What they needed was teaching on stewardship, not just one session, but a series. We did not do a good job of going there to teach. We needed to send people there for two or three months in order to give a good grounding.

Bishop Shenk probably has a point there. The brethren in Malawi were not absolutely destitute. The Macedonian churches (2 Corinthians 8:1-6) are said to have excelled in the grace of giving. Amidst severe trial and suffering, their overflowing joy and their extreme poverty welled up in rich generosity, and they gave as much as they were able, and even beyond their ability.

Bishop Shenk met with the Executive Board in Zimbabwe and it was agreed that the overseeing church should embark on a five year phase-out scheme. Meanwhile, many other leaders have emerged to support the BIC church in Malawi. Much progress has been made, although the church is not yet satisfied with the support from members for pastoral activities.

Brethren in Christ Church in Botswana

The Brethren in Christ church ministry in Botswana began in the early 1960s. Rev. George Bundy and Brother Bafanya Mlilo had been ministering to the San people in and around Phumula Mission, in the Gwayi area of Zimbabwe. In 1961, it was ascertained that across the border from Phumula Mission, at Simatapili in Botswana, there was a sizable community of the San people, "Bushmen" as they were then called. Rev. Bundy and Brother Mlilo took three San converts from Phumula and crossed the border to Simatapili. There were no roads or clear-cut paths, so the trekkers relied upon their San guides absolutely. It was not an easy journey. They spent a night in the bush and only arrived at the San settlement the following day.

The San people at Simatapili fled and kept their distance when they saw the visitors. It was the San companions that Rev. Bundy and Brother Mlilo took along who entreated their kinsfolk to return and assured them that no harm was meant. After putting them at ease, the Gospel was introduced to them, followed by a film that very evening. This was something new for the San people.

A second visit was made to Simatapili at a later date. This visit included Bishop David Climenhaga, Dr. R. Virginia Kauffman and Rev. Roy Mann. This time the inhabitants did not flee. When Dr. Kauffman played her accordion during the worship service, the San people were quick to grab their own musical instruments and joined in the playing. Over two hundred people attended that service. Unfortunately, the border with Botswana was closed and guarded closely by the authorities who feared infiltration into that country to training camps for the eventual liberation war in Rhodesia. Missionaries could not cross with ease as they had before. A rich harvest might have issued from those visits, but border closure forced the evangelists to divert their energies to the needs of the area in and around Phumula Mission in what was then Rhodesia (Zimbabwe).

It was not until the 1970s that interest in evangelizing in Botswana was revived. This mainly came about because of the growing numbers of refugees in Botswana, people fleeing the simmering political situation in Rhodesia. A great number of refugees were young people determined to get out of the country and train in ways that would enable them to come back and liberate their country from colonial rule. A number of those young people also were seeking opportunities to further their education.

Life in the refugee camps was not easy, and there was a great need to minister to those in exile. Rev. Jonathan Dlodlo was sent to Botswana to minister among the refugees. The BIC church needed to be registered in the country before any serious evangelism could take place. Bishop P. M. Khumalo, Rev. and Mrs. J. Dlodlo and Mr. Jacob D. Moyo travelled to Botswana in 1979 to try to accomplish this, but failed because there already was another church going by the name Christian Brethren Church. The BIC was not willing to change its name, resulting in a stalemate.

Meanwhile, there were many Zimbabwean professionals who had left Zimbabwe to work in Botswana. Some were lonely for church fellowship. Even if there were some churches around, there were those who still longed for their own church, the Brethren in Christ. Maggie Mpofu says, "Since there was no BIC church, we sought fellowship in other congregations, but it just was not the same." Just as there is no place like home, there is nothing to compare to the way one worships in one's home church. Therefore, around 1994/95 many Zimbabweans, then based in Botswana, began to push for a BIC church there.

A great landmark in the work of the mission to Botswana happened during the weekend of of November 5-7, 1999 when the first baptisms were held in Botswana. Mr. Cornelius Mathobela, who leads the Francistown congregation, gave the evangelistic messages during the baptism weekend. He challenged the baptismal candidates to seek to know God's truth, not the truth of the Pastor or BIC doctrine. He encouraged them to seek to know and relate to God.

The Botswana BIC church has not yet struck deep roots among the Botswana people. It has mainly ministered to Zimbabweans who are based there. But this is beginning to change. The members in the Botswana church have recruited a new pastor, Isaac Ntungwana. He is a national of Botswana, and a graduate of the University of Botswana, and no doubt his influence will strengthen the national church.

The Brethren in Christ Church in Mozambique

A number of efforts have been made to establish and support a Brethren in Christ church in Mozambique. The first recorded incident was in the early 1980s. During the Zimbabwe General Conference of 1979 special delegates from Mozambique were introduced. A story was shared that the guests represented a budding BIC church in Mozambique. While listening to the radio they had encountered the BIC radio programme "Amagugu Evangeli." They had felt drawn to the teachings presented by the church and had come to request the Zimbabwe BIC to consider taking them under its wing, to nurture and help them understand the BIC doctrine. The story was appreciated by the whole Conference, and it was recommended that some church leaders be sent to Mozambique to meet, encourage and work towards building a relationship with these Brethren.

The following year Rev. K. Q. Moyo travelled to Mozambique to strengthen the relationship which had been formed and to help set up structures to enable teaching. Representatives of World Missions made more visits. The late Rev. Jack Mclaine was particularly keen to support this new venture. Unfortunately the Zimbabwe church did not follow up consistently so a chance to expand missions to Mozambique was missed. But because this is God's work, not man's, the believers who call themselves Brethren in Christ continued to meet. The company of believers continued to reach out to others and to plant churches. God has rewarded their faith through the ministry of the Malawi Brethren in Christ church.

Over the last few years, Pastor Youngson Palibendipo and Evangelist Laston Bisani, two BIC graduates from the Evangelical Bible College of Malawi, have been ministering to the Brethren in Mozambique. Evangelist Bisani is assigned to the Milanje area, which is quite close to the border with Mozambique. There are about eight churches in this area already. He and Youngson have been conducting services, seminars on discipleship, and teaching on spiritual warfare. Rev. Ephraim B. Disi, the BIC church National Director for Malawi, has visited the Brethren to offer encouragement and to explore possibilities of leadership training and youth ministry. The Lord is at work in Mozambique

Brethren in Christ in South Africa

There are two BIC efforts in South Africa. The first one is led by Rev. Hamilton Madlabane. Rev. Madlabane was introduced to the BIC church by the missionary Anna Engle who lived in South Africa and worked on Scripture translations there. Rev. Madlabane has been the leader of the Soshanguve Brethren in Christ church for as long as it has been in existence. This congregation has not had much contact with other BIC churches in the region. A little effort was made to have a relationship with the BIC group in Hillbrow, but it did not work out well.

The second group of BIC believers in South Africa can be found in the Johannesburg area of Hillbrow. There are many Zimbabweans who over the years have left their homeland to seek jobs in South Africa and in the Hillbrow area, they formed a support group to help one another. They longed to worship together but there was no BIC church nearby. David Masuku and Patrick Sibanda made an effort to mobilize the other Zimbabweans residing in Hillbrow and surrounding areas for the purpose of worshipping together.

Unfortunately all efforts to get started did not bear fruit until 1990. It was in the following year, on January 22, 1991 that the first BIC service was held in the home of Buhle Ndlovu at flat number 204, Claim Towers. The following Sunday more people came and the service was held at number 902. The two services are memorable in that they were attended by both South Africans and Zimbabweans. A South African, Charles Maphosa, was very helpful in starting the church. An interim administrative committee composed of Patrick Sibanda, Buhle Ndlovu and Pride Thoko Zikhali was put in place. Three months later, when a full committee had been elected, Rev. Albert Ndlovu representing the Zimbabwe BIC Executive Board, travelled to South Africa especially to introduce the new BIC group to the older one led by Rev. Madlabane. In the first two years there was no Pastor at Hillbrow; the committee performed all the pastoral duties.

In more recent years the Zimbabwean church has been making more of an effort to nurture the Hillbrow group. Leaders from Zimbabwe have gone to South Africa to conduct revival sessions and to encourage the believers. Sending Benedict Macebo, who already has pastoral experience, is one way in which the church is trying to strengthen this sister church.

South Africa has been the field of service ministry through MCC for many people who belong to the Mennonite family. As they have come and gone something of who they are and what they represent has rubbed off on their local contacts. One of the mandates of the many Mennonite-related sending bodies has always been that they do not plant churches but relate to those already in existence in their areas of operation. This of course has put them in contact with people who worship in many varied styles. In spite of the differences in their backgrounds many lasting relationships have been formed.

Two of the notable communities where the strongest relationships were made were the Broken Wall Community of Reconciliation and the Grace Community Church in Cape Town, South Africa. The former was an effort at mending and building relations among people of different races and cultures. Considering South Africa's history of apartheid this was a good way to move forward and build the church. Graham Cyster and Xola Skosana from this community even attended an Africa Mennonite and Brethren in Christ Fellowship (AMBCF) meeting in Nairobi, Kenya in 1994. They wanted to learn more about the Mennonites.

The second group was made up of people from a variety of denominations with different views and worship styles. Most were scattered in the Philipstown farming community and so quite a number of them were farm workers. They had a zeal to learn and grow. Graham Cyster met most of the leaders at one time or another and developed a relationship. Later he became the link between both groups of South African believers and Mennonite congregations in the United States. Relations did not work out well and what had promised to be the core to Mennonite-related

217

churches in Southern Africa did not solidify. Cyster went his way and the other people carried on worshiping in their own way.

Tim Lind, who for many years was the MCC Connecting People representative in South Africa and is also the part of the MWC Global Gift Sharing Project, came across interested people in his travels. Realizing their desire to build strong churches with Bible-centred teaching he related closely with them. When these people under the leadership of Pastor David Makaleni showed a desire to have some of their leaders ordained, he helped them connect with the BIC in Zimbabwe. For that reason, during the Easter weekend of 2001 Bishop Jake Shenk of Zimbabwe and his wife Nancy travelled to Philipstown and spent a weekend fellowshipping with the brethren. There were about twelve couples needing to be separated for special service in the church.

It was a busy weekend for Bishop Shenk as he taught, then installed Deacons, commissioned Evangelists and ordained Pastors. During that weekend the leaders also baptized about seven people. Their greatest need was for further teaching, and that need remains. Unfortunately, neither the BIC nor the Mennonites of Africa have made any more efforts to relate and nurture these fellow believers, but they are still building their church and studying the Scriptures as best they can.

Notes

[1] "*Lifaqane/Mfecane* is a word denoting a state of migration not the ordinary movements of peoples, but the struggles of wandering tribes accompanied by their families, flocks and herds." Eileen Jensen Kringe, *The Social System of the Zulus* (Shutter & Shooter, 1950), 14.

[2] Even then the Boers made one unsuccessful attempt to invade the Ndebele State in 1837 under the leadership of Andreas Hendriek Portgeiter, called Ndaleka by the AmaNdebele. Phathisa Nyathi, *Igugu lika Mtwakazi* (Gweru: Mambo Press, 1994).

[3] Nyathi, *Igugu*.

[4] S. I. Mudenge, *Christian Education at the Mutapa Court* (Harare: Zimbabwe Publishing House, 1986).

[5] Hannah Frances Davidson, *South and South Central Africa* (Elgin, IL: Brethren Publishing House), 76.

[6] This was evidenced by the letter of introduction Rhodes gave to the missionaries. For many years it was displayed at the conference room at the Matopo Book Centre, BIC church headquarters.

[7] Terrence O. Ranger, *Voices from the Rocks: Nature, Culture and History in the Matopos Hills of Zimbabwe* (Oxford: J. Currey, 1999).

[8] The community in this area was moved in the late 1930s to make way for white farms.

[9] In some communities, Chisi is on Thursdays.

[10] The role of the *Sangoma* is played by the "prophet" in African Independent Churches.

[11] Nyathi says they use *isagenama,* another wild bulb. Nyathi, *Igugu.*

[12] H. Frances Davidson, *South and Central Africa* (Elgin, Il.: Brethren Publishing House, 1915), 190.

[13] Interview with Dorcas Kumalo by Barbara Nkala, June 3, 2002.

[14] *Celebrating the Vision: A Century of Sowing and Reaping*, Barbara Nkala, ed. (Bulawayo: Brethren in Christ Church, 1998).

[15] A representative, but limited list, would include the following. **Education:** I. N. Mpofu, Jack D. Ndlovu, Vivian Dube, Dr. Beatrice Ncube. **Civil Service:** Mtshena Sidile, Nathan Moyo, George Mlilo. **Law:** Lot Senda, Mordecai Mahlangu. **Health:** Mabel Sigola, Violet Senda, Dr. Dinginhlalo Dhlamini. **Radio Ministry:** Abbie Dube, Amon Nyamambi, Ferdinand Sibanda. **Agriculture:** Dr. Siboniso Moyo, Marko Dokotela Ncube, Dr. Henry Sibanda. **Commerce:** Ayanda Kumalo, Sithabile Majoni, Vulindlela L. Ndlovu. **Business:** Agrippa V. Masiye, Henry Mpumulo Ncube, Knight Ngwabi. **Evangelists:** Sitshokuphi Sibanda, Maria Tshuma, Ethel Sibanda. **Politics:** Daniel Nyamazana Dube, Johnson Ndlovu, George Ndlovu. **African Statesman:** Stephen N. Ndlovu.

[16] R. M. Sichala, "Keep the Light Burning," (unpublished paper completed in 1988 at the request of the Zambia BIC church), 34.

[17] E. Morris Sider, *Nine Portraits. Brethren in Christ Biographical Sketches* (Nappanee, IN: Evangel Press, 1978), see the chapter on Hannah Frances Davidson.

[18] *Ibid.,* 200.

[19] Sichala, "Keep the Light Burning," 38.

[20] Sichala, "Keep the Light Burning," 35, 37 – 39.

[21] Interview with Mukuwa Kalambo, November 26, 2002, Macha Mission, Zambia, by Barbara Nkala and Doris Dube.

[22] Sichala, "Keep the Light Burning," 42.

[23] *Ibid.,* 42.

[24] *Ibid.*

[25] *Ibid.,* 44.

[26] *Ibid.,* 50.

[27] The preceding is based on an interview with Bishop Enoch Shamapani, November 26, 2002, Choma, Zambia, by Barbara Nkala and Doris Dube.

[28] The preceding is based on an interview with Rev. Moses Munsaka, November 26, 2002, Choma, Zambia, by Barbara Nkala and Doris Dube.

[29] Sichala, "Keep the Light Burning," 20-21.

[30] *Ibid.,* 51-52.

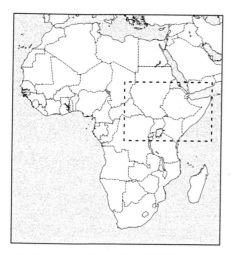

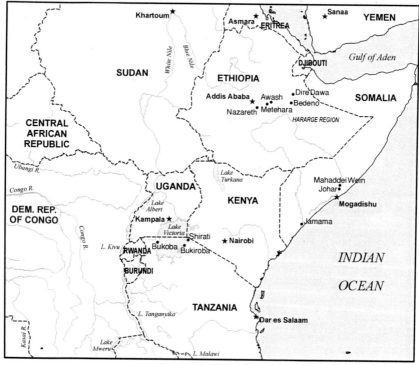

Eastern Africa

220

Mennonite Churches in Eastern Africa

by Alemu Checole, assisted by Samuel Asefa

Religion in Eastern Africa: An Overview

We live in Africa, and the best way to serve God effectively and productively is through the expression of our unique identity. God is our father, not a stranger. We must serve Him the way we know Him and understand Him, not as carbon copies of other people's experiments and styles, but as ourselves, creating our own forms of worship from our own perspective. The time to follow our own conscience is overdue.[1]

East Africa, a region comprised of Ethiopia, Eritrea, Djibouti, Somalia, Kenya, Uganda and Tanzania, was probably the home of the first human species. Geneticists and anthropologists have concluded that the earliest humans originated from a single common ancestor in East Africa about 150,000 years ago. Most likely, religion also originated along with humanity in Africa.[2] "African religion" is defined as the African understanding of God and African religious expression as it existed before the coming of western missionaries to the continent. The understanding of African religion has been refined in recent years. Traditional histories described African religion as polytheistic, but Africans scholars have begun to dispute this characterization, arguing that it was primal European religion that was polytheistic. The re-visiting of African theology is an important new develpment.

African Religion in Eastern Africa

African Religion: One or Many Religions

In his book, *African Religion: The Moral Traditions of Abundant Life,* Dr. Laurenti Magesa, an African Catholic theologian from the Jita tribe in Tanzania, speaks of African religion in its singularity as a universal religion.[3] He poses three important questions:

—Is African religion in fact one religion, or are there many religions?

—If it is one religion, is it in any case a world religion?

—If it is one religion, what is its one main unifying philosophy?

Most tribes in eastern Africa had many religious features in common. Many of them venerated their ancestors. In addition, they all believed in a supreme being who was the creator of life. They believed in an all-powerful, all-knowing God whose presence was felt in their songs, prayers, stories, proverbs, and in their religious rituals and ceremonies. Of course, they had their own deities and spirits, but the creator God was recognized everywhere. For instance Kisare, the first Tanzanian Mennonite bishop, writes in his autobiography of his childhood experience with the creator God, called Nyasaye Nyakalaga in the Luo language. He says,

How has this come about? How did I, Marwa, come to be a human being? How is it that I sit here feeling the warmth of the morning sun? The answer comes as an epiphany. If God would not have been, then I, Marwa, would not have been. God is both the purpose (why) and manner (how) of my existence.[4]

Many anthropologists, ethnologists and missionary scholars have asked if African religion is one religion or many religions. In the 1960s and 1970s, African religious scholars did not choose to speak out against the "plurality argument." African scholars were educated in the thought tradition of western Christianity, and though they had experienced political independence, many of them had not yet attained intellectual freedom. In his book *African Religions and Philosophy,* the renowned African theologian John Mbiti admitted that the variety of religious expressions among the various peoples of Africa would lead one to speak of religions in the plural. But he argued that the philosophy underlying and unifying these religions expressions is in fact a philosophy in the singular.[5]

Dr. Magesa also argues that African religion is one religion with one underlying philosophy, expressed in many ways. Dr. Magesa states emphatically that African religion is a universal religion like Christianity, Islam and other world religions in that it possesses "moral power that shapes and directs the lives of millions of people in their relationship with other human beings, the created order and the divine."[6] The ultimate justification for considering African religion to be a world religion, Magesa concludes, can be found in the meaning of religion itself. For Africans religion is a way of life where a distinction or separation is not made

Ethnic Groups in Eastern Africa.
Tanzania:
- The Bushmen were probably the earliest settlers in Tanzania.
- The Hamitic group were probably from early Egypt.
- The Nilo-Hamitic people, represented today by the Maasai, are thought to have come from the North. They were warlike and nomadic, moving often in search of grazing land for their cattle.
- The Bantu comprise the majority in Tanzania and the Mara region.
- Nilotic people, the Luos, are the most recent arrivals in Tanzania, thought to have originated in the Nile Valley and moved southward into Kenya, Uganda, and Tanzania.

Kenya:
- Bantus, Nilotes, Hamites, Arabs, Indians and a few Europeans make up the population of Kenya today.

Ethiopia:
- The population of northern Ethiopia and a portion of the newly-independent nation of Eritrea is mostly Semitic in language. The Agaw peoples still preserve their ancient Hamitic tongue in remote districts, and pockets of Oromo tribes have established themselves here and there. The southern highlands are inhabited by a mix of the Omotic and Oromo ethnic groups. Nilotic tribes live in the extreme southwest, while in the outlying southeastern highlands are found people belonging to the Afar, Somali and Oromo ethnic groups.[7]

between religion and other areas of human existence. For Africans, religion is life. How mistaken were some early European coastal traders who concluded, on the basis of superficial and insufficient evidence, that Africans had no religion.[8]

Major Characteristics of African Religion

The basic philosophy of African religion is founded on an understanding of good and evil: "good is that which promotes or enhances life. Evil is that which diminishes or destroys life. These two poles become the measure of all thoughts, words, actions, or even natural events."[9] Generosity is one of the most important tenets of African religion because it promotes the good. A related religious duty is hospitality to guests which is the opposite of greed. Hospitality helps to build community whereas greed hinders the well being of the community. In addition, generosity is demonstrated through maintaining extended family ties, including ties with the ancestors and those yet to be born. "Our traditional worship," says Kisare, was concerned with building up the village. It was important that village ancestors, two or three generations back, were pleased with our lives. From time to time we made sacrifices at our ancestors' graves so that they would know that we were respectful of them and that our lives were being lived in such a way that their village was being strengthened.[10]

Begetting children was a form of expressing generosity because it was viewed as a way of sharing life. Fertility was a sign of prosperity and blessing. Infertility, on the other hand, was a serious limitation to life. Esther Kawira states that "In the case of male infertility, a clansman may be asked to discretely come in and help out the couple. The underlying principle is that life, the ultimate good, be preserved and perpetuated in every way possible."[11]

According to Magesa's explanation, wrongdoing, illness and witchcraft are the three most dangerous enemies of life. Wrongdoing can inflict consequences on the wrongdoer or his community which may be life-threatening. Suppose a young man kills his brother, suppose a young man sleeps with his father's wife, or with his own mother. These are terrible sins which make it impossible for this man to live in his father's village. He is thrown out; he is outside the village covenant law. As Shenk puts it, "No matter how good a person he may have been or how much the people of the village have admired him, it is not possible for him to return unless a sacrifice is made which is powerful enough to undo the evil thing which he did."[12]

Christian missionaries from Europe and North America came to Africa with the aim of spreading the Christian Gospel. In their attempt to evangelize and civilize, they saw the need for education and modern health care. However, in trying to meet those needs, they overlooked the importance of respecting traditional practices and beliefs, thus creating rivalry between traditional cultures and "mission Christianity."

Christ Supreme in African Religion

In the traditional African religious experience, the expression of faith was never understood in universal terms. Beliefs and practices varied from one locality to another, from one tribe to another. Religious expression was always understood to be a Luo, Maasai, Turkana, or Zanaki expression of faith. African Christians accepted Christianity, however, because they saw in it a new way of life, one which was profoundly better than their traditional existence. For example, their hope for eternal life, assurance of the forgivenness of sins, peace and reconciliation with God and humanity assured them of security. The new Covenant sealed by the blood of Christ united them in a new universal community of faith.

A careful study of African religion will help us connect the Gospel's message to our traditional African faith. In the past, very few missionaries looked seriously at Africa's traditional faith because they were influenced by negative colonial attitudes. Strange as it may seem, we also simply accepted the missionaries' assessment of our traditional beliefs. But now we should be knowledgeable enough to see where traditional faith is in conflict with the Christian faith, and also see where the Christian faith is the fulfillment of traditional faith. Evidently, we do not and cannot find true salvation in ethnic religion, although ethnic religion may point the way to salvation. Salvation is found only through the sacrificial work of Jesus Christ.

The Gospel transcends all cultures and should challenge every cultural heritage. Because of the marvelous work of Jesus Christ, millions of Christians in Africa live in joyous hope and faith. Through Jesus the powers of death are defeated; victory is made certain because Jesus is Lord. The Gospel is the Good News for the whole person. Announcing this to his Jewish audience nearly two thousand years ago, Jesus said:

> The Spirit of the Lord is on me, because he has anointed me to preach good news to the poor. He has sent me to proclaim freedom for the prisoners and recovery of sight for the blind, to release the oppressed, to proclaim the year of the Lord's favor (Luke 4: 18-19).

Two Tribes That Never Intermarried

Rebecca Miringeri Kulwa, education secretary of Kanisa la Mennonite Tanzania (KMT), tells an interesting story about the marriage of her parents, Elisha Meso and Wakuru Mwangwa, illustrating the supremacy of Christian understanding over traditional practices. Elisha Meso was born in 1927 and Wakuru Mwangwa in 1932. When the missionaries came to Bumangi, they brought education along with the Gospel. Elisha was very much interested in education. His father wanted to send him to school.

Village woman outside Shirati, Tanzania.

Unfortunately his father died when Elisha was only twelve years old and so he was forced to take on his father's responsibilities.

Wakuru Mwangwa was living in one of the remotest villages in the Bumangi District; it had never been reached with the Gospel of Jesus Christ. Some of the girls in the Bumangi area became interested in hearing the Word of God and went to the mission station. After hearing the Word they received Jesus as their Saviour and went out to the surrounding villages to witness. Wakuru found not only the message of these girls appealing, but also their headscarves and their white garments. One day while looking after her father's cattle, she walked all the way from her village to the mission station, a distance of about twenty kilometers. The hilly and wild country Wakuru walked through was frightening territory for a nine-year-old girl, but she wanted to leave her cattle behind and go to the mission station. They welcomed her and she became a part of their fellowship.

When her parents heard where Wakuru was, they came after her. She was captured and taken back several times and given severe beatings. She promised she would never again leave the cattle and go to the mission station. But whenever she got the chance to slip away, she did. When her parents would come after her, she would run into missionary Shenk's bedroom and hide under their bed. Her father used to warn Wakuru's mother that she could not come into his compound till she had brought Wakuru from the mission station. So Wakuru's mother had to go all the way to the mission compound for her daughter, or else she was not allowed into her house.

Her mother appeared to be cruel, but she was actually being forced by her husband to be harsh. But Wakuru persisted in clinging to her new-found faith. Even though she was nearly maimed for life from the severe beatings she received from her parents, she recovered gradually and now she walks properly. Eventually, Elisha and Wakuru met at the Bumangi Mission School and got married at a very young age.

Elisha belonged to the ironsmiths clan and Wakuru to the pot makers. These two tribes never married one another. Their parents refused to let Elisha and Wakuru get married because they belonged to enemy tribes. They could not override that cultural barrier. The potters believed that ironsmiths had a history of leprosy, and the potters said that they could never marry lepers. When it became virtually impossible for Elisha and Wakuru to get married, they decided to go ahead and get married without the consent of their parents. So on the wedding day, neither Wakuru's parent's or Elisha's parents showed their faces.

On their daughter Miringeri's birthday, Wakuru's mother did not come to celebrate with the family. In fact, she had placed a curse on the parents so that their children might die—but Miringeri survived and grew up, followed by a second girl, and a third one as well. It was only after the third girl was born that Wakuru's mother came to remove the curse that had been placed on the family. Grandmother said, "Now, these are my grandchildren. I'm sorry for what I did! I now accept them into the clan!" In all, thirteen children were born into the Meso family, nine girls and four boys.

When the Meso children were born, their parents had already abandoned the tribal gods and had decided to believe in the one and only God. The people of the village also believed in the power of the witchdoctors. These tribal beliefs created fear among the people. However, daughter Miringeri says, "when we grew up, we were made not to fear. We were taught that God is all-powerful; there is no power greater than He. He made these witchdoctors. So, how can they be more powerful?" "I'm thankful for the kind of faith I was born into. We grew up healthy in body and mind."[13]

The Meso family had more girls than boys. There was a traditional belief that a girl was worth very little and was only good for marriage and bearing children. Consequently, people would come and laugh at Elisha saying: "Elisha, you are really nothing, you possess only three girls." But somehow faith in Christ created in Miringeri's parents the strength to stand up and challenge the negative things people said. Their parents helped the children with their schooling and made sure that the girls enjoyed an equal chance with the boys. "They even told us when we sat together to pray in the evening before we went to bed," continued Miringeri, "that we could do things just as well as the boys. We finished elementary school, went on to middle school, and some of us even went on to secondary school and college." And soon people found out that the Meso girls were successful and they began to say, "So, girls can do as well as boys!" This encouraged other villagers to send their girls to school.[14]

Islam in Eastern Africa

Islam in eastern Africa is a great religious and political force. It has penetrated the lives of many peoples in the coastal areas of Tanzania and Kenya, and all along the former slave trade routes in Tanzania. In Djibouti, Ethiopia and Eritrea there are also large areas inhabited by followers of Islam. However, in Somalia Islam has made its greatest impact.

According to Somali mythology, three clan chiefs (Isaac, Darood and Dir) emigrated from Arabia to Somalia, married local women, and established the Somali clan families in the tenth century AD.[15] Somalis began to push Oromo and Bantu tribes southward along the Shebele River and west into Ethiopia. Arab settlers established towns in Somalia along the coast of the Indian Ocean, introducing commerce and Islamic culture. Religious leaders followed the traders into the towns, conveying the teachings of the Prophet Mohammed. The Somalis accepted Islam, integrating it with their own traditions. Somalis say that "to be Somali is to be Muslim since the blood of the Prophet flows in Somali veins."[16] Social and religious ties are so binding in the Somali Muslim community that it is difficult for its members to follow another religion. When Somalis choose to become Christian, they are considered traitors and ostracized immediately.

It is an undeniable fact that Christianity has succeeded little, if at all, in penetrating Somali society with the Gospel. A few Protestant missions, including Mennonite missions, have witnessed and worked for many years among these people with little visible result. But the Gospel is a powerful message and the seed sown will not return void; it will bear fruit, much fruit, some day in the future.

Bringing Christianity to a clan-based, Islamic society such as the Somali society has presented its own particular problems. For instance, some Somalis posed as Christians and acted as spies for the government or for Islamic associations. Another problem for the Christian Somali fellowship was how to maintain a balance between nurturing believers who were rejected by their families and helping them overcome dependence on the church to grow into a mature Christian faith.

Part of the challenge of witnessing to Muslims is establishing a relationship of trust. As Bertha Beachy relates,

> In our witness to the Muslims we must have something to offer
> in the community, something that helps to build trust, like the
> schools, clinics or hospitals, something that they have a felt need
> for so that they learn to know us and the faith we hold on to;
> [we must] be holistic.[17]

Abdul-Cadir Wursame, one of the first Somali believers, recalls how he stumbled across Mennonite missionaries serving in Mogadishu in the early 1960s. To him the Mennonites seemed to be a unique community of believers blessed with the virtues of humility, love, compassion, gentleness and meekness. In their humility and meekness, he saw Christ.

> I was surprised to see a white North American bending low to
> wash the feet of a black Somali. It was something new and
> strange to me. It taught me the important lesson of the life of a
> servant dedicated to the service of his Lord and his fellow human
> beings."[18]

The Ethiopian Orthodox Church

The Ethiopian Orthodox Church has dominated the national religious life in Ethiopia for ages. In its growth the Meserete Kristos Church (MKC) has borrowed some ideas and practices – such as the *shibsheba*, a type of liturgical dance – from the Orthodox Church. According to historical records, Christianity came to Ethiopia in the second quarter of the fourth century when two Syrian boys, Frumentius and Aedisius, arrived at the court of Aksum (the ancient name of Ethiopia) and began to proclaim the Gospel to the monarch and his followers.[19] In 346 AD, Frumentius went to Alexandria and met with the great church father, Athanasius. After being told of the needs of the Christians of Aksum, Athanasius appointed Frumentius as the first bishop of Aksum.[20]

Syrian missionaries who arrived in the country in the fifth century converted Ethiopia to Christianity. They founded monasteries and translated the Bible into Ge'ez, the ancient Ethiopic language still used in the Ethiopian Orthodox liturgy. In succeeding centuries, monks played a major role in spreading the Gospel in the surrounding countryside of Aksum, rooting Christianity more firmly in Ethiopian society.

When Anabaptist leaders in the sixteenth century were dying as martyrs for freedom of conscience, the Ethiopian faithful were giving their lives to stop the onslaught of invading Muslims. The amicable relations between the Muslims and Christians in Ethiopia, which began in the seventh century, had come to an end with the invasions of the Muslim general nicknamed 'Gragn' (the left-handed). Between 1529 and 1543 Gragn devastated the whole of the Christian highlands, demolishing churches and monasteries. Spurred on by the dreadful havoc inflicted on the Christian kingdom, the Ethiopian monarch sought assistance from Portugal to save the country from fatal disaster. Soon after the defeat of the invading Muslims, however, Portuguese missionaries stayed on and worked to bring the Ethiopian Orthodox Church under the umbrella of Rome. Ethiopians saw this as an affront to their religious freedom. From that time onward all foreign Christians were classified as "Catholic."[21]

The Ethiopian Orthodox Church has developed its own distinctive form of the Christian faith, unique in Africa. It has survived because of physical remoteness and mountainous terrain, which served as protection and enabled Christianity to take root and become a national religion. Here, isolated from the rest of the world, the Orthodox Church thrived, mixing teachings from Christian, Jewish and even local traditions. Christianity in Ethiopia was virtually synonymous with the nation.[22] As Nathan Hege has noted, "Ethiopia has preserved its Christian faith up to our time through peril and threat. Its long history and its great contribution to both African and world Christianity, its wealth of tradition, liturgy and theology have given it a prominent place in the history of the Church."[23] To twentieth-century African Christians,the history of the church seemed a fulfillment of the promise of the psalmist: "princes shall come out of Egypt, Ethiopia shall stretch forth her hands to God" (Psalms 68:31).

The Ethiopian Orthodox Church has continued to dominate other expressions of Christian faith in Ethiopia. Ato Geber-Selassie Habitamu, a retired drugstore owner and a prominent church elder for many years, relates how Orthodox Church officials reacted against the Bible Churchmen's Missionary Society (BCMS). In the late 1940s, Geber-Selassie and his friends went into an Orthodox Church compound in the town of Fiche, 150 kilometers north of Addis Ababa. As they entered the compound they began to sing, "Hosanah, Hosanah." One angry Orthodox believer stood up and shouted at them saying, "In the name of Haile Selassie [the emperor ruling at that time] stop your singing." One of our group replied saying, "The Lord has told us to praise Him. If we keep silent, He will make the stones to offer Him praise." Hearing this, the Orthodox priests became angry, supposing that the term "stones" was intentionally used to blaspheme them. All sixteen of the BCMS members were arrested and imprisoned immediately. However, after paying a fine of 30 Birr (Ethiopian cash) they were released the next day.

The author himself remembers how he and his friends were insulted in 1960 on their way to a Billy Graham Crusade being held at the Addis Ababa Stadium. "You Catholics, how dare you defile our land," a priest screamed at us. "How dare you go to listen to this pork-eating infidel" (eating pork is a taboo in Ethiopian Orthodox practice).

Beginning with the intrusion of the Portuguese Jesuit missionaries in the seventheenth century, the Ethiopian Orthodox Church has been wary of foreign missions. For many years, and during Haile Selassie's reign especially, evangelical Christians were labeled as "enemies of Saint Mary" because they did not give sufficient veneration to the mother of Jesus. Evangelicals were also accused of following a foreign religion.

Another source of contention was the fact that Orthodox believers thought that their church was the only "true" church and the "straight" way to heaven. They despised and counted all other Christian denominations as heretical. Moreover, they used their numerical strength to suppress religious minorities, particularly Protestant denominations. Close to 59% of the population of the country is said to belong to the Orthodox religion, while less than 10% are members of evangelical churches.

The fact that it has been a national religion for centuries has given the Orthodox Church a reason to feel superior to Protestant groups. In the feudal land tenure system, one-third of the land belonged to the Orthodox Church. Not only did the church own much property, it also received tithes from all types of produce. The Orthodox Church became an economic as well as a religious power in Ethiopia, though its economic power was lost under the Marxist government.

Several spiritual awakenings have affected the Ethiopian Orthodox church. The first and most famous of these was led by Stephanos during the reign of Emperor Zara Yacob (1434-1468). Stephanos and his disciples ardently taught that salvation was only through Jesus Christ. They refused to do obeisance to the crucifix and the image of Saint Mary. Stephanos and his followers were severely persecuted and finally martyred for their religious convictions. Stephanos himself was arrested and sent from his native region of Tigrai into exile in Shoa.

In 1825 the Church Missionary Society (CMS) sent two missionaries to Ethiopia to promote revival. Samuel Gobat and Christian Krubler arrived in Tigrai in 1830, where a local ruler received them. They brought with them thousands of copies of Scripture. They had a rewarding ministry, but Krubler eventually died and Gobat's health forced him to retire in 1836. John Krapf, also from the CMS, served among the Shoa Christians from 1839-1842. He wanted to proclaim the Gospel to the Oromo. He later shifted his ministry to Kenya, Uganda and Zanzibar.

In 1855 Emperor Tewodros gave permission to J. M. Flad to establish schools and preach the Gospel. He began preaching and teaching the Gospel to Ethiopians and Falashas (black Jews living in Ethiopia), distributed Ge'ez and Amaharic Bibles, and established schools. In 1862 thirty-one Falashas were baptized.[24]

Under Emperor Menelik the Second, the Swedish Protestant Mission undertook mission work in western Wallaga in 1904. In 1920 the United Presbyterian Church began mission work among the Wallaga Oromo in western Ethiopia. The Bethel Evangelical Church of Ethiopia grew out of the Presbyterian ministry during the Italian occupation of Ethiopia, 1936-41. The largest Protestant ministry in the country grew out of the work of the Sudan Interior Mission in Ethiopia which began in 1927. The Bible Churchmen's Missionary Society (BCMS) of the Anglican Church sought to bring renewal to the Ethiopian Orthodox Church by teaching Bible and other subjects. Later, Lutherans, Baptists, Finnish Pentecostals, Full Gospel believers and, of course, Mennonites attempted to minister in Orthodox areas.

In the late 1950s and throughout the 1960s, the presence of evangelical Christians carrying out aggressive evangelism affected the Orthodox Church both positively and negatively. The effect could be said to have been negative, since large numbers of Orthodox members joined Protestant churches. This caused indignation among Orthodox officials, which led to punitive measures against Protestant denominations. Unfortunately, instead of recognizing the immediate need for reform, the Orthodox Church began to persecute the evangelical churches even more severely. Peter Cotterell notes, "Rather than cleaning their old and tarnished lamps, they were determined to extinguish the light of the new. Predictably they failed."[25] On the positive side, through the exemplary personal witness of dedicated Christians and the powerful testimonies of individuals in schools, at work, and in their neighborhoods, many Orthodox believers were persuaded to follow the way of salvation as revealed in the Scriptures. Many were compelled to form secret associations of believers while resolving to remain within their own church in order to bring spiritual awakening and transformation.

Meserete Kristos Church (MKC) has actively participated in offering religious instruction to the leaders of such associations at different times and in different places. For example, in 1978 Solomon Kebede, the chairman of the Nazareth MKC, Kedir Delchumie, then evangelist, Asefa Ketema, then Development Project Director, and other church leaders from the Nazareth MKC went to the famous sanctuary of Saint Mary in Woliso Town, about 125 kilometers southwest of Addis Ababa, to preach and teach. Abba Fiseha, the monk who had invited the MKC church leaders, was excited about the positive relations established. Unfortunately, some Orthodox officials discovered what was taking place and brought an abrupt end to the relationship.

Because of the interaction that had taken place, a number of changes occurred in many of the Orthodox churches: sound biblical teaching has been and is being offered at mass gatherings; youth choirs have been and are composing their own Amharic songs and singing them to worshippers on saints' days and other special occasions; there is much more attendance at church services than ever before. As Paul says in his letter to the Philippians: "But what does it matter? The important thing is that in every way, whether from false motives or true, Christ is preached. And because of this I rejoice" (Philippians 1:18, NIV).

Mennonite Missions to East Africa

The six Mennonite churches in East Africa, and their dates of origin.
-Kanisa la Mennonite Tanzania (KMT), 1935.
-Meserete Kristos Church of Ethiopia (MKC), 1951.
-Somalia Mennonite Fellowship (SMF), 1953.
-Kenya Mennonite Church (KMC), 1965.
-Djibouti Mennonite Fellowship, 1987.
-Meserete Kristos Church of Eritrea, 1989.

On December 2, 1933, Elam and Elizabeth Stauffer and John and Ruth Moseman were commissioned for mission service by the Eastern Mennonite Board of Missions and Charities (EMBMC). Soon afterwards Orie Miller, the first general secretary of EMBMC and director of Mennonite Central Committee (MCC), and Elam Stauffer went to London to seek counsel from Alexander McLeish, head of the Africa Inland Mission (AIM). McLeish suggested Tanganyika (now Tanzania) as a possible mission field. Miller and Stauffer proceeded to Tanganyika where Stauffer met veteran AIM missionary, Emille Sywulka; they began exploring the East Lake area for possible mission sites. They traveled on foot, by bicycle and canoe. At last Stauffer and Sywulka arrived in Shirati, about 110 kilometers north of Musoma town, and only 13 kilometers from the Kenyan border. This area was chosen as the site for the first Mennonite mission station. Stauffer then sent for his wife, Elizabeth and for John Moseman and his wife to come to the mission field.

In 1934 the four missionaries began setting up the first simple worship building; prior to its completion they held their services outdoors. Sharing the Good News was the first priority of the missionaries. Zedekiah Kisare, a young African Christian, became the interpreter for the missionaries at Sunday services, since the inhabitants of the area did not understand Kiswahili. The missionaries had come with a clear vision of the type of church they wanted to build. They entered Tanganyika hoping to avoid big institutions, wanting to plant a church by providing only basic education and medical care.

In September of 1934 the first service was held in the finished building, to which a crowd twice as big as usual came. In the early months of 1935 the number of believers at Shirati had been gradually increasing, but the missionaries were not so sure if all of them were real believers. Elam Stauffer commented that most of the worshippers were in earnest and learning the way of life. But he felt also that stricter measures needed to be adopted for disciplining those who were not serious. Those who had no desire for the new life needed to be weeded out. He talked over the situation with Mr. Sywulka and was told that the natives knew nothing of proving themselves but needed to be guided and ruled continually to make them prove their profession.[26]

A second mission station at Bukiroba was built in 1935, then the third, Mugango, was established among the Jita, related to the Ruris, who inhabited the area. Some believers from AIM joined the Mennonites at Mugango. On May 18, 1937 the Shenks and the Fersters opened the fourth station at Bumangi among another tribe. The fifth station, Nyabasi, was opened in January of 1940 near the Kenyan border. Simeon and Edna Hurst took responsibility for the building programme.

At each mission station a school was established with instruction up to the equivalent of third grade level. At first, missionaries taught the classes. Within a few years missionaries taught the higher classes while Africans taught the lower grades. A few years later, fourth grade was added at Shirati and Mugango, and more subjects, such as geography and hygiene, were included in the curriculum. Although in the beginning these were theoretical studies, they later became practical and made a slow and gradual impact on the lives of the people.

In addition to opening schools and performing medical work in order to promote evangelism and train African personnel, the mission opened a girls' home. They thought that the converted men would find it hard to be married to non-Christian wives. Moreover, they recognized the important role women played within families. Thus, to strengthen African Christian homes, they started a girls' home to which young girls came to live and learn to become believers. Eventually, most of them married Christian men. Shirati and Mugango remained shining examples of such institutions, where young women were taught cooking and baking, how to care for children, and many other skills. In addition to the girls' home, missionary women initiated womens' activities which included sewing classes, fellowship, reading the Bible together, praying and visiting the sick.

Although the mission board urged missionaries in Tanganyika not to involve themselves in large-scale institutional work, medical work began immediately in 1934. Medical work included evangelism. Every morning before medicine was dispensed, the Gospel was preached to the sick and afflicted, and some who heard became Christians. Missionary physicians arrived in 1940 and hospitals were established at Shirati and Mugumu (1980). These centres supported a network of local clinics. From 1954 to 1972 a leprosarium at Shirati became an important research centre. Training also was an essential part of the medical programme, including a school for nursing established in 1960. Managing and supporting these institutions has continued to be a major concern for the church.

In 1942 a revival began with the preaching of an African evangelist. The revival began at Mugango mission station and spread to Majita. There, two people were touched by the power of the Holy Spirit and were convicted of their sins. In August of 1942, people at Shirati were convicted of the ineffectiveness of their Christian lives. The fire of God swept through the group. Many people repented of their sins. There was confession of hidden sins and unworthiness and of a lack of willingness to follow the Lord and a new openness and frankness. During this time most of the African elders, bush school teachers and church leaders were touched and their lives changed. On the whole, this wave of revival in East Africa touched people from every walk of life. It brought unity between missionaries and Africans and created sympathy and understanding between the two races.

Bishop Kisare, speaking of his precious revival experience, wrote:
I was like a signboard, which shows the way but never took a step in that direction. I was telling people that Jesus is the way to heaven, but I myself had not yet met the Lord. I was like Naaman with bleeding leprosy hidden beneath beautiful garments, in my case, a leadership position. I was not free to take my wife with me when I served. I could not get along with her at home and I could not at all get along with the missionaries. I regarded them as proud people, seeing themselves as important overlords, and me as an ordinary black man. And then I realized that my fellow leaders were right there beside me, seeking God also. With deep sorrow we began to ask forgiveness of each other for the terrible sins we had committed. From this point onwards, I have had good fellowship with my brothers.[27]

The revival was also a big factor in rousing believers to spread the Good News far and wide. Chief Wilson Oguwada, now a retired chief residing in Migore, Kenya, tells of his revival experience:
I met Jesus in 1942 when someone called William Nagenda from Uganda came to Shirati, Tanzania for a convention. In November 1942 the Holy Spirit spoke to us in a special way and I confessed my sins and was empowered to go out to witness. When the revival meeting was over, God sent me back to my land, Kenya. With me was Nikanor Dhaji. We walked all the way to my birthplace. We preached the Word to many people who listened to us attentively. We were in Migore for three days preaching the Good News. Then we went to Nyarombo where we built a church, then to Kamkago-Katieno. When we went to Nyarombo, the Roman Catholics began to persecute us because many people turned away from them to us. Hence, they saw us as their enemies. Also, when we were at Sili the Seventh Day Adventists were against us. At Nyarombo we were severely beaten. Today, Nyarombo features a church which was planted during the time of revival.[28]

The revival of 1946 brought about by Gospel teams from Uganda to Rwanda touched the lives of both the Africans and the missionaries. They preached the Gospel of humbleness at the foot of the Cross and brokenness of spirit; these were educated people who preached against white superiority, pride and greediness. They emphasized that at the Cross there was not White or Black, educated or illiterate, missionary or African, pastor or layman. All needed to be released from sinfulness. A new relationship was born between missionaries and Africans.

Mennonite Relief Work in Ethiopia and the Establishment of a Church

Ethiopia was one of the first countries to suffer the horrific effects of Fascism when Italy invaded the country in 1936. Some forty years earlier, Italy had been badly defeated at the Battle of Adowa in 1896 by the backward and ill-equipped military forces of Ethiopia. But on the eve of the Second World War, Ethiopia was ill-prepared to counter the technically-advanced Italian military. Nevertheless, after five years of struggle the Italians were finally forced out of the country, and Ethiopia began to rebuild.

During this period of economic destruction the Mennonite Relief Committee (MRC) offered help. In August, 1945 Paul Hooley and Samuel Yoder, two Mennonites working in the United Nations relief program in Egypt, arrived in Ethiopia. The government of Ethiopia was very unwilling to admit mission organizations into the country, but since the Mennonites had not asked for permission to begin mission work, they were allowed to begin relief work in Nazareth, some sixty miles southeast of Addis Ababa. Hooley and Yoder renovated and converted an idle cotton-ginning mill into a hospital, an effort very much appreciated by the people. In April 1946 they signed a five-year contract with the Ethiopian government to extend their work. By 1947 this work included running a forty-bed hospital, the Haile Mariam Mamo Memorial Hospital, and an outpatient clinic. Besides medical work, MRC sponsored six teachers under the Ministry of Education; twenty dressers or nurses' aides were enrolled in the hospital school in 1947.

According to government guidelines some areas in the country—particularly those predominantly comprised of Orthodox believers—were designated as "closed" areas, off limits to evangelical witness. Nazareth was one such area, where missionaries were prohibited from preaching and teaching the Gospel. It was only in the Muslim and traditional religious areas that missions were allowed to evangelize. In 1947 Emperor Haile Selassie visited the Haile Mariam Mamo Memorial Hospital in Nazareth and gave encouragement to the workers. The royal visit and the remarks made by the Emperor prompted the service workers to request the expansion of their work to include mission status.

On June 7, 1948 Dorsa Mishler and Daniel Sensening were given an audience with the Emperor, at which time they obtained permission for permanent mission status. They were given the Hararge area in eastern Ethiopia in which to work. The two mission representatives travelled to Hararge to explore possible mission sites. Eventually they decided to start construction at Deder and Bedeno, where the majority of the population was Muslim. In February 1949, Sensening went to Deder and started putting up the buildings for a school and a clinic. In 1950 the school was opened, and the clinic in 1952. Thus Deder became the first mission station in Ethiopia, and Mennonite relief work was transformed into mission work.

The year 1951 was one of historic importance for Mennonite mission work in Ethiopia; in this year the work of the Mennonite Relief Committee was transferred to the mission board, the Bedeno school was opened and the first ten believers were baptized. These believers were taken to Addis Ababa in secret and baptized there, due to the prohibition to proselytize in and around Nazareth. These converts came to Christ as a result of testimonies from Ethiopian Christians. The baptism of these ten converts was described as the planting of ten trees.[29] Two of these believers were Bati Ensermo and Badi Tassew. The news of the baptism was heard by Nazareth government officials and even by the Emperor himself, and caused some consternation. The missionaries were rebuked and warned not to engage in such activities in a closed area. Nevertheless, the work of baptizing new believers continued to be performed by Ethiopians such as Gemeda Baruda and Geber Selassie Habitamu.

Educational work continued to grow. Following a request by the goverment, a school for the blind was opened in 1952 with Martha Keener as teacher and director. The school was dedicated and opened by the Emperor himself. Located in Addis Ababa, the school also served as the business center for the mission and became a most valuable focal point for young Christian men from various parts of the country to come for worship. By 1952 there were five mission stations in Ethiopia: Adis Ababa, Nazareth, Deder, Bedeno and Deredawa, nearly 450 kilometers east of Addis Ababa.

Most of the Ethiopians who worked in the hospital or in the schools came from other areas of evangelical Christian witness, and they often joined in midweek or Sunday worship with the missionaries. But as the testimony in the schools and hospital continued, and the Bible school students continued to visit surrounding areas to give their testimonies, more people began to show interest in the midweek and Sunday meetings. An annual Christian life conference was organized to bring all believers together. Dr. Beyene Chichaybelu is credited with having initiated the conference after asking Daniel Sensening, then mission director, "Why are you missionaries separating yourselves and holding annual meetings? Are you conspiring against us?" Daniel Sensening replied, "we are not conspiring against anyone, but trying to counsel and comfort one another. You can do the same thing if you want to."[30]

In 1956 the first spiritual life conference was held on the grounds of the Haile Mariam Mamo Memorial Hospital. In 1958 the conference was held in four different stations, and in the following year at all the mission stations, with large attendance. Councilors for each station were selected as lay leaders or elders representing local churches. They were not ordained pastors but assumed the same duties and responsibilities. In his report, Wenger says,

a milestone was reached on January 17-19, 1959 when these brethren with several Board-appointed missionaries met in the first organized Ethiopian-American council meeting. Matters concerning the doctrine and work of Christ were discussed. To those of us who took part in these discussions, the spirit and vision of our Ethiopian brethren was most heartening and their helpful suggestions appreciated.[31]

In one of the general council meetings held in 1959 the name of the emerging church, Meserete Kristos Church (Christ Foundation Church), was agreed upon. Nathan Hege, a long-time beloved missionary and pastor, has these memories about that meeting:

The name "Mennonite" was not adopted because of its foreignness, having no local cultural expression. By this time the church had grown not only in number but also in geographical areas. There were three sugar plantations in close proximity to Nazareth. Some of the believers, having left their home church in order to take jobs in the factory, were organized into a church. The first church building was erected in Wonji, about twelve kilometers south of Nazareth. The church also expanded in other ways. A Christian boarding high school, the Bible Academy, was built in Nazareth. Elementary and junior high schools were opened in a number of places. Literature ministry was started. Mennonite bookstores were opened at different locations throughout the country. Livestock of good breeding was introduced.

The Somali Mennonite Mission

In 1953 Wilbert and Rhoda Lind arrived in Mogadishu, capital of Somalia, to begin Mennonite mission work in that country. At the time Somalia was under Italian occupation, although the Somali spirit remained fiercely independent and rebellious. The Mennonites took a step of faith when they decided to launch their evangelical ministry.

By 1954 Lind was ready to recommend that the Somali Mennonite Mission start mission work in Mahaddei Wein, approximately 120 kilometers north of Mogadishu, to provide educational services and health care, and in August of the same year Jamama was suggested as the third mission station site.

English classes were the chief means of evangelism employed by the missionaries in Mogadishu. Classes began in 1953 with 100 young men enrolled for the evening classes. The missionaries testified that it was in these English classes that they learned to know and love the Somali people. Toward the end of 1954 there were three classes for men and two for women in Mogadishu. On November 4, 1957, Victor and Viola Dortsch began English language classes in a rented facility in Jamama village. Eighty-nine men and eleven women enrolled. Portions of the Bible were used to teach the students in the classes, and the students were invited to come to Sunday worship services. In spite of these open attempts to interest people in the Gospel, not one Somali joined the missionaries for Sunday worship services in the early going.

During the period from 1955 to 1960 Orie Miller showed interest in developing the (MCC) PAX agricultural programme, believing that the programme would contribute to the total discipleship witness of the Mennonites. The programme provided training services in housing, health, sanitation, agriculture, trades, community cooperatives, small-scale industries, marketing, child care, maternity services, family welfare, food preservation, nutrition and education.

The first Mennonite church members in Somalia were Bantus who had been converts of the Swedish Mission in the Juba Valley. By 1961 there were ten active members.[32] In 1960 the first ethnic Somali became a Christian believer,[33] and near the end of 1960 the first baptismal service for new converts was held. Two men and two women were baptized.[34] The converts began to witness boldly to family and friends. As a result, many were disowned and rejected from their homes. News of the conversions aroused opposition, even though there was a clause in the 1961 Somali constitution guaranteeing religious freedom.

These new conversions created much tension between the Mission and the Somali government, culminating in the closure of the Mission in March of 1962. This was brought on by the distribution of Arabic Christian literature by some zealous young Christians on the streets of Mogadishu. The Mission was forbidden to conduct its regular Saturday evening meeting with the Somali Christians. So, when the Somali Christians came, the missionaries met outside for a few minutes with them and explained the situation, suggesting that they try to meet by themselves elsewhere. The Somali Christians met and discussed how they would conduct their fellowship in the future and informed the missionaries which one had been selected to be their leader.

"This experience surely touched my heart," Harold Stauffer wrote. Here was a group of young intelligent fellows who accepted Christ only after long, hard consideration of the implications, which such a decision would have. Quite suddenly our relationship with them is drastically altered. They're enthusiastic and want to reach their own people with the Gospel, and yet they must be tactful and move carefully in order not to antagonize them to the extent of spoiling what possibilities for witness they do have.[35]

By 1962 the number of believers had grown to about twenty-five.

In July 1962 Merlin Grove was stabbed to death as he was registering students for the Mogadishu adult evening classes. Dorothy, his wife, was also seriously wounded but recovered soon afterwards. Apparently the attacker was a fanatical Muslim. Strange as it may seem, the temporary closure of the mission in 1962 and the death of Merlin Grove, instead of

Dorothy and Merlin Grove and their children.

slowing church activity, seems to have roused rapid church growth. Among the first believers were Abidi Dahir, Said Smatar (now Professor at Rutgers University, New Jersey, USA), Herze Ahimed (now living in Seattle, Washington) and Abdul-Cadir Wursame (now living in Nairobi, Kenya). The believers in Mogadishu, Johar, and Mahaddei Wein held weekly fellowship meetings and formed the Somali Christian Association.

In 1963 the mission was required to allow Islamic and Arabic instruction in its schools. Allowing the Somalis to teach Islam in mission schools helped create a lot of trust. Even after this imposition, Mennonites stayed on in Somalia, even though workers of another Protestant denomination chose to leave. The Mennonite missionaries left behind a strong positive impression among the Somali, who consider them people who have worked hard for Somali progress.

The Socialist revolution changed many things. According to Aden Matan,

> before the Socialist revolution of 1970 the Somali brothers were not brothers by clan but by faith in Christ Jesus. When they held fellowship meetings in Jamama, Johar, Kismayo and Mogadishu, they were very close to each other. But when the revolution broke out some of the top church leaders joined the security and after that the fellowship became weaker and smaller."[36]

The money, sweat and blood that the Mennonite missionaries expended in Somalia during their twenty-three year stay (1953-1976), however, was not in vain; it created a small but strong Christian fellowship. Moreover, their presence left an indelible impression on the hearts and minds of many Somalis. Mennonites still enjoy a positive reputation which should serve as a strong foundation for future relationships in Somalia.

The Mennonite Church in East Africa, 1960-1970

As East Africa moved towards independence from colonial rule, missionaries discovered their old network for making programme decisions was disappearing. An African frame of reference was taking its place, and Africans were moving to the top of the leadership pyramid. The transition was difficult and often painful. Many "old-time white folks" were concerned that their lives' efforts would get lost in history's trash bin. Jack Shellard, an Australian missionary and World War II army officer, succinctly voiced the missionaries' feelings: "The things we were always afraid would happen are happening now."[37]

Educational work continued. By the end of the 1960s there were 35 primary schools and four secondary boarding schools sponsored by the church. During the peak of the revival period there was a lot of sharing and fellowshipping between the Anglicans, Lutherans, Moravians and Mennonites in Tanganyika in the areas of evangelism and education. Together they built the famous Katoke Teachers' College near Bukoba, Tanzania and participated in the preparation of teaching material and the provision of religious instruction in the various schools of the country. There was sustained church growth from 1945 to about 1965. For many years the Mennonite Church in Tanganyika was a lighthouse for revival. The revival story was compiled, printed and released from the press in Bukiroba. During this period the Tanganyika Mennonite Church (TMC) was declared a free conference in 1960. TMC grew very rapidly in the early part of the '60s because of revival and autonomy.

The Life and Growth of TMC, 1950–1970

The Mennonite Mission intended to build a strong African church based on the three principles of "self-propagation, self-support and self-governance." However, in the early years of the church there were separate conferences for missionaries and for African church leaders. The African church leaders saw no reason why the mission ought to insist on the three principles while at the same time not giving them more responsibility. As yet, they had not been ordained as pastors; they had not been given sufficient education to enable them to become efficient councillors.

In their 1948 annual conference, the missionaries discussed two items of major significance to the future relationship of the mission and the church: the type of church organization to be established, and the procedures for ordaining African pastors. They wanted to build an indigenous African Mennonite Church with an organizational structure based on three ministry offices: bishops, pastors and deacons. Furthermore, as Josiah Muganda noted,

> They wanted the African Church to have a line of demarcation between church and state. They did not expect African Mennonites to hold posts in the civil service or work for a company. Such practices were incompatible with the Mennonite faith or way of life. At that time they were not open to cultural and local differences.[38]

Tanzanian Pastor and wife.

Ezekiel Muganda and Andrea Mabeba were ordained on October 4, 1950 to become the first two African pastors in the Mugango-Majita area; Zedekiah Kisare and Nashon Kawira Nyambok were chosen to become pastors in the Shirati area and were ordained on December 10, 1950. The Tanzanian church had come of age with its own African leadership. After serving as lay preachers for more than fifteen years, these men had become ministers in their own right with authority to baptize new converts, administer the Lord's Supper, excommunicate the recalcitrant and perform marriage ceremonies.

In 1956 Jona Itine was ordained pastor and Elisha Meso deacon in the Bumangi area. In the same year, Nathanael Robi Nyamari and Yusuf Wambura were ordained pastor and deacon in Nyarero area. Before this, four deacons had been ordained in the Mugango-Majita area: Paul Chai and Aristarko Masese among the Bajita people, Daniel Maato Sigira and Hezekiah Saria among the Baruli people. In the Shirati area the ordained deacons were Zefaniah Migire, Koja Dishon Masogo and Esayo Obiro.

In 1955 the General Church Council created an executive committee, named the "Kamati Kuu," whose first African members were pastors Nashon Kawira and Obiro from North Mara, Ezekiel Muganda and Jona Itine from South Mara. The Kamati Kuu oversaw the work of the education, marriage problem-solving and Pastors' committees among others. In July, 1957 the Kamati Kuu approved the first draft of the organizational plan of the African church.

The sense of oneness in the Spirit, the joy and appreciation at finding national pastors, aroused great interest in the work of evangelism. The number of new converts increased significantly and many were baptized. According to Mahlon Hess, "Whereas from 1943 to 1950 three churches were opened each year, from 1951 to 1960 seven churches were opened every two years."[39]

In the Shirati area, Zefaniah Migire was the leading evangelist at this time, and helped to establish twelve new churches. As the evangelists moved from place to place preaching the Gospel, they faced many difficulties such as shortage of money, inadequate clothing and, sometimes, lack of food. Despite these difficulties, the ministries produced a remarkable growth in membership. Again according to Hess, "From 1935 to 1943 [new membership numbered] an average of 25 per year, 1943 to 1950 an average of 40, 1951 to 1960 an average of 178."[40]

During this period many primary schools were opened in the Mara Region. The Bumangi boarding school was opened in 1954 and the Shirati boarding school in 1955. Middle schools not only offered academic training but also training in handicrafts and agriculture. Altogether eleven schools opened in Tarime district and sixteen in Musoma District. Musoma Alliance Secondary School was opened in 1959, from which the church recruited some of its teachers.

Independence Celebrations

When national independence came in 1961, the question arose of how involved Christians should be in the political life of the new nation. Some Tanganyika Mennonite church members were under pressure to become village leaders. Should they accept such responsibilities? The principles by which the Tanganyika African National Union (TANU) party was led were those of equality and justice, which were appealing to Christians. The party leader and the first president, Mwalimu Julius Nyerere, was considered a father to the nation. He was popular with the people for his forthrightness, devotion, sincerity and humility. He was a devout Catholic and encouraged Christians of all denominations to pioneer in the act of nation building. Christians rejoiced over gaining political independence and realized their responsibility as citizens to set an example of good leadership. They were determined to build a strong nation, and as a result they answered the call to fight ignorance, disease and poverty. It was expected of Christians to clearly demonstrate self-reliance and national unity. Communities usually chose Christians to hold positions as chairmen or treasurers in local government.

Autonomy in the church and independence for the nation prompted Mennonite leaders to inculcate in their youth the value of handling leadership responsibilities in their church. Shemaya Magati (now leader and founder of the Free Church of Africa in the Shirati area) was chosen as youth leader in 1960 and thereafter worked hard to direct the energy and enthusiasm of the youth toward building the church. In 1962 the Tanganyikan Mennonite Church Youth League (TMCYL) was organized with Daniel Matoka assisting Magati in the leadership. People up to the age of forty were placed in the youth category. Each congregation formed a branch of the TMCYL. Youth activities in the church included cleaning the church, receiving offerings, helping with Sunday school programmes, bringing messages in song, cultivating gardens, building temporary shelters during spiritual life conferences and taking care of guests who came to such conferences.

The First National Bishop of TMC

In the year 1964 the Tanganyikan church was struggling to choose its first African bishop. There were two candidates, but one was Bantu and the other was Luo, and there was serious tribal strife concerning who should be the national bishop. When it became clear that Zedekiah Kisare from the Luo tribe was going to be appointed bishop, it called for Ezekiel Muganda (from the Bantu tribe) to rise to a level of holiness that only a handful of men attain. "Let us move beyond our differences. Jesus is our head," said Ezekiel Muganda after Zedekiah Kisare had been chosen as

(R to L) Margaret and Bishop Zedekiah Kisare, President Julius Nyerere, and Bishop Salmon Butenge, at the retirement celebration of Bishop Kisare.

the first national Mennonite bishop of Tanganyika. Tribal tensions could have split the church, but there were a few people like Muganda who stood in the breach and made peace. Ordination took place on January 15, 1967.[41]

From 1967 onwards African socialism was proclaimed in Tanzania. Land was nationalized and schools taken over by the government. Churches were asked to get involved in religious instruction in all schools so that moral character would be developed along with the mind and the body. There are varying opinions about the effect of the mission effort in this area. For instance, Kembo Migire, founder of the Shirati Secondary and High School, and a polygamist who also calls himself a Mennonite, asserts that the "missionaries who came to Tanganyika in the 1930s ruined our culture completely." He goes on to say that

nothing of us was really good in their eyes; our food, clothing, system of marriage. In order to be a Mennonite one had to succumb to everything they claimed was right. And they didn't want anybody with education. No shoes, no long trousers, no watches, no moustache! If an African went to their house, they wouldn't let him in, but met him at the door and talked to him there.[42]

On the contrary, Chawachi Migire, Mwanza Diocese secretary and brother to Kembo says "some people tell stories with a political bias, but the missionaries did the best they knew was right. They had no evil intentions."[43]

Meserete Kristos Church (MKC) before the Socialist Revolution

The Gospel spread in Ethiopia as Christians shared their faith wherever their occupations took them. In the early 1960s Million Belete, who had a degree in electronics from Western Michigan University, was sent by the government to run a new high school in Mekele. He started and strengthened believers' groups in Baher-Dar as well. Fanatic Orthodox Christians destroyed the chapel in Baher-Dar.

The appointment of a constitution revision committee at the general church council meeting in 1966 was the beginning of a movement to make MKC a truly Ethiopian church. Eight Ethiopians, but no Americans, were appointed to the committee. However, independence for the church came in incremental steps, and not as quickly as many desired. Shemsudin Abdo was elected church administrator in 1968; later it was determined that the missionaries were to be directly responsible to MKC, which would correspond directly with Eastern board. In August 1969 the Eastern Board decided to discontinue electing members to the executive committee of MKC.

Analysis and Vision for the church of twenty young MKC brothers, 1966.
—The church is too dependent on the mission.
—The church's programmes are a continuation of the missions' programmes.
—The articles of faith are based on foreign customs.
—They decided to strengthen their unity through times of fellowship, eating, singing, praying and discussing together frequently.
—They decided to re-study the articles of faith as related to the Bible and to customs of the culture.
—They agreed to examine carefully the church's programmes to provide for the training of church members and to start organizations which would produce income for the church.

In 1970 the MKC board of education was organized to manage the six remaining elementary schools and the Nazareth Bible Academy. By the early 1970s MKC had increased its budget for development, created a new development and rehabilitation board and appointed a full time

The ordination of Million Belete.

Ethiopian director to lead the program. An evangelism board, organized in 1970, stimulated the congregations to focus on establishing outreach centers. In 1971 an evangelism seminar for church leaders was held at the Bible Academy.

The socialist revolution in 1974, which overthrew the Haile-Selassie government, changed the context in which the church functioned. In the feudal land tenure system before the revolution, almost two-thirds of the land was owned by absentee landlords who demanded high rental fees and up to a fifth of the harvest. After the outbreak of the revolution, land reform was accomplished so that for the first time peasants tilled their own little plots for their own use. Rents for houses were reduced; private businesses were curtailed; younger men replaced incompetent district governors; local associations known as "Kebele" assumed judiciary rights to try criminal cases. During this period the Ethiopian Orthodox Church lost much of its power, but most Protestant denominations continued their work. The government did not interfere with the churches as long as they did not become politically active. Nevertheless, some local associations troubled Christians from time to time.

A common feature of the socialist revolution in its early days was the weekly two-hour session of political indoctrination. Most early attendees found these sessions enjoyable because they were instructive and informative, but later people hated them because the sessions became boring and frustrating. People sat through those sessions as if they were sitting in a funeral home. Every session was wrapped up by chanting revolutionary slogans. A number of Christians were intimidated, flogged or imprisoned for not shouting the slogans with the other people, especially the slogan, "Nothing is above the revolution!" They asserted instead, "Jesus is above the revolution!"

Revolutionary Slogans:
—Nothing is above the revolution!
—We shall bring nature under our subjection!
—Everything to the war front!
—Motherland or death!
—Down with reactionaries!
—Death to counter revolutionaries!
—Forward with our revolutionary leader!

In the 1960s there were two historical forces at work for social change in Ethiopia: Pentecostalism and the students' movement. The spiritual awakening or Pentecostal movement was a radical movement, as far as mainline Protestant churches were concerned. From the very beginning, the leaders of this movement experienced much suffering. They had to pay a heavy price for what they believed to be true. But as the ancient saying goes, "the blood of martyrs is the seed of the church." And so it was with the lives of these Christians. The spiritual renewal yielded much fruit in all the mainline evangelical churches.

The second force at work was the revolutionary political movement spearheaded by the university students. Unlike the first movement, the second one appears to have caused great harm to the church. Nevertheless, the Lord used it to expand his kingdom and strengthen his church. As the Psalmist puts it, "Praise be to the Lord, who has not let us be torn by their teeth" (Psalm 124: 6).

The Pentecostal Movement

The Pentecostal movement affected the MKC. It came both from within and from outside the church. In 1959 six young men,[44] students at Atese Gelawedios school, approached Dr. Roher Eshleman, then medical director of Haile Mariam Mamo Memorial Hospital, and asked him to teach them English. Seizing this opportunity to share his faith, Roher

Church prayers, Nazareth.

expressed his willingness to teach them English every Saturday evening using the Gospel of John as their textbook. While continuing their lessons they began to focus their attention on getting Bible knowledge rather than on simply learning English. As the doctor expounded the Gospel message, the truth was revealed to them. Although they got the truth, they did not wish to be identified with the missionaries because the people understood the missionaries to be "enemies of Saint Mary." People also accused the missionaries of not fasting on Wednesdays and Fridays and also said that their religion was something foreign, imported into the country.

Roher's students knew full well that eternal life was obtained through faith in Christ. They therefore accepted Jesus as their only Saviour. As a result, they began to witness in their school and invited their fellow-students to come to church. At the 1964 annual spiritual life conference, Solomon Kebede (Moderator of MKC) discussed the baptism of the Holy Spirit with Zeleke Alemu (now a pastor in the United States). Zeleke had already discussed the matter with Getachew Mekere, a frequent visitor at the Finnish Pentecostal mission in Addis Ababa. Again, Zeleke shared thoughts with Solomon Kebede. When the conference was over Solomon and Zeleke agreed to wait on the Lord in prayer and fasting for Holy Spirit baptism.

When the school year commenced, Zeleke went back to Harar Teachers Training Institute and Solomon continued with his secondary school education at Gelawedios. The Lord gave them what they asked, they were filled with the Holy Spirit. This was the first experience of the special anointing of the Holy Spirit in the history of the Meserete Kristos Church. Subsequently, they prayed earnestly for the manifestation of the Spirit in the gifts of prophecy, healing, and discerning of spirits. On several occasions they even raised the question among themselves "how could Alemu (the writer of these words) be a Christian and remain blind at the same time!?" They expected the Holy Spirit to heal infirmities of all kinds.

These young men completed high school and went on to university and there they shared their new experience with people like Bedru Hussein (now Vice President of MWC), Mekonen Tesema (Administrator at the Finnish mission) and Solomon Lulu (a successful business man). They received the baptism of the Holy Spirit and became strong church leaders. The movement spread to other parts of the country. The new Charismatic Fellowship in Addis came to be known as the Full Gospel Believers' Churches which grew in strength until 1972, when it was closed by government order. In Nazareth the charismatic fellowship was called "Heavenly Sunshine." Relations were established with MKC and Ato Geber-Selassie serving as a bridge of peace between the two groups. In 1973 people in Nazareth began to confess their sins openly, pleading for forgiveness. People started to flock to the church and trust in spiritual work increased dramatically. Many zealous young Christians gave their lives and time to God's work, and the church allocated a large percentage of its budget to evangelistic work. Each congregation has its own story to tell of how God started to move among its members in the person of the Holy Spirit, but what started in Nazareth seems to have spread to other parts of the country like wild fire. The Lord used the charismatic movement to bring dynamism and vitality into his church.

The Emerging Mennonite Churches of Kenya (1965-1977)

The Kenya Mennonite church had a unique beginning. It grew up as an extension of the Tanzanian Mennonite Church and therefore did not have the normal external structure that national churches usually have. Consequently, the church has lagged behind in establishing those structures.

Scarcely aware of the political boundary between Kenya and Tanzania, families have traditionally moved back and forth within their tribal areas. In the intervening years between the 1942 revivals and the 1960s, Zefanya Migre, Dishon Ngoya, Zedekiah Kisare and others made regular visits to Kenya to witness and nurture believers groups emerging at Bande, Nyangwaye and other places. In 1960, Kenyan residents asked the colonial government to allow to them set up a Mennonite station, but the government refused permission. Requests were repeated in 1962 and 1964, but they were also refused. Finally in 1965 the Kenyan government recognized the Mennonites as a church body. In the same year many Luo people from Kisaka, Tanzania, uneasy about the new government, returned to Kenya. Groups led by Naman Agola (now bishop) and Elifaze Odundo went to Songhor and Kigoto.

To lead the emerging churches, TMC sent Helon and Joyce Amolo to Suna in 1966, and in 1968 Clyde and Alta Shenk were transferred to Migore. The work expanded to central Nyanza. "Within the Suna area we planted six churches," comments Helon Amolo. "Then in the Kadema area we established four more churches, and in Mbewa we planted two more."[45] Musa Adongo and Naman Agola had returned to Kenya from Tanzania and settled in the Kisumu area.

The mission board felt strongly that the Kenyan government already had enough institutions of its own, so the mission did not see the need to set up institutions of social care. Helon Amolo, on the other hand, was of the opinion that the church needed its own institutions rather than depending on government or other denominations for education and medical care. According to Amolo, after Clyde and Alta Shenk left,

> disunity appeared in the Kenya Mennonite churches because of tribalism. Perhaps we may not call it "tribalism" as they are all Luo, but because of political influences from the various parties, there are factions within the same geographical area that spill over into the church. We praise God that church leaders are now coming to the realization that these political divisions should not divide the church."[46]

The Kenya Mennonite Church remained a part of the Tanzania Mennonite Church until 1977, when bishop Kisare met the pastors of the

Kenya churches to set up a Kenyan Mennonite central committee to bring the church in Kenya under its own structure. From that time on, the Kenya Mennonite Church (KMC) has had direct contact with EMBMC (now EMM) through its central committee.

Recreation at Eastleigh.

The Eastleigh Fellowship Center in Nairobi was opened and dedicated on June 8,1980. It is a very valuable community centre whose facilities include two classrooms, an assembly hall, a library, a study room, and a basketball and volleyball court. Its objectives include the provision of a Christian witness and presence, offering an opportunity for conversation and sharing between various religious communities, providing constructive recreation and help for low-income families and students, thus improving the quality of their lives.

Another important service given to Muslims by the Kenya Mennonite Church is the correspondence course "People of God Service to Muslims."The basic work of the People of God course is distributing and handling correspondence with over a thousand students. The course was written to introduce Muslims to the Christian faith. Bishop Joash and his wife Rebecca Osiro along with Daren Schaup, a Mennonite missionary, are the field staff who visit churches to give seminars on Islam.

Ogwedhi is on the border of two tribal areas occupied by the Maasai, a nomadic pastoral people, and the agricultural Luo tribe. In the past there has been a lot of conflict between the two tribes. When Wilson Oguwada, a Luo, was chief, he talked to a Maasai chief asking how they could bring peace to the area. When Wilson suggested that only a church could end the bloodshed in the area, the Maasai chief asked him if he knew of a church capable of bringing peace. Wilson replied that he knew "a peace-loving church," the Mennonite Church.[47]

The Kenya Mennonite Church was called to this situation to bring peace and reconciliation. Originally the call came as a request from the

Border Committee, a group of elders from both tribes. The Border Committee asked that a mission be established to minister to the varied needs felt within the community. The first need on their list was the establishment of a church. They also asked for agricultural, educational and medical development. After several months of prayer, visiting the site and holding meetings with the Border Committee, the Kenya Mennonite Church decided that God was leading them to this area of service. Paul Otieno began the work of evangelism and started a good working relationship with the community, traveling eighty kilometers every week from his home in Mohuru Bay, a village on the shores of Lake Victoria.

Mennonite Churches in Eastern Africa, 1970-2000

Kanisa la Mennonite Tanzania and its Service Organizations

Beginning in 1974 Tanzania experienced a series of crises, which reduced per capita income significantly: agricutural productivity was significantly reduced due to migration to village settlements; the global oil crisis limited the power of Tanzania and other developing nations to buy oil; and in 1978 war erupted in Uganda at a great cost to the Tanzanian government. Following these crises, Tanzania also experienced two consecutive years of famine. These factors brought great difficulties to the nation. Some factories had to reduce production while others were closed down altogether. Transportation became difficult and national income dropped sharply resulting in lower food production and fewer manufactured goods. Staple foods were available at inflated prices or by paying bribes. Fuel shortages hampered medical services. In the midst of these shortages many people compromised their integrity to meet their basic needs. But many brothers and sisters committed themselves to continue their walk with Jesus. They refused to purchase on the black market and refused bribes.

The war in Uganda of 1978 involved the Mennonites of the Mara Region. When Iddi Amin attacked Tanzania, some church members volunteered to join the Tanzanian armed forces, contrary to the Mennonite understanding of the Scriptures. Others, however, stood firm in their religious conviction of non-resistance. "When we had to fight Iddi Amin in 1979," says Christopher Ndege, "our first president, Julius Nyerere gave the order that all Tanzanian young men enlist in the army to go to the war front." Ndege, however, decided to stand up for the biblical principle of non-resistance. As a result, he was taken to court as someone who had rejected the national call.[48]

In 1990 when Nyerere spoke of the wisdom of solving conflicts through dialogue instead of war, Ndege wrote a letter to Nerere to tell him that in 1979 he had refused to go to war because it was not the right solution. At that time he was going to be thrown in jail, but he had visited Nyerere in the early 1960s and had explained to him the Mennonite stand on the peace issue. Nyrere told him then that it was not possible to give a blanket exemption to Mennonites from the military, but that a way should be found to grant alternative service to individual conscientious objectors. When Ndege refused to participate in the Uganda War, Tanzanian officials asked about his church membership. When they found out that he was Mennonite, they let him go free.

Conflict in the Leadership Structure

During the late 1970s more leaders were needed to fill church positions all over Tanzania because the Mennonite Church had spread beyond the Mara Region. Consequently, Pastor Hezekiah N. Saria was elected bishop on November 22, 1977 and ordained on February 18, 1979. The church was now divided into two dioceses, North and South Mara. Tribal conflicts were increasing throughout the nation at this time, affecting Mennonites as well as other denominations. After the ordination of Saria as bishop, disunity in the KMT increased because political considerations had heavily influenced his selection. In the United States, Eastern Mennonite Board of Missions expressed the view that the church in Tanzania should be governed by more than one bishop. It became clear at this time that Bishop Saria did not have that much respect for the authority of the Lancaster Mennonite Conference. He interacted with the local ecclesial culture, with groups like the Anglicans and the African Inland Church.

From 1984 to 1986 there was a power struggle between the younger leadership and the older leadership in the South Mara Diocese. After the jubilee celebrations in 1984, growth and membership declined; the bookshop was closed and the Mennonite Guesthouse in Musoma deteriorated to the extent that it could no longer offer effective services.

Even more worrying was the fact that members of the church and community did not consider these institutions as church property, and they were mismanaged in many ways. In 1989, the problems came out into the open. In the following year the EMBMC tried to resolve the conflict. Doctors had meanwhile diagnosed Saria's illness as heart disease and told him he had only two alternatives: one was to start medication and discontinue any strenuous and stressful work like preaching, teaching and chairing meetings. The other was to continue what he was doing before and face the physical consequences.

A Mennonite brother from Lancaster who was in the area at the time, told Saria that he was most welcome to come to the United States to receive medical treatment and relax for a while. "Send the money to me and I will decide what to do with it," Saria said. Saria's poor interpersonal skills were a factor in many people distancing themselves from the Mennonite Church: he made decisions without consulting his fellow church leaders and claimed to be the final authority of the Mennonite Church in the South Mara Diocese. On one occasion he tried to have the names of seventeen people read out on Radio Tanzania and have them pronounced as rebels in the church.The radio announcer demanded that Saria bring a supporting document, such as the minutes of an official meeting, identifying and charging these people. Saria took this refusal as an affront to his authority as bishop. He flew from Dar es Salaam to Musoma and asked the district police commissioner to help him remove all the rebels from the church premises. Again, the district police commissioner said that they could not do such a thing without the suport of a legal document. Then Saria went to President Nyerere to seek some advice on the matter. The President told him to go back to the church and resolve the matter with his fellow church leaders.

From the medical point of view, all of this was probably a symptom of an illness which had stricken Saria. Other observers, however, perceived this as an ethnic problem. After Saria's death in 1992, interested people who had earlier been ordained by Saria, continued to argue the case in court up until April 2001, when the court dismissed the case stating that it was, "dismissed with expense [meaning, that every expense incurred by the Buteng'e group should be paid in full by Saria's group]."

The conflict within the Tanzania Mennonite Church was definitely harmful and resulted in a spiritual decline which divided the church in two. Some members joined Saria and others joined the opposing group. Some Mennonites who had been working for the government came into the church as leaders and also took positions on one side or the other in the dispute; church business began to be done from a political perspective. A "spiritual malnutrition" and "the disease of ethnicity" seriously affected the church. There was tension between North Mara and South Mara; Luo versus Bantu. Through this traumatic period, serious Christians prayed for revival to take place.[49]

After the conflict of the 1980s, there was a kind of stagnation in church growth. However at the time of this writing, there is an entirely new leadership that is trying to bring peace and reconciliation to the KMT.

Profile of the Upanga Mennonite Church,
Dar Es Salaam, Tanzania

Upanga Mennonite church is located close to the centre of Dar es Salaam, Capital of Tanzania. Upanga Mennonite church is the mother of four smaller congregations within the city itself and of daughter churches in other localities.

Upanga Mennonite church was established in 1964 under the leadership of Mahlon Hess, one of the early Mennonite missionaries and the first education secretary of the Tanganyika Mennonite church. Mahlon and his wife Mabel were transferred to Dar es Salaam in April 1963 with the aim of handling pastoral careresponsibilities. They quickly had the names of a hundred young Mennonites, the basis of a strong fellowship. In May 1963 the fellowship held its first worship service. Within a year the church was given a plot of land adjacent to the college. In addition to pastoring Upanga Mennonite church, Hess had other responsibilities which took up a lot of his time, so he had to hand over pastoral care and leadership to Daudi Mahemba, now a retired bishop residing in Musoma town.

Within the past thirty-seven years Upanga Mennonite church has grown and become a large congregation with a membership of well over 450 people, with women making up 60% of its members. This church has a strong family base comprising nearly eighty households.

Upanga Mennonite church has one leading pastor, an associate pastor, two evangelists, and twelve elders who make up the elders' committee. The elders assist the pastor in planting new churches, teaching

A typical worship service.

Bible to new converts, planning and implementing development programs (such as pre-school education and HIV-AIDS prevention), preparing spiritual life conferences and crusades, and planning and managing church finances. In short, the elders are instrumental in administering the church.

The youth in the Upanga Mennonite church are integrated into the activities of the church. Some of them participate in the church choir, serving not only their own congregation but travelling to different churches to convey the Christian message in song. Now and then the choir records songs in Swahili on cassette tapes and sells them to church members to generate additional income. Others form Gospel teams and travel to places as far away as Morogoro, some 200 kilometers west of Dar es Salaam. There they camp for several weeks, helping the weak and the needy, and preaching the Good News. As a result of their missionary efforts, a local church has been planted. The youth of Upanga Mennonite church have made contacts with young Christians of other countries, such as those in South Africa.

The women in this church have played a significant role as deaconesses, providing assistance to destitute people housed in government shelters. The Christian women of this church distribute clothing and food items to these needy people. On Friday afternoons they have their own special meetings at which time they discuss issues of particular interest and undertake practical activities like sewing, knitting, gardening, and taking care of children as ways of supporting their church.

As is common in most evangelical churches, Sunday worship in Upanga Mennonite church begins at 10:00 a.m. and ends at 12:30 p.m. with Sunday school starting at 9:00 a.m. Usually, the pastor brings the Gospel message, but occasionally an elder, a deacon or someone from another church is invited to preach. The choir sings before and after the sermon. The choir uses guitars, drums and keyboard instruments.

Until recently, the use of such musical instruments was not a common practice in the Mennonite churches in Tanzania because of the residual influence of the missionaries of the 1940s and 1950s. Today, the choir prepares its own compositions while the congregation sings North American songs translated from English in the early missionary days. The worship pattern is gradually changing in that today the women ululate and worshipers clap and shout "hallelujahs." There is much more exuberance and fervor in the worship service now than was the case some decades ago.

Baptism, the Lord's Supper and foot washing are ordinances practiced in the Upanga Mennonite church. Baptismal instructions of three to six months are offered to new believers. The catechumens are baptized upon the completion of the course. Generally speaking, the form of baptism used is sprinkling but sometimes, if baptismal candidates declare a preference for immersion, the church is open to performing baptism that way. A significant number of members partake of the Lord's Supper, which is administered four times a year. Foot washing used to be observed in all of the Mennonite churches of Tanzania, but because of the spread of HIV/AIDS, it is no longer practiced. Only the Scripture portion from the Gospel of John is read to remind believers of the ordinance.

Marriage ceremonies are conducted according to church procedures. Both young men and young women are given instruction on marriage for three weeks before their wedding day. Currently, the church requires that young people be examined for HIV/AIDS before final approval for marriage is given.

Upanga Mennonite Church is a good example of a self-supporting congregation. Many of its members are willing to give of their time and money to the Lord's work. Members pay their full-time workers, operate a nursery and kindergarten school, support various programs and undertake vigorous missionary activity. The members of Upanga Mennonite church are a composite of different ethnic groups, which have migrated from various parts of the country in search of employment, education and other opportunities. Obviously, the majority of members are from the Mara region. Many of the members are gainfully employed as civil servants, some in high positions as members of the diplomatic corps; some serve as political party officials, and some even serve in the military.[50]

Upanga Mennonite Church is a well-organized cosmopolitan congregation with a significant number of members enlightened spiritually and intellectually dedicated to the service of their Lord and their fellow countrymen. The Upanga Mennonite congregation has contributed a great deal to the growth and expansion of the Tanzanian Mennonite Church in the past and will continue to do so in the years to come.

Most of the Mennonites in Tanzania—between 75% and 90%—live in the area between Mwanza town and Shirati village, near the Kenyan border on Lake Victoria, and to the east into the Serengheti Plains. Most of this area is in the Mara Region, one of Tanzania's twenty administrative regions. Therefore, North Mara Diocese and the Lake Diocese, although the smallest geographically, have the highest concentration of Mennonites. Mwanza Diocese and Eastern diocese are very large geographically, but have a lower density of Mennonites. There are two major concentrations of Mennonites in Eastern Diocese, especially in Arusha town and in the coastal city of Dar es Salaam. Mwanza Diocese is growing quite rapidly in recent times.

The Impact of the Socialist Revolution on the Meserete Kristos Church

From 1977 onwards the Marxist regime forcibly prevented the church from performing any activities anywhere in the country. As a result of this brutal repression, the church was forced to conduct its programmes in a clandestine fashion. In those days it was not possible to meet with more than five people without getting permission from officials of the local political associations. Church leaders concluded that they should gather their members into small cell-group fellowships. Five people were assigned to each group, and suitable meeting places were chosen. On holidays larger groups could gather under the guise of celebrating Saints' days.

Despite adverse conditions, the church grew rapidly between 1974 and 1981, with new converts joining the church in large numbers. For example, in Addis Ababa alone fifty people made personal decisions to follow Christ every week, and hundreds of people were baptized at one time.[51] One of the reasons for this phenomenal growth was the work of the Holy Spirit. The healing ministry of evangelist Daniel Mekonnen, now pastor of a church called Gospel Light Church, had reached its peak at this time. Many people were healed of asthma and a variety of internal diseases. Handicapped people were restored to full health, and demons were cast out of many people. What was amazing at this time was the fact that demon-possessed people were unable even to enter the church compound. They would cry out loud at the entrance gate before they stepped into the church grounds. During this time people who had lung problems, spinal disorders, short legs, and hearing and vision problems were healed. The hand of the Lord was clearly demonstrated for its miraculous delivering power. The testimonies of some who were healed were published in Berhan Magazine (the Ethiopian Evangelical Fellowship Churches' magazine), a very popular Christian publication even among unbelievers. This aroused many to go and seek healing, although some went merely to satisfy their curiosity. Wednesday mornings and Sunday early mornings were set aside primarily to pray for the sick.

Later, when the eyes of the people turned from God to Evangelist Daniel, he gave some of the programmes to other evangelists. The work of the Holy Spirit was clearly manifested in the ministry of these evangelists. The church also organized committees such as Youth-for-Christ, Prayer, and Choir. The Jimma, Nazareth and Addis Ababa choirs were well known among Christians of Southern Ethiopia. Solo singers like Dereje Kebed, Tamirat Wolba from Addis Ababa and Shewaye Damte from Nazareth attained great popularity and their singing is still held in high regard among evangelical Christians.

This renewal did not come without difficulty. Groups calling themselves "prophets" caused many problems in the church, particularly in the choir ministry. Confusion and instability emerged because there was no responsible pastor to take care of the flock. This became quite evident in Addis Ababa after the departure of Dagne Asefa to the United States in 1977.

Among the strong features of the MKC during this time was the training program for lay leaders. Every year solid teaching was offered at the Bible Academy in Nazareth. Many naïve Christians had viewed socialism as a benign system that would turn Ethiopia into the "bread basket of Africa." However, some of the enlightened church leaders exposed Marxism's anti-Christian practices and beliefs.

Before the closure of the church, especially between 1976 and 1981, there were conventions and seminars for the church leaders of the various evangelical churches which contributed to the strengthening and unity of these denominations. The annual leadership conferences were designed chiefly for MKC members although the majority of the participants were from other denominations.[52] Leaders who were involved in producing materials and giving seminars were Solomon Kebede, Bedru Hussein, Shimelsẹ Retta and Pastor Syume G/Tsadik. The materials were written in handout form and distributed to participants. If found in the hands of any person, these materials were considered counter-revolutionary and the person possessing them was arrested; some were even imprisoned.

When pressure from the Marxist government intensified, Daniel Mekonnen left for the United States. Daniel claimed God had given him a vision to minister to those who lived abroad. Had he remained in Ethiopia, his imprisonment would have been a certainty. When he was in Addis, he had been harrassed by the "Kebele" (town dwellers' associations). Daniel's departure from MKC left a shadow of sorrow on the hearts of many members. He was a prominent person who had helped the church to be recognized in many ways. Many lost heart when he went abroad.

In 1982 the Marxist government confiscated MKC's institutions, including its head office, worship buildings, bank accounts, etc. At the time, MKC had five thousand members throughout its fourteen congregations. The official closure of the church and the expulsion of the missionaries placed serious obstacles in the path of the national leaders of the young church. It was a difficult time, requiring the church to go underground; it had to support its full-time workers and provide sufficient numbers of church leaders, adequately trained to minister to the underground cell groups. A mechanism had to be put in place to connect all the existing local churches and create normal working relations among them. All these tasks required strong and committed leadership.

On February 21, 1983 the first council of the underground church met in pastor Kasa Agafari's home in Addis Ababa. There were representatives from all the local churches. Pastor Kedir Delchumie of Nazareth was instrumental in organizing the underground council, taking the initiative of gathering the leaders of the various local churches. The first underground council agreed to meet twice a year and chose its executive committee.

In spite of all the risks involved, the underground executive committee decided to visit the scattered members of the Meserete Kristos Church wherever they might be found and to organize them into small underground cell groups. In addition, the committee decided to divide any local churches which had more than five hundred members into two, to create more local churches and render them more amenable to pastoral care. Hailu Cherenet gives the reason for the division as follows: "We started implementing the above vision because our main idea was that the daughter churches reproduce themselves and make disciples by giving birth to other churches."[53] Evangelist Kedir Delchumie and Seyoum Gebre-Tsadik from Nazareth began to meet with representatives from other local churches which made up the seven-member underground executive committee. These seven men started to meet every month at Nazareth. They met at

Aster Debose, underground cell group organizer, MKC, Nazareth.

night using candlelight to hide their gathering from the close surveillance of the regime's cadres.

In the initial stages of their work, the committee had to find someone to represent the local churches in the Awash Valley region. It was particularly difficult for Christians from this area to communicate with the people in Nazareth and vice versa, because cadres easily identified them if they were seen with others. The committee looked for someone who resembled the people in the Awash Valley region, who could easily disguise himself. He was expected to serve there and act as a liaison officer between Nazareth and the Awash Valley region. The local Nazareth church was asked to finance Zeleke Dadi, the man picked to serve in that difficult place.

The Nazareth church leaders agreed and began paying one hundred Birr (about forty U.S. dollars at that time) every month. The executive committee worked together to reorganize the disintegrated church on their own because no local church had appointed them as representatives. They discussed and decided to implement nine ministries: Children's Ministry, Visitation Ministry, Group Bible Study, Women's Ministry, Prayer Ministry, Worship Services Ministry, New Believers Ministry, Pastoral Care Ministry, and the Counselling Ministry.

From that time forward the executive committee members followed through with the implementation of the nine ministries at each local church. After some time these seven men began to report their progress and confer with the rest of the unimprisoned church leaders. Evangelist Kedir Delchumie was chosen to be chairman of this committee. Meetings were held at Babogaya (Debra Zait), Finnish Children's Center (Debra Zait), Kasa Agafari's house (Addis Ababa), Langano, Dire Dawa, etc. The result of these meetings was the establishment of the Evangelism Committee, headed by Pastor Kasa.

A subcommittee named the Christian Education Committee played a significant role in the survival and growth of the underground church.[54] The major concerns of this committee included preparing educational materials and choosing training centers, which were set up in Addis Ababa, Nazareth, Metehara and Dire Dawa. Teaching materials were prepared and sent to these centers in order to train mature, responsible members who could, in turn, train others. This laid the foundation for the small underground cell groups. Ever since, MKC has been clearly distinguished from all other evangelical churches for this solid training programme and pastoral care ministry.

Because of the political situation at the time, two or more people were not allowed to sit together repeatedly in the same place. If they were found doing so, they were considered terrorists or threats to the young revolution, or perhaps members of the EPRP (Ethiopian People's

Revolutionary Party). This situation directly affected the small group ministry. To overcome this problem a method was devised by which no more than five people were allowed to attend a Bible study programme. Each of the attendees was assigned a specific arrival and departure time at three-minute intervals. No singing, clapping of hands or shouting of halleluiahs was allowed at such gatherings. Speaking in a very low voice was a requirement.

New converts were handled in a very special way for a period of at least six months, the time needed to prepare them for baptism. Since coming to the programme with a Bible in hand would serve as a "dead give away," no one was allowed to carry a Bible to programmes. Bibles were provided at the meetinghouse. Worship services were conducted every month and governed by the same rules. In addition, the time for those monthly worship services was intentionally made to coincide with the time Orthodox Church-goers went to mass on Sunday morning, at 6:00 a.m. to 8:00 a.m. MKC members dressed in the style of Orthodox believers and mingled with them. The monthly worship service was the time when believers were introduced to each other; fellow Christians longed to see the faces of their brothers and sisters. The lack of mature ministers to serve at such meetings forced the churches to prepare written sermons which were read at worship.

One important programme that emerged was the "One Month for Christ" service. People who participated in this program were principally students who had completed high school. Their service focused on visiting believers who had been in the church before the persecution era started, but were unaware of what was being done in the church since then. So, the purpose of these visits was to help such people join the underground fellowship groups.

Something unexpected and marvelous came out of the efforts to reorganize the disintegrated church. One would have expected the relatively young church to collapse from the intense pressure exerted by the repressive government, but with God's help the church emerged triumphant: success replaced failure; maturity replaced immaturity. The church became stronger than it had been before the revolution. Before the official closure of the church in 1982, there were five thousand members. Nine years later, in 1991 when the church resurfaced, membership had risen to thirty-four thousand. The number of local churches had increased from fourteen to

Solomon Kebede, chairman of the Executive Committee, MKC

fifty-three. It is true, the church had lost buildings, property, and money, but it had gained devoted hearts suitable for God's dwelling.

The persecution also helped produce a good number of committed leaders. Although the church lost some of its key leaders because they were jailed, it managed to identify multiple leaders in spite of all the difficult circumstances. For example, in Addis Ababa, there were only seven elders in the local church at the start of the persecution. But the small group ministry and the home cell worship services forced the church to divide into six local churches. Each local church needed to have seven elders, which resulted in forty-two elders. This meant that the number of leaders grew from seven to forty-nine. The number of deacons grew in the same proportion, as did Bible study leaders, prayer group leaders, and preachers.

Though difficult to measure, spiritual maturity was one of the positive results of the persecution era. The vision of the seven men who were responsible for the implementation of the "nine ministries" influenced the lives of many believers, leading them to love and be committed to the church. When church members were assigned or transferred to new areas where there were no MKC local churches, they were encouraged to join other evangelical churches in the area. Usually they preferred to keep their ties with the mother MKC church. Even though they lived far away, they kept in touch and planted MK local churches wherever they went. Ministers (visitors) were sent even to individual members wherever they were. In this manner the Jimma MKC was founded, as was the Arba Minch local church and many others. With God's grace and power the church emerged victorious.

There were also negative aspects of the persecution experience. Besides the material losses and the loss of dedicated leaders languishing in prison, participants were deprived of their right to sleep at night. Because the same male and female participants met regularly at the same place, some personal problems emerged. Due to the secret nature of each church activity, church workers failed to provide receipts for tithes and offerings, which led to occasional misuse of money.

Compared to the blessings the church enjoyed during the dark period, however, the negative aspects of church life were indeed insignificant. What the Marxist government thought it had killed and buried in fact survived and multiplied through the resurrection power of our Lord. The event reminds us of the saying of Jesus in John 12:24: "I tell you the truth, unless a kernel of wheat falls to the ground and dies, it remains only a single seed. But if it dies, it produces many seeds."

The reopening of the church in 1991 brought a sense of freedom to all nationals who had endured Marxist rule. Freedom of religion, finally granted to the nationals, was indeed a great relief, but the resultant economic crisis had a great effect on the growth of the church. Leaders of the church responded to the new situation by undertaking a holistic ministry. Since the new religious freedom placed no restriction on evangelism, the church took advantage of this situation.

In general, the young people of the nation had been attracted by the propaganda of the Communists, which promised a non-religious, egalitarian society. However, when the Communist regime was overthrown, these young people found themselves empty-handed and disillusioned. The church sought to satisfy this hunger with the Good News of Christ by conducting large crusades and conferences as a form of mass evangelization. Because of these efforts large numbers of people responded to the call of the Gospel. Secondly, the leaders of the church considered the political instability of the country an opportunity to encourage politically bankrupt former party members to repent and become members of the Kingdom of God.

Inclusion and Exclusion of the Nakuru Happy Church

"We see ourselves as Mennonites, as Anabaptists. We are in a different conference," says Bishop Joseph Kamau, the leader of the Nakaru Happy Church, begun in 1983. Its leader claims to have a membership of fourteen to fifteen thousand baptized people in about fifty congregations. A few of their leaders were trained at Rosedale Bible Institute in Ohio, USA. They consider themselves Mennonite in doctrine and ecclesiology but they are demonstrably charismatic in their worship style. Bishop Kamau states emphatically that Nakuru Happy church is "by principle Anabaptist, but it does not mean we cannot relate with any other evangelical group. We want to relate to the Body of Christ at large; we don't want to be bound by denominational barriers."[55]

Happy Church congregations grew out of fellowships comprised of some ten members each. These fellowships are not accorded congregational status until the fellowship consists of fifty members and is able to sustain its own pastor or elder, demonstrating ability to send tithes to church headquarters and to pay rental for its meeting place. Then and only then is it called a congregation. At this point in the life of the congregation, the pastor is ordained. Higher contributions payments are requested when the congregation grows economically.

"We don't want to have a bishop just for the sake of carrying the title," says Bishop Joseph Kamau. As Bishop Kamau puts it, there were leadership wrangles in the KMC structure between the years 1989 and 1992, when bishops could not see eye to eye on a number of issues. According to Kamau and his colleagues, they were trying at the time to restore relationships among the various KMC bishops, noting how important it was for church officials to work together of one accord. However, as retired Bishop Musa Adongo puts it, the real reason for Bishop Kamau's wish to join the Kenya Mennonite Church may have been for the purpose of legal registration.

Bishop Kamau noted, "People who came to our church and saw us worship the way we did, gave us the name 'Happy Church.' They observed that our worship was very expressive and joyful. Most probably, too, we overused the word 'happy': 'Happy for meeting this Sunday! Happy for being saved! Happy for God's blessings to us!' So people said, 'I go to a church where people seem to be so happy. So let's call it Happy Church.'"[56]

As of 2001, the Happy Church is no longer affiliated with the Kenya Mennonite Church but is separately registered with the Kenyan government.

Mennonite Presence in Djibouti

Djibouti is strategically positioned in the Horn of Africa at the entrance to the Red Sea with its more powerful and populous neighbors, Ethiopia and Eritrea, to the north and west. It consists largely of two ethnic groups, the Afar and the Somali, who are almost totally Muslim in their religious practice. Djibouti has been a society of rapid change and a place of much opportunity; it continues to be a cultural crossroad and centre of communications where new ideas are given a fair hearing.

In this country Mennonites have been involved in different areas of service. The principal ministry has been education, teaching in schools in partnership with the Ministry of Education. Over the years, Mennonite personnel have built many bridges establishing individual friendships and relationships with people working in governmental and non-governmental organizations.

Djibouti continues as one of the original foreign mission sites in the overall missionary enterprise of the Meserete Kristos Church of Ethiopia. Since 1986 the Dire Dawa Meserete Kristos Regional Church Administration has taken responsibility for following up and organizing Ethiopian Christians who settled in Djibouti, fleeing the Marxist repression. At the beginning, the fellowship consisted of a tiny group which met in the French Protestant church building on Fridays. This group continued to witness to unconverted Ethiopian refugees. Now the fellowship has fifty-nine baptized members, including seven converts and two children.

The Small but Growing Meserete Kristos Church in Asmara, Eritrea

In 1987, a few years before Eritrea achieved political independence, several Christian brothers were working in the hinterland of Ethiopia. Because of the severe political persecution imposed on Eritreans by the Mengistu regime (the military leader during the Marxist repression), these brothers had been forced back to Eritrea. Since these young men were MKC members, the church sent an evangelist to Asmara to find out how they were doing in their Christian life. By this time, there were eight believers in Asmara who identified themselves as MKC members.

In 1988 Tesfaye Seyoum (now an evangelist in the Asmara MKC) came to Addis Ababa to participate in the "one-year-for-Christ" training program. He planned to go back to Asmara to minister to believers there. Then came the end of the Marxist regime and the ushering in of the new nation of Eritrea. Tesfaye continued to serve the Tigrignya- speaking people in Eritrea and Tigrai.

Baheta Haile, a fulltime minister in the Asmara, MKC, left Ethiopia in 1994 and joined the MKC fellowship that had already been established in Asmara. This fellowship met once every two weeks. In 1995 the Asmara MKC was warmly accepted into the Ethiopian MK family. Baheta was immediately elected and began serving in the new church. He was employed with an NGO but gave all his spare time to the Lord's work. In 1997 the person who was doing full-time work in the church was relieved of his responsibilities because of wrongdoing he had committed in the church, and someone had to be called to fill the vacancy. When he was asked to serve, Baheta quit his job with the NGO. "Tesfaye Seyoum was studying at the MK Bible Institute (now called the Meserete Kristos College) in Addis Ababa, and so, when the request came from the Elders' committee, to give myself full-time to church work, I did not have the heart to say no," said Baheta. Then he added, "I told myself I wouldn't be committing an offence if I surrendered to the church's call for service."[57] He had no definite call to be an evangelist or pastor at that time, but after one year of service he had a clear confirmation of his call to full time ministry.

There are now 160 baptized members in the Asmara Meserete Kristos Church. The church follows the guidelines set forth in the constitution of the Meserete Kristos Church of Ethiopia. The church members are devoted in that they give of themselves and their money to the work of God's kingdom. Believers tithe faithfully and are able to support two full-time workers by collecting 1,800 Naqfas (Eritrea's currency: about 180 US dollars), per month, which includes payment for the rent of a meeting house and other functions of the church.

Asmara MKC operates under the umbrella of some of the larger, long-established Protestant churches like the Society of International

Mission, the Full Gospel Believers Church, The Presbyterian Church, etc. "We have been conducting worship services and carrying out other church activities without any difficulty although there are rumors going around that they're going to close our meeting house," said Baheta.[58]

Tesfaye and Baheta praise God for sending many strong leaders to Eritrea from numerous parts of Ethiopia after the outbreak of hostilities between the two nations. In a sense, this has been a blessing in disguise for the Asmara Meserete Kristos Church. The church is thriving and expanding to places outside the city of Asmara.

The Development of Local Mennonite Churches in Eastern Africa

It has been said that religion, if it is real, cannot be a part-time thing; it cannot be a mere Sunday thing. Christian leaders recognize that one of the primary emphases of God is the development of local churches. God has called them to this important task of building His church. What is God's purpose in building local churches? How are local churches built?

It is not just the individual who is the temple of God; the local church is also the temple of God. In Ephesians 2:21-22 Paul says: "And in Him you, too, are being built together to become a dwelling in which God lives by His spirit." We as a people are being built together. God works in the local churches among people who are inhabited by His Spirit. In 1 Peter 2:4-5, Peter says: "As you come to Him, you also like living stones are being built into a spiritual house." This is not referring to individuals; this is the local body, a group of people. We also, like living stones, are being built into a spiritual house. God by His Spirit is building us together to become His holy temple, a people through whom He can manifest His presence in this world. Through prayer, God's plan for the local church can be discovered. How does God establish this distinct group of people into "local churches?"

One way of building the local church is through theological training. The theological training offered in KMT, KMC and MKC supports the structure and organization of these churches, their missionary enterprises, relations within the Mennonite family and other Christian groups.

Paul Baru, student at MCSEA, Bukiroba, with his wife and family.

Theological Education in KMT, KMC, and MKC

The first Mennonite missionaries who came to Tanganyika opened a Bible School at Bukiroba already in 1937, under the direction of John Leatherman. All the students came from the Shirati area, among them the first Tanzanian bishop and his wife, Zedekiah and Susana Kisare.[59] The School was centrally located for the tribes living in North and South Mara, although no students in that first class came from South Mara. Courses offered at the Bukiroba Bible School included: Old Testament, New Testament, Church History, Doctrine, and Church and Leadership. "I found Catherine Leatherman's Old Testament courses particularly interesting, for I found so many parallels between our Luo society at Kiseru and those ancient people of God," says Kisare.[60]

With independence on the horizon, the Mennonite Church in the Mara Region was facing a crisis in leadership training. True, they had the Bible School at Bukiroba but it did not meet the more immediate needs of the church. Consequently, the Mission asked the government of Tanganyika to release Don Jacobs from his responsibilities as acting principal at the Alliance Teachers' Training College at Katoke to work instead with the leadership programme at Bukiroba.

Emebet Mekennon, Dean of Students, MK College, Addis Ababa.

The Bukiroba Bible College was opened on August 7, 1962 under the leadership of Don Jacobs and Dorothy Smoker. Sixteen students enrolled. The students found Jacob's theology class particularly interesting. "By laying the Scriptures alongside the teachings of African traditional religion, they discovered larger dimensions of truths, relevant approaches to tribal customs, and sometimes a third way between African and Western cultures."[61]

Following the conflict in the 1980s, the Theological College at Nyabange near Musoma was closed. It reopened in the early 1990s under the name, "Mennonite Theological School of East Africa" to serve students from Mennonite churches in Kenya and Ethiopia. However, this plan has not materialized as originally planned; the College has not made much progress, although it has been in existence for quite a long time. Two Ethiopian and several Kenyan students have graduated from this Bible College. Many KMT leaders have expressed the view that the College has adequate space in a beautiful setting, suitable for a much larger institution of higher learning and therefore, the KMT leaders conclude, the education secretary should plan to upgrade all aspects of the College.

Bedru Hussein notes that in the experience of the Meserete Kristos Church, there is a high level of lay mobilization in all local churches and church-planting centers. As much as possible members are assigned discipleship programmes in home cell groups and according to their gifts members are asked to serve within the structure. Due to the solid leadership training they get through its educational system, many members of MKC are serving not only in MKC but also in other evangelical churches. For example, there are many members of MKC who are chosen to be leaders of various committees directing evangelical church fellowships, Para-church organizations and student fellowships. In most cases the members are lay leaders, not full-time workers.[62] With the ever-increasing number of churches and church planting centers, administration in non-formal theological education must constantly be expanded. In order to accommodate such growth and expansion and to reflect the message of Jesus Christ, the administrative as well as the educational structures (the pastoral care structures) are being re-worked continuously.

With the establishment of the Nazareth Bible Academy in 1959, MKC has also been providing formal

Kena Dula, Professor at MK College.

theological education. Alongside academic subjects the school offered religious courses such as Bible doctrine, Christian ethics, New Testament, Old Testament, etc. As a result, many of the church leaders who have graduated from the Bible Academy have been equipped with the necessary Biblical knowledge, which has helped them become morally strong human beings and effective church leaders.

In collaboration with Eastern Mennonite University, MKC established its own Bible Institute in 1994 under the leadership of Pastor Seyuom Gebre-Tsadik, Director, Hailu Cherenet, Coordinator and Emebet Mekennon, Student Dean. The Institute has been upgraded to become Meserete Kristos College, with the following programmes: "One Year for Christ," Certificate Diploma, Associate Degree and Degree.[63]

The College's plan calls for developing a liberal arts programme offering degrees in science, business administration, computer technology, nursing and pharmacology besides offering a variety of courses in biblical and theological studies. MK College hopes to move in a few years to a town called Debere Zeite, about thirty miles outside Addis Ababa.

Structure and Organization

How are the Mennonite churches in Eastern Africa structured and organized? In the Tanzanian and Kenyan Mennonite Churches the highest

277

executive body is the General Church Council consisting of bishops, pastors and church elders. There is a General Church Council for the entire KMT and KMC which meets once every three years. The day-to-day activities are in the hands of the National Executive Committee consisting again of bishops, pastors and elders. On the diocesan level, the bishop is the chairman with a pastor serving as deputy chairman. The diocesan Executive Committee includes the secretary of the diocese while church elders come under district congregations. This is where committees discuss budgeting and planning for the local church. Finances are collected and dispersed under the secretary of the General Conference, diocese or district. Neither bishops nor pastors have the authority to manage finances.

The smallest unit of administration in the Meserete Kristos church structure is the local church. In the local church there are a number of small committees, led by seven to nine elders. Discrete ministries function through the following committees:

—Pastoral Care Committee deals with spiritual matters including preaching.

—Education Committee conducts and supervises Bible study groups for various age groups, and conducts periodic informal training.

—Youth Committee looks after the interests and problems of the youth, and promotes youth activities in the church.

—Prayer Committee organizes prayer groups throughout the week.

—Sunday School Committee organizes Sunday school education for adults and children.

All the various committees are answerable to the elders' committee, which in turn is accountable to the executive committee of the region. Representatives from the local churches form the Regional Council. Elected members from the council make up the regional executive committee. The regional coordinator is responsible for the regional administrative office. Several regional committees form the regional representative council. The General Church Council, which is the highest organ of the church, consists of regional representative councils, the executive committee and two members from each local church.

The administrative structure of MKC is quite elaborate, but the fact that the highest organ, the General Church Council, includes two members from every local church provides representation in the decision-making process while keeping members in touch and informed all the time. Also, involvement in church affairs is not restricted to just a few powerful personalities.

The non-participation of women in the administration of the church leaves much to be desired. Not only is this the case in Ethiopia, but also in Kenya and Tanzania. The head office of MKC does not to allow women to assume a high position in the leadership until "there is light." It seems that on this question the church has largely been influenced by cultural norms.

Inter-Church Relations

The Tanzania Mennonite Church was well known for its deep involvement in the East Africa Revival Movement. In the late 1950s and early '60s Mennonites were leading other denominations in revival activities. Before the conflict of the '80s, the Tanzania Mennonite Church was regarded as a model spiritual church by the other evangelical churches. In recent inter-denominational meetings, representatives of other churches have repeatedly mentioned the fact that Mennonites were pioneers in the advancement of the spirit of brotherhood, peace, justice and reconciliation. Maticku Nyatambe, the current General Secretary of KMT, remembers what some of these representatives said, "You were a peace church, but now you are fighting among yourselves. We're very much disappointed. What happened?"[64]

KMT used to be very active in CCT, the Christian Council of Churches of Tanzania. "KMT was among the four founders of CCT," says Maticku.[65] After a long absence, KMT was able to send a large delegation to the annual CCT conference in 2001, bringing great joy to the delegates from the other denominations. Relations between the Kenya and Tanzania Mennonite churches are quite good. Together they operate the Mennonite Theological College of East Africa located at Musoma, Nyabange. The bishops from the two sister churches are in conference every year to discuss matters related the College and other issues of mutual concern. They also collaborate in the Council of East African Mennonite Churches.

In 1962 the Mennonite Church of Tanganyika began to get acquainted with Mennonites of Ghana, Nigeria, Zaire (now the Democratic Repulic of the Congo), Zambia, Rhodesia (now Zimbabwe), Ethiopia and Somalia. Delegates from these churches met in Limuru, Kenya, for a time of mutual admonition. They discussed how to live as people of peace in a restless

Retired Pastor, Nashou Kwira, KMT.

continent. In 1965 these churches formed the African Mennonite and Brethren in Christ Fellowship, (AMBCF) in Bulawayo, Zimbabwe, agreeing to meet every four years. Million Belete from the Meserete Kristos Church of Ethiopia became the first general secretary of the Fellowship. It was the belief of the founders of the Fellowship that a strong relationship of interdependence would help the entire African church community. They hoped closer cooperation in such areas as evangelism, nurture, discipleship, theological training, peace and justice, relief, and development would foster solidarity among Mennonite and Brethren in Christ churches and agencies on the continent and throughout the world. These objectives have not been met as intended due to lack of commitment and financial constraints.

In 1976 Mennonite churches in Eastern Africa with long-standing links to Eastern Board, began to meet every two years to exchange experiences and share concerns and vision. Here, too, there is need to strengthen relationships. The Meserete Kristos Church is a founding member of the Evangelical Churches: Fellowship of Ethiopia, created in 1971 in the context of a crusade. The Fellowship continued to hold mass gatherings every two years, except for some ten years when the Communists prohibited such meetings. The Fellowship gives high priority to evangelism and leadership training seminars. It includes 12,248 local churches, seventeen denominations with ten million members, nineteen parachurch organizations as associate members, and ten fellowships based outside Ethiopia.

We recall with gratitude the accommodating spirit of the Catholics toward MKC during the underground years, 1982-91. For example, in February 1984 and again, one year after that, they allowed the MKC to hold underground general church council meetings in their facilities. We conducted those conventions without much apprehension, thanks to their hospitality. During those same years, the Lutherans also provided an umbrella for repressed evangelical churches to conduct weddings and funerals. It was an act of solidarity with their suffering Christian brothers and sisters. On many occasions different Mekane Yesus Churches (Lutheran Churches) in Addis Ababa opened their doors for a good number of MKC members for these special worship services.

Not only did the Lutherans open their church doors to MKC members, they also opened their homes and arms in an expression of Christian love and compassion. Reverend Asfaw Kalborie, a retired clergyman of Lideta Mekane Yesus (Lutheran), remembers with joy the excellent relations enjoyed with MKC members and how the council of clergymen of the Addis Ababa Lutheran churches agreed to commit themselves to serve the body of believers suffering repression under the Marxist regime, even risking the closure of their own churches.

The Lutheran pastor acknowledged the gratitude of Beyene Mulatu, an MKC church leader, who said that if the Lutheran churches had been closed and MKC had remained open, Mekane Yesus members might not have enjoyed such privileges. These actions by the Lutherans were a significant expression of solidarity and demonstrate the interdependence of all churches on one another.

Stewardship

KMT, KMC and MKC started out insufficiently prepared to manage their financial resources, but they gradually learned the importance of becoming self-supporting. Since financial assistance was flowing to these churches from Eastern Board for a long time, they remained dependent on outside funding for most of their activities. When the Mission Board began cutting back funding, the nationals felt they were being deserted.

Retired bishop Musa Odongo says that when he returned to Kenya in 1975, the situation there was somewhat different from that in Tanzania. Even though the Kenya Mennonite church was still under the leadership of KMT, the missionaries from North America made it clear from the start that they would not give the Kenyan Mennonites any financial assistance; they did not wish to repeat the mistakes they had committed in Tanzania. They wanted the Kenyan Mennonite church to be financially independent. However, with some prompting from Bishop Kisare, the Mission Board agreed to help in supporting some of the Kenyan pastors and to cover expenses of office supplies and roofing for church buildings for a specified period of time. "I see this [approach] as a positive measure because it taught us a lesson in giving. It was good because it taught us the importance of depending on God and on our congregation for meeting our needs," remarked Musa Odongo.[66]

Doctor Ziki Makoyo, a highly qualified Tanzanian Mennonite surgeon who runs his own private hospital in Shirati, Tanzania, tells a story which may illustrate the lack of giving in many churches throughout Africa.

One day I met a missionary from South Africa at a conference in Nairobi. This fellow was called Schwartz, a man from Lancaster, Pennsylvania, not a Mennonite though. The missionary told me [Ziki] that they had a very good purpose for mission when they first came out to Africa. But things turned out differently later on.

When Schwartz left for South Africa, he took a small bag of money with him. That bag was very useful. When he went back for furlough, he made the little bag bigger and when he went back to the mission field, he found out that the bag was even more useful. After finishing out his second term of service, he went back to his homeland and made the bag much bigger. He came out to the mission field and set up institutions—a bookstore, a hospital, a school—but what he didn't do was teach the people stewardship. When the people came to church on Sunday, they threw in their coins knowing that there was a big bag somewhere behind which would cover their needs. He found out that the entire church did not trust him and did not trust anybody with the bag. He had to bring someone from the States to run the various institutions.

So, there came a time when this man had to leave and go back to America. After returning home he discovered there was nobody to work in the institutions he had started. He stopped and thought why there was lack of personnel. He came to realize that he had not trained anybody who was trustworthy to take over. Now he is back talking differently and the missionaries don't like him. This is what happened to us, too. The bookstore collapsed when the missionaries left; the printing press stopped functioning; the theological school quit operations.[67]

Today an entirely new group of leaders is trying to encourage members to be more faithful in their giving. These leaders realize that they've become very dependent on outside assistance for too long a time.

Bedru Hussein, Vice President of MWC, in a book entitled *Stewardship In The Self-supporting Church*, writes the following about the Meserete Kristos Church experience with regard to giving.

In 1975 MKC was in crisis. The Marxist-Leninist government of Ethiopia was threatening to expel all missionaries and threatening to refuse any foreign money from the West. The MKC-affiliated mission, which had been supporting the church since 1948, had been gradually cutting back its funding. But there was no corresponding increase in giving from the churches.

Many ideas were discussed to resolve this problem. It was decided that the biblical way was to train the members in tithing. This has been done on a regular basis ever since. All new members, during their discipleship training, are also taught the biblical concept of stewardship. This teaching, along with having a good accountability system and leaders of integrity modeling giving, has enabled the MKC to be a financially healthy church able to carry out Christ's Great Commission without undue outside help.[68]

As churches in developing countries, we still need financial assistance from sister churches in the developed countries in such areas as education, health care, relief and development. But we should aim toward becoming self-supporting in such areas as out-reach ministry, local church administration, paying pastors and evangelists, and helping the poor.

283

Bedru Hussein,Vice President, MWC.

Something is happening in this direction. As the African historian, John Mbiti has noted, Christian Africa is not just feeding on borrowed grain alone. It is also cultivating its own grain. Perhaps the first harvest may not be sufficient, but the process is at least underway. The Gospel has, and continues to be proclaimed to African peoples.[69]

Concluding Reflections

The writer and his assistant, Samuel Asefa, visited many Mennonite churches in Tanzania, Kenya and Ethiopia and interviewed many dedicated servants of the Lord. We noticed how devoted many of them were to the work of the Kingdom of God, in spite of the great challenges facing them. Meeting the physical and spiritual needs of their people is their daily concern.

These believers in Eastern Africa strive to demonstrate in their daily living that Jesus is the foundation of faith and life in all cultures. Witnessing for Christ in both word and deed is their guiding principle and their reason for living in this world. Mennonites in Eastern Africa are mission-oriented, witnessing boldly, unafraid of what might follow. This is why they are growing so quickly, and expanding into new frontiers.

We found worship services in these churches meaningful and joyful. Congregational singing is particularly warm. We came to understand that spiritual music is certainly a vehicle of communication that brings together Christians from different cultural and linguistic backgrounds. Even though we did not understand the Swahili language, for example, we were able to appreciate their singing very much. Singing in four parts seemed quite natural to believers in Tanzania and Kenya Mennonite churches. This is not so in the Meserete Kristos churches of Ethiopia. Many of the songs from Tanzania and Kenya seemed to be translations from hymnbooks of the early missionary days. This reminded us of the type of singing which was popular in Meserete Kristos congregations in the early 1950s, but no longer in use today. In the majority of Mennonite churches in eastern Africa, choirs compose their own songs. This is indeed a very encouraging trend.

The first venture of the Lancaster Mennonite Church to Tanzania in 1934 was certainly a learning experience for the sending church. Church leaders sent out missionaries with the intention to evangelize, not to build institutions. But soon they came to realize that the ministry of serving the body as well as the spirit was also important. They also learned that it was difficult to mould a new church in a different culture according to their own old traditional patterns. With the Mission came schools, health centres, the teaching of skills such as carpentry, brick-making, and so on. Not only did they preach the Gospel but they passed on technical know-how as well.

There is a continuing concern for evangelism and church growth. Members of KMT have become doctors, teachers, judges, engineers, and administrators. Some have turned out to be excellent witnesses for Jesus Christ. Kenya Mennonite Church is the daughter church of KMT and in many ways it resembles its mother church. As Kenya is a highly-churched nation, there is a lot of enthusiasm among the Mennonite groups in Kenya. However, many of the church leaders we interviewed stressed the importance of providing solid Bible training for pastors and church elders. This will help them nurture the great number of people joining the church. In a country where the government encourages church activity, it is important to warn people of the dangers that a close state-church relationship might entail to the work of Jesus Christ.

Some of our interviewees suggested that political parties in Kenya have created a sense of division among the different ethnic groups. The church must give witness to its mission, and not yield to political pressure. Church leaders sometimes appear to relate more to the government rather than standing firm for God's Kingdom. Most church leaders do not seem to differentiate sufficiently between the state and the church.

KMC was registered in the National Council of Churches of Kenya in 1989. Missionaries working in Ethiopia from very early on, focussed on promoting national leadership in administration and church economy. This was successfully carried out with those who wished to pursue higher education. After church autonomy had been achieved, missionaries accepted service roles in the church as servants of the local church. Another positive factor was the missionaries' attitude toward political events. During the change of government in the 1970s in Ethiopia, the Eastern Board workers did not panic and fly home immediately; they stayed as long as the situation permitted.

The Meserete Kristos Church that God built in Ethiopia has miraculously survived through peril and threat and become one of the fastest-growing Protestant churches in Africa. With such rapid growth, there are bound to be "aches and pains." How can we cope with such problems? True, we have our "cell" leadership training structure, but that is not enough. To nurture such a huge number of new believers and continue with our discipleship training programs effectively, we need to train a host of pastors, evangelists and other church leaders.

Mission enterprise is cross-cultural; we learn from each other. The plain suits, prayer head coverings, and cape dresses have long vanished. Through mission work, members of other races and ethnic groups have joined the Mennonite brotherhood—Africans, Latinos, Asians. These groups are not Swiss-German or Dutch Mennonites or Russian Mennonites, but we are all brothers and sisters, one family in Christ. The Mennonite denomination has increased numerically, enriched with varieties of cultural heritages which have, in turn, enriched the Mennonite concept of the church and Christianity. There are now more Mennonites in Africa than in North America, and the Mennonite Church is now found throughout the world.

The material resources of our brothers and sisters in the North are indeed substantial, but our spiritual resources in the South are equally as great. We want people in the North to connect with the spiritual depth of the churches in Africa. There is an awakening, an exciting sense of being alive. The Spirit of God is being unleashed among us. Reading and praying in isolation is not the answer.

We feel there is a need for a spiritual awakening in North America and Europe. It is our firm conviction that Mennonites will pioneer in that, because they are people-oriented, and that is a great advantage.

Notes

[1] Kawami Bediako, *Christianity in Africa: The Renewal of a non-Western Religion* (Maryknoll, NY: Orbis Books, 1995), 32.

[2] Esther Kawira, "Life Syncopated," Unpublished paper (March, 2001).

[3] Laurenti Magesa, *African Religion: The Moral Traditions of Abundant Life* (Maryknoll, NY: Orbis, 1997).

[4] Joseph C. Shenk, *Kisare: a Mennonite of Kiseru*, (Salunga, PA: Eastern Mennonite Board of Mission and Charities, 1984), 36.

[5] John Mbiti, *African Religions and Philosophy* (New York: Praeger, 1969).

[6] Cited in Kawira, "Life Syncopated," 3.

[7] Merle W. Eshleman, *Africa Answers,* (Scottdale, PA: Mennonite Publishing House, 1951), 30.

[8] Kawira, "Life Syncopated," 8.

[9] *Ibid.*, 9.

[10] Shenk, *Kisare*, 72.

[11] Kawira, "Life Syncopated,"10.

[12] Shenk, *Kisare*, 80.

[13] Interview with Rebeka Kulwa, Mwanza, Tanzania, Nov. 19, 2001.

[14] *Ibid.*

[15] Interview with Aden Matan Hassan (one of the early Somali believers now residing near Toronto, Canada), Nairobi, Kenya, Feb. 7, 2002.

[16] David W. Shenk, "A Study of the Mennonite Presence and Church Development in Somalia from 1950 through 1970," Unpublished paper (1972), 361.

[17] Interview with Bertha Beachy, Elkhart, IN, June 26, 2001.

[18] Interview with Abdul Cadir Wursame Omar, Nairobi, Kenya, Feb. 6, 2000.

[19] A. H. Jones and Elizabeth Monroe, *A History of Ethiopia,* (Sebeta, Ethiopia: Haile Selassie I Braille printing press, 1969), 33.

[20] Adrian Hastings, ed., *A World History of Christianity* (Grand Rapids, MI: 1999),197.

[21] Nathan B. Hege, *Beyond our prayers* (Scottdale, PA: Mennonite Publishing House, 1998).

[22] *Ibid.*, 199-200.

[23] *Ibid.*,

[24] Calvin Shenk, "The History of Christianity in Africa," Unpublished paper (2000), 38. These black Jews living in Ethiopia were taken to Israel in 1990 and 1991 by operation Moses and Solomon.

[25] Peter Cotterell, *Born At Midnight* (Chicago: Moody Bible Institute, 1973), 153.

[26] *Missionary Messenger* (July 7, 1935) , 14.

[27] Cited in Mahlon Hess, *Pilgrimage of Faith* (Salunga, PA: Eastern Mennonite Board of Mission and Charities, 1985), 61.

[28] Interview with Wilson Oguwada, Migori, Kenya. Feb. 11, 2000.

[29] Fikru Zeleke, "The Trees of God," Unpublished paper (2000), 3.

[30] Interview with Beyen Chichaybelu, Debra-Zait, Ethiopia. Sep. 29, 2000.

[31] Yeshitela Mengistu, "The Story of the Meserete Kirstos Church," Unpublished paper (1983), 5.

[32] *Mission Yearbook*, (1962), 66-67.

[33] *Missionary Messenger* (Nov., 1973), 6.

[34] *Mission Yearbook* (1961), 62-63.

[35] Omar Eby, *A Whisper in a Dry Land* (Scottdale, PA: Herald Press, 1968), 138.

[36] Interview with Aden Matan Hassan, Nairobi, Kenya, Feb. 7, 2000.

[37] Joseph Shenk, *Silver Thread: The Ups & Downs of a Mennonite Family in Mission* (Intercourse, PA: Good Books, 1996), 140.

[38] Josiah Muganda, "The Impact of Mennonite Mission on Mara Region Tanzania," unpublished paper (1978), 117-18.

[39] Mahlon Hess, *Pligrimage of Faith* (Salunga, PA: Eastern Mennonite Board of Mission and Charities, 1985), 96.

[40] *Ibid.*, 98.

[41] *Ibid.*, 119.

[42] Interview with Kembo Migire, Shirati,Tanzania, Nov. 10, 2001.

[43] Interview with Benjamin Chawachi Migire, Muwanza, Tanzania, Nov.15, 2001.

[44] Zerehun Gebrehana, Gebeyehu Weldeargay, Ashen Getachew, Tilahun Yilema, Tilahun Abera and Girma Asfaw.

[45] Interview with Helon Amolo, Musoma, Tanzania, Nov.13, 2001.

[46] *Ibid.*

[47] Interview with Wilson Oguwada, Migori, Kenya. Feb. 11, 2000.

[48] Interview with Christopher Ndege, Muwanza, Tanzania, Nov. 19, 2001.

[49] *Ibid.*

[50] Interview with Joram Mbeba, Bulawayo, Zimbabwe, July 31 and August 1, 2002.

[51] *Misikir* (MKC official magazine), vol. IV, no. 11, 1989.

[52] Courses offered included: "Christianity and Socialism," "Creation and Evangelism," "The Church, a Community of Love," "Spiritual Man," "Guard your Fortress," "The Second Coming of Christ," "Let Nature Testify," and others.

[53] Hailu Cherent, "Multiplication by Division," Unpublished paper (19??), 2.

[54] Kedir Delechumie, Taddsse Negewo, Yeshitela Mengistu, Seyoum Geber-Tsadik and Shimeles Regga were members of the Christian education committee.

[55] Interview with Joseph Kamau, Niarobi, Kenya, Feb. 29, 2001.

[56] *Ibid.*

[57] Interview with Baheta Haile and Tesfaye Seyoum, Nairobi, Kenya, Feb.14, 2001.

[58] *Ibid.*

[59] Also students were Yacobo and Elisaba Agwanda, Daniel and Susana Opanga, Samuel and Esta Ngoga, Tadeo and Julia Makori, and Zephania and Ruth Migire.

[60] Joseph C. Shenk, *Kisare: A Mennonite of Kiseru* (Salunga, PA: Eastern Mennonite Board of Mission and Charities, 1984), 68-69.

[61] Mahlon Hess, *Piligrimage of Faith* (Salunga, Pennsylvania, 1985), 132.

[62] *Mission FOCUS*, (Annual Review, vol. 5, 1997), 38.

[63] The "One Year for Christ" programme is a six-week training programme designed to train workers for church planting centers and outreach ministry. The Certificate Programme is a one year programme designed to raise the level of Bible knowledge of ministers, so that they can teach and serve their church members more effectively. The Diploma Programme is a two-year programme for equipping students with knowledge of the Bible. It offers courses such as Systematic Theology, Church History, Evangelism and Church planting, Anthropology, etc. The Associate Degree programme is designed to prepare students for the four-year Degree programme.

[64] Interview with Maticku Nyatambe, Musoma, Tanzania, Nov. 15, 2001.

[65] *Ibid.*

[66] Interview with Musa Odongo, Kisumu, Kenya, Feb. 10, 2001.

[67] Interview with Dr. Ziki Makoyo, Shirati, Tanzania, Nov. 9, 2001.

[68] Bedru Hussein, *Stewardship in the Self-Supporting Church*, (Muwanza, Tanzania: Inland Publishers, 1998), 20.

[69] John Mbiti, *African Religions and Philosophy* (New York: Praeger, 1969).

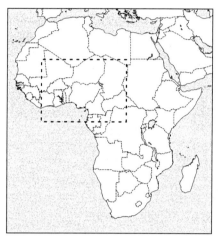

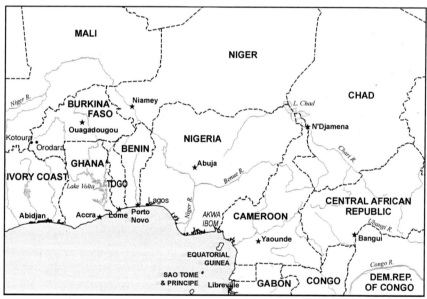

Western Africa

Mennonite Churches in Western Africa

*by Michael Kodzo Badasu, I. U. Nsasak,
and Erik Kumedisa*

Compared to the churches described in other sections of this volume, the churches located in Western Africa are younger, smaller, and perhaps more intimately related to neighbouring Christian bodies. Few of these churches were founded by western missionaries. Each of them existed in some form, some as independent bodies that sought out a relation with the Mennonite Church. While this chapter highlights only three of these churches, Mennonites continue to relate intensely with other churches in Benin, Cote d'Ivoire, Togo, Liberia, Senegal, and Mali. Since this history is so much in process, the following sketches primarily indicate the vitality of bodies whose full story still requires a chronicler.

One of the best ways of understanding Mennonite churches in Western Africa is to read Edwin and Irene Weaver's *The Uyo Story* published in 1970. This short account of learning to work with already-established congregations and churches is one of the most significant statements of contemporary Mennonite missiology. The work of the Weavers inspired additional work with existing independent groups in Southern and Eastern Africa where the goal has been cooperation and reconciliation rather than the establishing of new churches.

Ghana

by Michael Kodzo Badasu

The Ghana story doesn't begin in Ghana but in London, England, where a Ghanian named George Thompson was baptized at the London Mennonite Fellowship. Thompson felt called to begin a Mennonite Church in his own soon-to-be independent country in 1956. Mennonite Board of Missions appointed missionaries to assist Thompson in establishing congregations, rural schools, health clinics and agricultural projects. From its beginning Mennonites in Ghana played an active role in the Ghana Christian Council.

Currently, the Ghana Mennonite Church has twenty-three congregations in six districts. Twenty of the congregations are in the southern part of the country. The total membership of the church is about four thousand. The church has nine trained pastors working as full-time pastors as well as twenty-three trained local leaders serving congregations.

The church has established several committees that guide its affairs. The executive committee is comprised of members from all of the six districts in the church. The chairman of the executive committee is the moderator of the church. The general secretary of the church is the vice chairman as well as the executive committee secretary. Other committees that also take part in the decision-making of the church include Evangelism, Finance, Women, Youth, and a Standing Committee consisting of the moderator, the general secretary, and the church treasurer.

The church meets in an annual conference of delegates to discuss reports from the various committees and to vote for new leaders selected by the executive committee. Each congregation elects two persons to represent them in the annual conference.

The main languages spoken by our church members are Twi, Ga, Ewe, Krobo, English, Hausa, and Dagbani.

Inspired by a missionary spirit, a number of Ghanian pastors crossed the border into the Republic of Togo to found congregations there beginning in 1993. This ministry work continued for three years and as a result of this, three congregations were planted in the Republic of Togo in the year 1997. The Togo Mennonite Church has five congregations in five towns with five trained pastors. The leader of the pastors is Rev. Leopold Houmey, a dynamic, hard working pastor. The people of Togo speak Ewe, which is the same language spoken by the people of the southern part of the Volta Region of Ghana. The total population of the Togo Mennonite churches is about 1,000 members. Living conditions in Togo are very hard so many people are moving from rural areas to work in the cities.

The situation in Ghana is well expressed in a description of the congregation known as Gbenuakope Mennonite Church. It is located in the Lower Volta District of the Ghana Mennonite church. This

Gbenuakope congregation has a total membership of ninety-three. These members are small-scale farmers who rear animals and cultivate food crops such as maize, yam, cassava, vegetable, fruits and beans to feed their families. Normally these local farmers have two seasons for farming, depending on the rains. Although the largest man-made body of water in the country is called Lake Volta and passes through this village, farmers in this area find it extremely difficult to practice irrigation farming because they do not have the money to buy irrigation machinery. If these local farmers were trained and given financial assistance, they could become one of the largest food producers in the country.

The main occupation for women is mat weaving. Mat weaving is very difficult work which requires one to sit in a particular place for more than six hours without getting up in order to complete the work. The most unfortunate thing is that the mats do not bring a good price. Two mats now sell for less than one American dollar. When all expenses are taken out, the profit is less than fifty American cents. This means that to make and sell twelve mats the profit is only three dollars. It takes about six days to weave the twelve mats. The indication is that if one weaves forty-eight mats in a month, the profit for the month is only twelve dollars. The youth also engage in this mat weaving job.

Lack of employment makes it difficult for the youth to stay in the village. They go to the big cities for employment and that has affected the church's attendance at every worship service. Out of the ninety-three members, only twenty-seven can be described as full-time members since the rest have travelled to the cities for better jobs.

This congregation meets under something we call in our local language "kporgha." It is made of long grasses and branches of palm and coconut trees. The grasses are used to stand upright while the branches of either palm or coconut trees are used to support them by tightening them with strong nylon ropes. The top of the chapel is also covered with grasses. This type of building does not last long, especially in the rainy season. These grasses are scarce during the dry season. Due to this, there are no church activities during these days.

In a typical worship service, there is a lot of dancing and shouting of praises to the Most High God. There is singing of Pentecostal songs and hymns from the Ghana Mennonite Church Hymn book. They use our locally-made instruments like konka, malacas, dondo, and so on to praise

God. The congregation does not provide any income for the pastor. They rather depend on the pastor for their needs. As the people are very poor, the regular Sunday service offering amounts to less than one dollar. A pastor therefore cannot depend on that money as income. He has to do other jobs to get his income to feed himself and his family. A trained pastor is called "Osofo" by these local people. Both men and women can serve as pastors but at the moment, the Ghana Mennonite Church has no female pastor.

A typical church service could last for as long as five hours. A congregation relates to other Mennonite congregations in all aspects as Mennonites; the only difference may be their language, which differs from district to district. With other Christian groups, the only relation a church has is worshipping God through Jesus Christ with different beliefs. The Ghana Mennonite Church has only six built chapels out of the twenty-three congregations.

Nigeria

by I. U. Nsasak

As in Ghana, the Mennonite Church in Nigeria developed from churches already existing. These churches heard about Mennonites through the international broadcasts of the Mennonite Hour. Following their inquiry, Mennonite Board of Missions in Elkhart, Indiana, sent missionaries first in 1959. These missionaries worked in cooperation with the existing churches as well as with Scottish Presbyterians in education, medicine, and agriculture until the late 1980s.

The Mennonite Church in Nigeria is primarily located in Southeastern Nigeria. It is an area evangelized in the second half of the nineteenth century. More than 95% of the population calls itself Christian. But the Christian movement is deeply torn by tensions between churches—especially those who represent "northern" or Western denominations and the increasing numbers who represent the African independent church movements. Forty years ago Edwin Weaver noted the discrimination, and even hatred between these groups.[1] The Mennonite church has been conspicuous in working between these groups in a ministry of reconciliation.

The Mennonite Church in Nigeria was established in 1959. Currently we have sixty-eight congregations with 11,024 members. These churches are in the Akwa Ibom State of Nigeria. In 1968 a Mennonite congregation was established in the city of Lagos.

The problem that we are facing in Nigeria is not that of reaching and Christianizing non-Christians or heathen, but of faithfulness to Christ. There are two major religions in Nigeria—Christianity and Islam. The Muslim religion dominates northern Nigeria; Christianity dominates eastern Nigeria, while western Nigeria has 50% Christians and 50% Muslims. Akwa Ibom State, where the Mennonite church is mostly found, is predominantly Christian in population. The problem is, what percentage of baptized Christians are really Christians by faith? Faith adulteration is our major problem. Traditional forms and practices, witchcraft, jumu and fetish religions infiltrate the faith of baptized Christians. These other forms are not practiced openly, but in secret. Efforts to rid our Christian community of these demonic forms and secret practices have engaged the born again Christians in a great spiritual battle that goes far beyond ordinary orthodoxy.

Several of the old established orthodox churches, including the Catholics, are now embracing the new wave of Holy Spirit manifestation and life. We Mennonites in Nigeria come within this new wave of Holy Spirit exposition and practice. We do fast, we do engage in long prayers, and we do believe in the baptism of the Holy Spirit. However, we do give a spiritual examination and control of any spiritual manifestation during worship. In so doing we fulfill a special need of helping already-baptized members build faith in Jesus Christ and to eschew all trust in other forms of non-Christian power.

Our general experience is that without a proper knowledge of the Bible we will not succeed in battling with the hidden, non-Christian forces that deceive our faith and trust. It has therefore been our desire to increase our mission efforts through training and re-training of workers to stand the test of time in the Lord's vineyard. The Church has found out that if she does not embark on the training of her workers, there will be limited chances for expansion. Therefore, some of our pastors are encouraged to enroll in theological colleges and read courses which lead to the awarding of degrees in Theology and Christian Education. Our preachers are also encouraged to register and read for a Diploma in Theology.

At present we are concentrating efforts to renovate and reactivate our Bible School so that the church may train more workers. Periodically camp meetings, retreats, and short-term Bible studies are organized. We engage in a series of revivals and tarry-nights to bring converts and non-converts to the Word of God and to assure them of Christ's spiritual help. These efforts help bring new adherents to the Church.

It is our hope that within the next few years the Mennonite church will spread to towns and cities. All along we have been working in rural areas. We plan to start church planting in a number of urban areas, both in Akwa Ibom State and in other states. We are struggling to give life to our little congregation in Lagos.

We need to set up a special Ministry for Peace and Love Witness in this country, especially now that inter-tribal and Muslim/Christian conflicts constantly threaten the peace of our country. This special ministry requires specially-trained human resources and funding. Our conference is giving special consideration to this matter in relation to Nigeria and to set up a powerful Anabaptist teaching and proclamation on Christian faith, love, peace, and non-resistance.

This report will not be complete if we do not mention MCC working in Nigeria. Though in the years we had not worked very closely with them, we have now awakened to the need for working together, and relating more and more closely. Recently the MCC has been of immense help in our communication link between the church here and the Mennonite World Conference.

We have a God-equipped, trained theologian, a spirit-filled, honest and truthful Christian who can share our Christian experiences with other churches in and outside Nigeria. We have been trying to send him to Lagos. With the kind of work God is using him to do, we trust we can plant Mennonite churches in every urban town in Nigeria.

Burkina Faso

by Eric Kumedisa

"Burkina" is the Mossi word for integrity or honesty. "Faso" is the Dioula word for the land of our forefathers. The "be" of Burkinabe is from the Peul language meaning someone from Burkina Faso. Burkinabe are, therefore, people of "frank speech." Until August 4, 1984, the country was known as Upper Volta. Burkina Faso is a Sahel country without access to the sea. It has a tropical climate with two seasons: a dry season from October to May and a rainy season from June to September. Like most of the land-locked countries of West Africa, Burkina Faso has an economy based on agriculture. Subsistence crops such as sorghum, millet, corn, rice, peanuts, potatoes, and yams prevail over cash crops. Cotton and live cattle are the primary exports. Livestock breeding and related industries also constitute an important part of the country's exports, despite the drought conditions. The population of Burkina Faso is essentially rural and depends on subsistence agriculture, despite the intermittent rains and the dryness of the soil. It is this situation that pushes most Burkinabe, especially the young people of working age, to leave the country and live in neighbouring countries where they exercise their professions to support their families back in Burkina Faso.

Burkina Faso gained its independence from France in 1960. It has gone through several successive governments, such as the revolutionary government of 1983, but the military coup d'etat of 1987 put an end to the extreme measures adopted by this regime. The policies of the present government approve of evangelism and Christian assistance programs.

Forty percent of the Burkinabe population is Muslim and about ten percent of the population is Christian. The remainder of the population is animist and practices traditional religions. Many Burkinabe still engage in traditional religious practices. Secret societies and traditional religious practices are deeply rooted among the Lobiris of the south-west, the Gourmas of the east, the Gurunsis, the Senoufos, and the Bobos of the west.

Two important factors contributed to the birth of the Evangelical Mennonite Church in Burkina Faso. The first was the great famine that the country experienced in 1973-74 and MCC coming to participate in alleviating the suffering of the people. It was through this assistance that contacts were made and Africa Inter-Mennonite Mission (AIMM) missionaries arrived. The Evangelical Mennonite Church in Burkina Faso (EEMBF) was born after the arrival of several AIMM missionaries and also with the help of Burkinabe Christian brothers from other Christian traditions who had come to live in the Kenedougou Province. The first AIMM missionaries arrived in 1978 and the church was planted in 1983.

God used two Burkinabe brothers for the work in Orodara: Siaka Traore and Paul Ouedrago. Siaka came to faith from a strong Muslim background, whereas Paul was trained in agriculture. It was Siaka's vision, coming from a strong commercial Muslim family, to evangelize Kenedougou province by selling Christian literature. In 1984 Siaka and Paul opened a bookstore that is the most visible sign of Mennonite presence in Kenedougou to this day. With the assistance of other Christian brothers, civil servants living in Orodara, the nucleus of the Evangelical Mennonite Church of Burkina Faso was formed.

When AIMM arrived in Burkina Faso, the missionaries did not impose their organizational structure, with the result that much of the church governance today resembles that of the Christian Alliance Church. The Mennonite missionaries purchased the existing church building in Orodara. Places of worship have been built in Kotoura, Kangala, Banzon, Djigouera and Samoghohiri. EEMBF has a general assembly that meets once a year and an executive committee that meets three times a year. Each congregation is led by a pastor. Until 1997 there were only two trained pastors: Abdias Coulibaly and Siaka Traore. Since 2000 two more trained pastors have been added to the team.

The purpose of AIMM in Burkina Faso has been to plant churches throughout the province of Kenedougou. It seemed necessary to reach people in their respective languages. A programme was developed to translate portions of the Bible into four languages spoken in Kenedougou province. Missionary teams worked to bring these languages into written form. Today the Bible is being translated into the Tagba (Senoufou) language at Kotoura, the Nanerigue (Senoufou) language in N'Dorola, the Siamou language in Tin, and the Dzuun (Samogho) language in Samoghohiri. Believers meet together in two of these locations for worship.

The goal of translation work has been to plant churches, but some members of the local churches in Orodara, Djigouera and Banzon (many of whom moved into the area from northern provinces) have some reservations concerning the work of AIMM. The first is that the Christians in Kenedougou Province relating to the Mennonite Church are outsiders to the province, according to a 1991 study. To make the work of evangelization dependent upon translation work in effect requires those who have migrated to the area to learn a new culture and language in order to work with the AIMM missionaries in reaching the new groups with the Gospel message.

Another concern is that if this sort of programme continues, one might end up with a situation where each linguistic sub-group in Kenedougou will have its own church, its own pastors, and its own liturgy. In that case, rather than planting a united Mennonite church in Burkina Faso, one will have given birth to ethnic tensions as expressed in church communities where tribal identities predominate, and the maintenance of a national church structure will be problematic.

The internal tensions in the Mennonite churches in Angola and Congo can also serve as a lesson for the missionary work in Burkina Faso. Let us not plant the seeds of future conflict between historical leaders who, in ten or twenty years, will point to current AIMM methods as the cause. This method of work needs to be reviewed in such a way as to resolve tomorrow's problems today. As we say in Africa: "Solve the problems of your generation. The children and grandchildren will have their own. They will solve their problems as they are able and according to their generation."

Notes

[1] Edwin and Irene Weaver, *The Uyo Story* (Elkhart, IN: Mennonite Board of Missions, 1970), 24.

Afterword

by Siaka Traore

Although history is the narrative of past events, its primary goal is to help those concerned better know their identity. While helping us take a retrospective look at past events, history also invites us to learn the lessons of our strengths and weaknesses in order to better handle the present and better plan the future.

The goal of the historical task that has been accomplished here is to highlight God's sovereignty. We strongly affirm that God is the Master and Creator of the universe and, therefore, the Master of history. The human person, created in God's image, is the crowning achievement of His work. The human species, regardless of geographical location, colour, or particularities, constitutes the object of God's attention. God did not send his only Son for the angels (Heb. 2:16). The peoples of all the continents are His treasure on earth. In an expression of his diversity he created them black, white, red and yellow. Wherever they are they have the same basic needs. As the song by Helen and Samuel Grandjean puts it, " He loves them all equally."[1] That is, His love is the same for all peoples. The love of God in its fullness is discovered in Jesus Christ. We as Mennonites claim to follow this love, which is the basis of our existence and our identity. We are a part of the great universal family of those who have been redeemed by the Lamb of God. In this wide family we have our particular history, a history of God's faithfulness throughout the centuries.

This history started during the first years of the Reformation in 1525 in Zurich, Switzerland. At the beginning the group was called Anabaptist for the simple reason that they baptized adults. Due to the excesses of certain leaders, the group changed its name to Mennonites in recognition of the influence of Menno Simons.[2] Persecuted because of their faith, a number of Mennonites emigrated to North America and established

Mennonite churches. Others went from Russia and North America to South America in search of arable land. With the coming of the missionary era, inaugurated by William Carey in 1792, Mennonite churches in North America began to undertake mission work in Asia and Africa. It is in response to the Lord's commandment in the Scriptures (Matt. 28:18-20; Acts 1:8) that his people who call themselves Mennonites and Brethren in Christ came to Africa.

Even today many westerners still see Africa as a uniform whole. It is necessary to say one more time that Africa is a continent and not a country. From north to south, from east to west, and in the centre there is a diversity of peoples and cultures. Africa is not one, but many and diverse in its richness. In any region including several countries, the differences between countries are enormous. In two African countries like Benin and Mali, for example, customs, food, and clothing are very different. Within the same country differences are also visible. In Burkina Faso, the traditions and customs of the Lobi are different from those of the Gourmantché. It is into this diverse and multiple Africa that Mennonite and Brethren in Christ groups decided to bring the message of peace and reconciliation between God and humanity.

The first Mennonite contacts with Africa go back to the 1890s in Congo-Leopoldville which is now the Democratic Republic of Congo (DRC).[3] In 1911 and 1912 the Congo Inland Mission sent missionaries to establish Mennonite churches. Today, the DRC is the country with the largest Mennonite community in Africa. Throughout the twentieth century North American Mennonite churches continued to send missionaries to different African countries. The Mennonite Central Committee, even though it was the social arm of North American Mennonite churches, often worked as a precursor to Mennonite mission agencies. The Mennonite Church in Burkina Faso is an example of this.

The Brethren in Christ branch of the Anabaptist family began their African ministry in Zimbabwe and Zambia in 1897.[4] One century later, the entire global Mennonite/BIC family was invited to Bulawayo, Zimbabwe in August 2003 under the Mennonite World Conference to share with each other.

Mennonite churches in Africa, like the other churches that came out of western mission work, were influenced by western culture. Consciously or unconsciously, western missionaries mixed the Gospel with their culture.

Presenting the Gospel in this way did not favour the development of an indigenous or African theology. This situation created long-term dependency at all levels in African churches. There is also the fact that Mennonite missions did not emphasize Mennonite identity in the beginning. After more than half a century, several churches born of Mennonite work do not know who the Mennonites are or what their particularity is within the larger Christian family. Not knowing their identity, many of these churches have conformed themselves to those churches that are dominant in their context. They embrace the theology or doctrine that is dominant in their country. This explains the Pentecostal tendencies in Mennonite churches.

These historical realities present big challenges to the Mennonite Church in Africa today. The first challenge is to make the message of the Bible our own, that is, to develop our own theology while taking into consideration the contributions of others. We can get inspiration from the experiences of the African independent churches (AICs). These churches have a natural interpretation of the Scriptures, despite their limited knowledge. Their members do not feel a distance between the message and their reality. They are developing a contextual theology. Mennonite and Brethren in Christ churches should not become consumers without discernment. Like the believers in Berea, we must verify the teachings that have been given (Acts 17:11).

The missionaries of Africa Inter-Mennonite Mission in Burkina Faso seem to have learned the lessons of the past. They understood that in order to build a strong and well-rooted church, it was necessary to take socio-cultural values into account. It serves no purpose to get rid of customs and traditions that enable those who hear the Word of God to feel God's proximity. The message must not be distant from the intended audience because of the colours [i.e. western] that come with it.

The mistakes made by yesterday's messengers are sometimes now being repeated by those who criticize them. Our churches are paternalistic in their efforts at cross-cultural evangelism. As soon as a new local church is started, the leaders do not allow the new Christians to learn about God. Everything is ready for consumption. Existing church traditions are transmitted to the newly-converted as the norm and the leaders substitute themselves for the Holy Spirit. There is a dependence on the founding church. Such attitudes do not permit the new communities to be creative and put their gifts and talents to good use, but rather everything is done in the image of those who brought the Gospel.

Everywhere today the church agrees that the time for mission has come for the churches of the South (Asia, Africa, Latin America). In the countries of the North there is a crisis of missionary vocation. Fewer and fewer persons from the North are deciding to come to the South for missionary work. This is also the time for the Mennonite churches of Africa. It is important, therefore, that we make accepted missiological principles our own in order to undertake missionary action. The quantitative and qualitative growth of a church is tied to its missionary engagement.

For churches in Africa the mission task is urgent, since Islam is growing rapidly in the continent. In addition to the strategies that it already had, Islam is imitating Christian methods for its expansion by organizing youth camps, creating NGOs for social services, and multiplying FM radio stations for Islamic programmes.

In Burkina Faso in the 1980s animists were in the majority, but today Muslims are more numerous than animists. Estimates show that Muslims number approximately 50%, animists 35%, and Christians 15% of the population. Islam is a challenge for the churches in certain West African countries where Muslim leaders have asked a number of times for the country to be governed according to Islamic laws. Niger has tried several times—unsuccessfully—to proclaim itself an Islamic state. In Nigeria the introduction of Sharia law in several states was intended to make things difficult for President Olunsegun Obasanjo who is a Christian. Senegal, another West African country, is more than 95% Muslim. It is enough to spend one night there to realize this when one hears the calls of the mullahs that crisscross each other in space. In that country the Mennonites (AIMM) have started a ministry called "Friends of the Wolof." There are more than 3,000,000 Wolof and they are almost 100% Muslim. Among them there are fewer than 200 Protestant Christians. Mennonites have joined with others in a partnership to reach the Wolof. It would be desirable to create partnerships between Mennonite churches of Africa and other parts of the world to carry the message of reconciliation to the multitudes that have not yet heard.

As Mennonites and Brethren in Christ we have a heritage that must be preserved and transmitted to all those with whom we have contact. As part of the Reformation, the Anabaptists conformed their lives to the teachings of Scriptures. This return to the Word of truth allowed them to forge an identity founded on biblical values that they transmitted from generation to generation to their descendants.

In North America it is not rare to hear testimonies to the moral and ethical principles of Mennonites and Brethren in Christ. I was a witness to such testimonies on the good morals of Mennonites during my six-month stay in Canada. If others discover that you are a Mennonite, they see you as a person with integrity, one who is upright, and a pacifist. Mennonites have even influenced governments in adopting laws concerning social programmes and the environment.

It is a curious fact that when the Mennonite and Brethren in Christ churches of North America started their missionary enterprises they did not transmit these biblical and moral values to the newborn churches of Africa. Perhaps the missionaries believed that these values could not be transferred to people with a culture different from theirs. Everywhere in Africa Mennonite and Brethren in Christ churches do not know their history and the fundamental aspects of their identity. This deficiency must be corrected.

After more than eighty years as Mennonites, the churches of the DRC did not know much about their identity. It was necessary for them to organize forums on Anabaptism in the year 2000 and again in the year 2002. The goal of these forums was to learn to know their heritage from the time of the Reformation. The second forum was open to other Mennonite churches of Africa. In the various gatherings of the association of African Mennonites, Mennonite leaders have talked about the development of a theology for the churches and educational institutions of Africa.

Historically, Mennonite and Brethren in Christ churches are known as peace churches. This particularity has been the strength of Anabaptist descendants in history, and is still necessary today. The entire world is sick because of wars and rumours of war. Everywhere peace is fragile. Churches—particularly Mennonite and Brethren in Christ churches—must be actively engaged in fostering a culture of peace.

This commitment to peace is all the more pressing for the Mennonite churches of Africa. In front of our eyes the DRC, which has the largest Mennonite population in Africa, has sunk into a war that has been going on for more than four years. What has been our role as peacemakers in the DRC? Will history remember our actions for peace in the DRC in twenty-five years? What is our contribution in the midst of the political crisis in Zimbabwe? Do we accept the way in which land is being taken and redistributed in Zimbabwe? Should our peace-building be passive or active? Admittedly, throughout history we have stayed on the margins of politics. Does that mean that we have to maintain this position?

In our day, African populations no longer have confidence in their political leaders. They see the hope of African nations in the church. We are not advocating that the church as an institution should be involved in politics like the political parties, but she should be ready to play a positive role in the life of our nations when the sons of the nations come to her for help. In Benin, the Sovereign National Conference was led by a Christian religious leader to the satisfaction of all parties. In Burkina Faso, church leaders have been chosen two different times to preside over the National Independent Electoral Commission. When the church is prepared to bring its contribution to the governing of the nation, it is well placed to denounce all forms of social injustice. God includes us in the management of time and events so we must not simply be subjected to history; we must make history. We must influence history in the direction God wants.

Notes

[1] Helen and Samuel Grandjean, *Si tu chantais* (Geneva, 1970), 2.

[2] Jules-Marcel Nicole, *Précis d'Histoire de l'Eglise* (Nogent-sur-Marnes: Institut Biblique de Nogent, 1996), 157-58.

[3] Cornelius J. Dyck, ed., *An Introduction to Mennonite History* (Scottdale, PA: Herald Press, 1981), 360.

[4] Peter Falk, *La Croissance de l'Eglise en Afrique* (Kinshasa, 1985), 154.

Mennonite and BIC Conferences in Africa

Compiled by Elisabeth Baecher,
MWC, Strasbourg, France

Organization Name	MWC Membership	Est.
Igreja da Comunidade Menonita em Angola	Full member	1992
Igreja Evangélica dos Irmãos Menonitas em Angola	Full member	1980
Ireja Evangélica Menonitas em Angola	Non member	
Eglise Evangélique Mennonite du Burkina Faso	Assoc. Member	1980
Communauté des Eglises de Frères Mennonites au Congo	Full member	
Communauté Evangélique Mennonite	Full member	1962
Communauté Mennonite au Congo	Full member	1912
Meserete Kristos Church	Full member	1959
Ghana Mennonite Church	Full member	1963
Eglise Protestante Anabaptiste L'institution Chrétienne	Non member	
African Christian Church of East Africa	Non member	1964
Christian Believers Fellowship	Non member	1992
Kenya Mennonite Church	Full member	1965
Brethren in Christ Church (Malawi) Mpingo Wa Abale Mwa Kristu	Non member	1986
Igreja Evangélica Menonita em Moçambique	Non member	
Evangelical Church of Mennonite Brethren in Namibia	Non member	
Chuch of God in Christ Mennonite (Nigeria)	Non member	1963
Mennonite Church Nigeria	Full member	1959
Grace Community Church in South Africa	Full member	1989
Soshanguve Brethren in Christ Church	Non member	1987
Kanisa la Mennonite Tanzania	Full member	
Eglise Mennonite de l'Assemblée des Fidèles du Christ	Non member	1998
Brethren in Christ Church (Zambia)	Full member	1906
Brethren in Christ Church Ibandla Labazalwane ku Kristu e Zimbabwe	Full member	1963

City	Country	Number of Congregations	Number Baptized
Luanda	Angola	10	3760
Sao Paulo	Angola	58	3200
Luanda	Angola	21	4216
Orodara	Burkina Faso	7	230
Kikwit	Dem. Rep. of Congo	629	85, 648
Mubuji/Mayi Kasai Oriental	Dem. Rep. of Congo	160	21, 871
Kinshasa	Dem. Rep. of Congo	531	86, 600
Addis Ababa	Ethiopia	275	98, 025
Accra-North	Ghana	26	4101
Abdijan	Ivory Coast	15	1300
Thika	Kenya	238	15, 300
Kisumu	Kenya	6	341
Suna-Migori	Kenya	108	15, 915
Blantyre	Malawi	30	3500
Tete-Tete	Mozambique	3	100
Oshakati	Namibia	5	180
	Nigeria	14	349
Uyo, Akwa Ibom State	Nigeria	68	11, 024
Philipstown	South Africa	5	750
Pretoria	South Africa	4	200
Musoma	Tanzania	280	50, 000
Lome	Togo	5	144
Choma	Zambia	150	15, 374
Bulawayo	Zimbabwe	272	29, 213
	Total Africa	2920	451, 341

Subject and Name Index

Index of Mission Stations and Major Centres by Country

Index of Church Institutions by Country

Authors and Editors for
A Global Mennonite History. Volume One: Africa

Samuel Asefa, Nazareth, Ethiopia, is a student and church worker with youth and street children.

Michael Kodzu Badasu, Accra, Ghana is a pastor, evangelist, and Moderator of the Ghana Mennonite Church.

Bekithemba Dube, Gwanda, Zimbabwe, is a writer, a teacher of religion and morals at Joshua Mqabuko Teacher's Training College in Gwanda, and consultant in AIDS education.

Doris Dube, Bulawayo, Zimbabwe, is an author, the Africa editor for Mennonite World Conference, and co-director of the Mennonite Central Committee programme in Zimbabwe.

Alemu Checole, Nazareth, Ethiopia, is a writer, retired English teacher, and a long-time leader in the Meserete Kristos Church.

Erik Kumedisa, Kinshasa, Democratic Republic of Congo, is a teacher, writer and pastor in the Mennonite Brethren Church of the Congo (CEFMC).

John A. Lapp, Akron, PA, is a retired historian and church administrator, and coordinator of the Global Mennonite History Project for Mennonite World Conference.

I. U. Nsasak, Uyo, Akwa Ibom State, Nigeria is a pastor who serves as Bishop of the Mennonite Church Nigeria.

Barbara Nkala, Harare, Zimbabwe, is an author, editor, and director of the International Bible Society of Zimbabwe and Malawi.

C. Arnold Snyder, Kitchener, Ontario, Canada, is professor of church history at Conrad Grebel University College, managing editor of Pandora Press, and general editor of the Global Mennonite History project.

Siaka Traore, Ouagadougou, Burkina Faso, is a pastor, theologian, administrator for Mennonite Central Committee, and Vice Moderator of the Mennonite Church of Burkina Faso.

Pakisa Tshimika was a health administrator in the Congo and now serves as the Associate Executive Secretary for Global Networks and Projects of Mennonite World Conference in Fresno, California.

About Pandora Press

Pandora Press is a small, independently owned press dedicated to making available modestly priced books that deal with Anabaptist, Mennonite, and Believers Church topics, both historical and theological. We welcome comments from our readers.

Visit our full-service online Bookstore:
www.pandorapress.com

Karl Koop, *Anabaptist-Mennonite Confessions of Faith: the Development of a Tradition.* (forthcoming) ISBN 1-894710-32-0

George F. R. Ellis, *A Universe of Ethics Morality and Hope: Proceedings from the Second Annual Goshen Conference on Religion and Science.* (Kitchener: Pandora Press, 2003; co-published with Herald Press.) Softcover, 148 pp. ISBN 1-894710-36-3

Donald Martin, *Old Order Mennonites of Ontario: Gelassenheit, Discipleship, Brotherhood.* (Kitchener: Pandora Press, 2003; co-published with Herald Press.) Softcover, 381 pp., includes index. ISBN 1-894710-33-9

Mary A. Schiedel, *Pioneers in Ministry: Women Pastors in Ontario Mennonite Churches, 1973-2003.* (Kitchener: Pandora Press, 2003) Softcover, 204 pp., ISBN 1-894710-35-5

Harry Loewen, ed., *Shepherds, Servants and Prophets.* (Kitchener: Pandora Press, 2003; co-published with Herald Press.) Softcover, 446 pp., ISBN 1-894710-35-5

Robert A. Riall, trans., Galen A. Peters, ed., *The Earliest Hymns of the Ausbund: Some Beautiful Christian Songs Composed and Sung in the Prison at Passau, Published 1564.* (Kitchener: Pandora Press, 2003; co-published with Herald Press.) Softcover, 468 pp., includes bibliography and index. ISBN 1-894710-34-7.

John A. Harder. *From Kleefeld With Love.*
(Kitchener: Pandora Press, 2003; co-published with Herald Press.)
Softcover, 198 pp. ISBN 1-894710-28-2
[Letters from Russian women to Canadian relatives, ca. 1925-1933.]

John F. Peters. The Plain People: A Glimpse at Life Among the Old Order
Mennonites of Ontario
(Kitchener: Pandora Press, 2003; co-published with Herald Press.)
Softcover, 54 pp. ISBN 1-894710-26-6
[A pictoral history of the old order mennonites of Ontario.]

Robert S. Kreider. *My Early Years: An Autobiography.*
(Kitchener: Pandora Press, 2002; co-published with Herald Press.)
Softcover, 600 pp., index ISBN 1-894710-23-1
[Autobiography of a prominent scholar and churchman]

Helen Martens. *Hutterite Songs.*
(Kitchener: Pandora Press, 2002; co-published with Herald Press)
Softcover, xxii, 328 pp. ISBN 1-894710-24-X
[A study of the oral tradition of Hutterite songs]

C. Arnold Snyder and Galen A. Peters, eds. *Reading the Anabaptist Bible:
Reflections for Every Day of the Year.* Introduction by Arthur Paul Boers
(Kitchener: Pandora Press, 2002; co-published with Herald Press.)
Softcover, 415 pp. ISBN 1-894710-25-8
[A devotional book of daily readings]

C. Arnold Snyder, ed., *Commoners and Community. Essays in Honour
of Werner O. Packull*
(Kitchener: Pandora Press, 2002; co-published with Herald Press.)
Softcover, 324 pp. ISBN 1-894710-27-4
[Essays on Anabaptism, Reformation, and tradition]

James O. Lehman, *Mennonite Tent Revivals: Howard Hammer and Myron
Augsburger, 1952-1962*
(Kitchener: Pandora Press, 2002; co-published with Herald Press)
Softcover, xxiv, 318 pp. ISBN 1-894710-22-3
[A History of Christian Laymen's Association Based in Ohio]

Lawrence Klippenstein and Jacob Dick, *Mennonite Alternative Service in Russia*
(Kitchener: Pandora Press, 2002; co-published with Herald Press)
Softcover, viii, 163 pp. ISBN 1-894710-21-5
[Diaries and photographs from Russian Mennonite COs]

Nancey Murphy, *Religion and Science*
(Kitchener: Pandora Press, 2002; co-published with Herald Press)
Softcover, 126 pp. ISBN 1-894710-20-7
[Proceedings of the 2001 Goshen Conference on Religion and Science]

Biblical Concordance of the Swiss Brethren, 1540. Trans. by Gilbert Fast
and Galen Peters; bib. intro. Joe Springer; ed. C. Arnold Snyder
(Kitchener: Pandora Press, 2001; co-published with Herald Press)
Softcover, lv, 227pp. ISBN 1-894710-16-9
[Previously untranslated Anabaptist biblical resource]

Orland Gingerich, *The Amish of Canada*
(Kitchener: Pandora Press, 2001; co-published with Herald Press.)
Softcover, 244 pp., includes index. ISBN 1-894710-19-3
[Third printing of this definitive history of Amish of Canada]

M. Darrol Bryant, *Religion in a New Key*
(Kitchener: Pandora Press, 2001)
Softcover, 136 pp., includes bib. refs. ISBN 1-894710-18-5
[Explores dialogue between religious communities world-wide]

Trans. Walter Klaassen, Frank Friesen, Werner O. Packull, ed. C. Arnold
Snyder, *Sources of South German/Austrian Anabaptism*
(Kitchener: Pandora Press, 2001; co-published with Herald Press.)
Softcover, 430 pp. includes indexes. ISBN 1-894710-15-0
[A wide spectrum of newly-translated Anabaptist sources.]

Pedro A. Sandín Fremaint y Pablo A. Jimémez, *Palabras Duras: Homilías*
(Kitchener: Pandora Press, 2001).
Softcover, 121 pp., ISBN 1-894710-17-7
[Spanish. Reflections on the "hard words" of Jesus in the Gospels.]

James C. Juhnke and Carol M. Hunter, *The Missing Peace: The Search for Nonviolent Alternatives in United States History* (Kitchener: Pandora Press, 2001; co-published with Herald Press.) Softcover, 321 pp., includes index. ISBN 1-894710-13-4
[Focuses on each of the principal periods of United States history.]

Ruth Elizabeth Mooney, *Manual Para Crear Materiales de Educación Cristiana* (Kitchener: Pandora Press, 2001).
Softcover, 206 pp., ISBN 1-894710-12-6
[Spanish. Manual for creation of Christian education programs.]

Esther and Malcolm Wenger, poetry by Ann Wenger, *Healing the Wounds* (Kitchener: Pandora Press, 2001; co-pub. with Herald Press).
Softcover, 210 pp. ISBN 1-894710-09-6.
[Experiences of Mennonite missionaries with the Cheyenne people]

Pedro A. Sandín Fremaint, *Cuentos y Encuentros: Hacia una Educación Transformadora* (Kitchener: Pandora Press, 2001).
Softcover 163 pp ISBN 1-894710-08-8.
[Spanish. Stories and discussion questions for Christian education]

A. James Reimer, *Mennonites and Classical Theology: Dogmatic Foundations for Christian Ethics* (Kitchener: Pandora Press, 2001; co-published with Herald Press)
Softcover, 650pp. ISBN 0-9685543-7-7
[A theological interpretation of Mennonite experience in 20th C.]

Walter Klaassen, *Anabaptism: Neither Catholic nor Protestant*, 3rd ed (Kitchener: Pandora Press, 2001; co-pub. Herald Press)
Softcover, 122pp. ISBN 1-894710-01-0
[A classic interpretation and study guide, now available again]

Dale Schrag & James Juhnke, eds., *Anabaptist Visions for the new Millennium: A search for identity* (Kitchener: Pandora Press, 2000; co-published with Herald Press)
Softcover, 242 pp. ISBN 1-894710-00-2
[Twenty-eight essays presented at Bethel College, June, 2000]

Harry Loewen, ed., *Road to Freedom: Mennonites Escape the Land of Suffering* (Kitchener: Pandora Press, 2000; co-published with Herald Press) Hardcover, large format, 302pp. ISBN 0-9685543-5-0
[Life experiences documented with personal stories and photos]

Alan Kreider and Stuart Murray, eds., *Coming Home: Stories of Anabaptists in Britain and Ireland* (Kitchener: Pandora Press, 2000; co-published with Herald Press)
Softcover, 220pp. ISBN 0-9685543-6-9
[Anabaptist encounters in the U.K.; personal stories/articles]

Edna Schroeder Thiessen and Angela Showalter, *A Life Displaced: A Mennonite Woman's Flight from War-Torn Poland* (Kitchener: Pandora Press, 2000; co-published with Herald Press) Softcover, xii, 218pp. ISBN 0-9685543-2-6
[A true story: moving, richly-detailed, told with candor and courage]

Stuart Murray, *Biblical Interpretation in the Anabaptist Tradition* (Kitchener: Pandora Press, 2000; co-published with Herald Press) Softcover, 310pp. ISBN 0-9685543-3-4
[How Anabaptists read the Bible; considerations for today's church]

Apocalypticism and Millennialism, ed. by Loren L. Johns (Kitchener: Pandora Press, 2000; co-published with Herald Press) Softcover, 419pp; Scripture and name indeces
ISBN 0-9683462-9-4
[A clear, careful, and balanced collection: pastoral and scholarly]

Later Writings by Pilgram Marpeck and his Circle. Volume 1: The Exposé, A Dialogue and Marpeck's Response to Caspar Schwenckfeld Translated by Walter Klaassen, Werner Packull, and John Rempel (Kitchener: Pandora Press, 1999; co-published with Herald Press) Softcover, 157pp. ISBN 0-9683462-6-X
[Previously untranslated writings by Marpeck and his Circle]

John Driver, *Radical Faith. An Alternative History of the Christian Church*, edited by Carrie Snyder. Kitchener: Pandora Press, 1999; co-published with Herald Press) Softcover, 334pp. ISBN 0-9683462-8-6
[A history of the church as it is seldom told – from the margins]

C. Arnold Snyder, *From Anabaptist Seed. The Historical Core of Anabaptist-Related Identity*
(Kitchener: Pandora Press, 1999; co-published with Herald Press)
 Softcover, 53pp.; discussion questions. ISBN 0-9685543-0-X
[Ideal for group study, commissioned by Mennonite World Conf.]

 Also available in Spanish translation: *De Semilla Anabautista*,
 from Pandora Press only.
John D. Thiesen, *Mennonite and Nazi? Attitudes Among Mennonite Colonists in Latin America, 1933-1945.*
(Kitchener: Pandora Press, 1999; co-published with Herald Press)
 Softcover, 330pp., 2 maps, 24 b/w illustrations, bibliography,
 index. ISBN 0-9683462-5-1
[Careful and objective study of an explosive topic]

Lifting the Veil, a translation of *Aus meinem Leben: Erinnerungen von J.H. Janzen.* Ed. by Leonard Friesen; trans. by Walter Klaassen
(Kitchener: Pandora Press, 1998; co-pub. with Herald Press).
 Softcover, 128pp.; 4pp. of illustrations. ISBN 0-9683462-1-9
[Memoir, confession, critical observation of Mennonite life in Russia]

Leonard Gross, *The Golden Years of the Hutterites*, rev. ed.
(Kitchener: Pandora Press, 1998; co-pub. with Herald Press).
 Softcover, 280pp., index. ISBN 0-9683462-3-5
[Classic study of early Hutterite movement, now available again]

The Believers Church: A Voluntary Church, ed. by William H. Brackney
(Kitchener: Pandora Press, 1998; co-published with Herald Press).
 Softcover, viii, 237pp., index. ISBN 0-9683462-0-0
[Papers from the 12th Believers Church Conference, Hamilton, ON]

An Annotated Hutterite Bibliography, compiled by Maria H.
Krisztinkovich, ed. by Peter C. Erb (Kitchener, Ont.: Pandora Press, 1998).
(Ca. 2,700 entries) 312pp., cerlox bound, electronic, or both.
 ISBN (paper) 0-9698762-8-9/(disk) 0-9698762-9-7
[The most extensive bibliography on Hutterite literature available]

Jacobus ten Doornkaat Koolman, *Dirk Philips. Friend and Colleague of Menno Simons*, trans. W. E. Keeney, ed. C. A. Snyder (Kitchener: Pandora Press, 1998; co-pub. with Herald Press). Softcover, xviii, 236pp., index. ISBN: 0-9698762-3-8 [The definitive biography of Dirk Philips, now available in English]

Sarah Dyck, ed./tr., *The Silence Echoes: Memoirs of Trauma & Tears* (Kitchener: Pandora Press, 1997; co-published with Herald Press). Softcover, xii, 236pp., 2 maps. ISBN: 0-9698762-7-0 [First person accounts of life in the Soviet Union, trans. from German]

Wes Harrison, *Andreas Ehrenpreis and Hutterite Faith and Practice* (Kitchener: Pandora Press, 1997; co-published with Herald Press). Softcover, xxiv, 274pp., 2 maps, index. ISBN 0-9698762-6-2 [First biography of this important seventeenth century Hutterite leader]

C. Arnold Snyder, *Anabaptist History and Theology: Revised Student Edition* (Kitchener: Pandora Press, 1997; co-pub. Herald Press). Softcover, xiv, 466pp., 7 maps, 28 illustrations, index, bibliography. ISBN 0-9698762-5-4 [Abridged, rewritten edition for the non-specialist]

Nancey Murphy, *Reconciling Theology and Science: A Radical Reformation Perspective* (Kitchener, Ont.: Pandora Press, 1997; co-pub. Herald Press). Softcover, x, 103pp., index. ISBN 0-9698762-4-6 [Exploration of the conflict between Christianity and Science]

C. Arnold Snyder and Linda A. Huebert Hecht, eds, *Profiles of Anabaptist Women: Sixteenth Century Reforming Pioneers* (Waterloo, Ont.: Wilfrid Laurier University Press, 1996). Softcover, xxii, 442pp. ISBN: 0-88920-277-X [Biographical sketches of more than 50 Anabaptist women; a first]

The Limits of Perfection: A Conversation with J. Lawrence Burkholder 2nd ed., with a new epilogue by J. Lawrence Burkholder, Rodney Sawatsky and Scott Holland, eds. (Kitchener: Pandora Press, 1996). Softcover, x, 154pp. ISBN 0-9698762-2-X [J.L. Burkholder on his life experiences; eight Mennonites respond]

C. Arnold Snyder, *Anabaptist History and Theology: An Introduction*
(Kitchener: Pandora Press, 1995). ISBN 0-9698762-0-3
  Softcover, x, 434pp., 6 maps, 29 illustrations, index,
  bibliography.
[Comprehensive survey; unabridged version, fully documented]

Pandora Press
33 Kent Avenue
Kitchener, Ontario
Canada N2G 3R2
Tel./Fax: (519) 578-2381
E-mail:
info@pandorapress.com
Web site:
www.pandorapress.com

Herald Press
616 Walnut Avenue
Scottdale, PA
U.S.A. 15683
Orders: (800) 245-7894
E-mail:
hp@mph.org
Web site:
www.mph.org